RECONSTRUCTION
AND
MORMON AMERICA

RECONSTRUCTION AND MORMON AMERICA

EDITED BY
CLYDE A. MILNER II
AND
BRIAN Q. CANNON

UNIVERSITY OF OKLAHOMA PRESS : NORMAN

Publication of this book is made possible in part by a subvention from the Charles Redd Center for Western Studies at Brigham Young University.

Chapter 7, "Why Don't Mormons Have a Lost Cause?" by Clyde A. Milner II, previously appeared under the same title in *Journal of Mormon History* 44(2) (April 2018): 36–54, published by the University of Illinois Press.

Library of Congress Cataloging-in-Publication Data
Names: Milner, Clyde A., II, 1948– editor. | Cannon, Brian Q., editor.
Title: Reconstruction and Mormon America / edited by Clyde A. Milner II and Brian Q. Cannon.
Description: Norman : University of Oklahoma Press, [2019] | Includes bibliographical references and index.
Identifiers: LCCN 2018059451 | ISBN 978-0-8061-6353-6 (hardcover) ISBN 978-0-8061-9010-5 (paper)
Subjects: LCSH: Mormon Church—History. | Church of Jesus Christ of Latter-Day Saints—History—19th century. | Mormon Church—History—19th century. | Reconstruction (U.S. history, 1865–1877)
Classification: LCC BX8611 .R423 2019 | DDC 289.3/7309034—dc23
LC record available at https://lccn.loc.gov/2018059451

The paper in this book meets the guidelines for permanence and durability of the Committee on Production Guidelines for Book Longevity of the Council on Library Resources, Inc. ∞

Copyright © 2019 by the University of Oklahoma Press, Norman, Publishing Division of the University. Paperback published 2022. Manufactured in the U.S.A.

All rights reserved. No part of this publication may be reproduced, stored in a retrieval system, or transmitted, in any form or by any means, electronic, mechanical, photocopying, recording, or otherwise—except as permitted under Section 107 or 108 of the United States Copyright Act—without the prior written permission of the University of Oklahoma Press. To request permission to reproduce selections from this book, write to Permissions, University of Oklahoma Press, 2800 Venture Drive, Norman, OK 73069, or email rights.oupress@ou.edu.

Contents

Preface
    by Brian Q. Cannon and Clyde A. Milner II   vii

Introduction
Measuring Reconstruction
    by Elliott West   1

Part I: Background Issues

Interlude 1
Wrestling Practice
    by Anne Hyde   15

1. There Is No Mormon Trail of Tears
Roots, Removals, and Reconstructions
    by Angela Pulley Hudson   19

2. Constructing a National Marital and Sexual Culture
Reconsidering the "Twin Relics of Barbarism"
    by Christine Talbot   52

3. Disciplinary Democracy
*Mormon Violence and the Construction
of the Modern American State*
    by Patrick Q. Mason   88

Part II: The Context of Reconstruction

Interlude 2
Racial Dimensions
by Cathleen Cahill and Crystal N. Feimster 111

4. The Application of Federal Power in Utah Territory
by Brent M. Rogers 116

5. "To Merge Them into More Wholesome Social Elements"
The Greater Reconstruction and Its Place in Utah
by Brett D. Dowdle 150

6. The Case for Containing Reconstruction
Rethinking and Remeasuring
by Rachel St. John 181

Part III: Aftermaths

Interlude 3
Reckoning with Lost Causes
by Brian Q. Cannon 195

7. Why Don't Mormons Have a Lost Cause?
by Clyde A. Milner II 202

8. Whither Mormons' Lost Cause?
Collective Historical Memory in Comparison
by Eric A. Eliason 219

9. The Mormon Cause, Lost and Found
by Jared Farmer 235

List of Contributors 245

Index 249

Preface

Brian Q. Cannon and Clyde A. Milner II

Many generations of students at Yale University, including one of this book's coeditors, participated in Howard Lamar's beloved two-semester survey of the history of the American West. In one of his lectures, Professor Lamar advocated the recognition of three examples of "reconstruction" in the post–Civil War United States—reconstruction of the secessionist South through military occupation and political reform, reconstruction of American Indians through removal to reservations and assimilation to Christianity and farming (also supported by the military), and the reconstruction of Latter-day Saints (i.e. Mormons) to force the end of polygamy through new laws and federal court actions with the threat of disestablishing the church if necessary. These efforts sought to bring rebellious white Southerners, uncontrolled American Indians, and nonconformist Mormons into the American mainstream. The failures of the first two examples of federal reconstruction are well known to scholars of the American South, African American history, American Indian history, and American military history, whereas the connections to Mormon history are not as well recognized.

In 2002 both coeditors participated in the Western History Association conference where Elliott West delivered his presidential address, "Reconstructing Race," published in the Spring 2003 *Western Historical Quarterly*. West talked about a "Greater Reconstruction" that he dated from 1846 to 1877. His award-winning book, *The Last Indian War: The Nez Perce Story*, applied this concept more extensively to American Indians after the Civil War. Elliott West, as will be seen in this volume, also expanded his idea of the "Greater Reconstruction" to Latter-day Saints. Inspired in part by Howard Lamar's insights but most directly influenced by Elliott West's ideas, the purpose of the essays in this book is to consider and debate the concept of "reconstruction" as it may apply to Latter-day Saints with thoughtful comparisons in terms of what happened to white and black Southerners as well as American Indians.

Some key questions stimulated our thinking. Why did the federal government need to "reconstruct" Latter-day Saints, and when did such efforts begin? Compared to what happened in the South and with American Indians, were these initiatives successful? What did reconstruction mean for Mormon identity and sense of history? For example, why do Latter-day Saints not have a Lost Cause? Why are Latter-day Saints not like latter-day white Southerners? And do Mormons share a resentment for the loss of sovereignty and demands for "Americanization" that can be found among many American Indian peoples? What of the racial dynamics of reconstruction in the South and toward American Indians in terms of Mormons? Were nineteenth-century Mormons considered to be on the "wrong" side of a religious "line," but not a "race line"? Indeed, beyond the period of federal policies directed at the South after the Civil War, how useful is the term "reconstruction" in regard to federal actions toward American Indians and Latter-day Saints?

―――

The Charles Redd Center for Western Studies at Brigham Young University played a pivotal role in the creation of this volume. Not only was the center's director at the time one of the two coeditors, but the center also hosted a seminar for the book's contributors in June 2017. This occasion allowed a set of scholars to consider both the central topic and the way key ideas could be explained. It was an exciting two days of discussion that helped our authors focus their concepts. In addition, our participants agreed that an "interlude" essay could help expand the historical context at the start of each section of the book.

In our work on this project, the coeditors wish to acknowledge the following people. John Mack Faragher and Thomas Alexander enriched both the seminar and this volume through their incisive comments and recommendations. Chuck Rankin of the University of Oklahoma Press provided vital encouragement and support for this project, meeting with the coeditors at critical junctures and representing the press at the seminar. Amy Carlin, office specialist at the Redd Center, arranged for transportation, meals, and lodging for the seminar participants and standardized the manuscript for submission to the press. Brenden Rensink, assistant director at the Redd Center, attended the seminar and contributed to the discussion, offering suggestions and insights regarding the papers. Two anonymous readers for OU Press provided very useful suggestions; Kerin Tate did excellent copyediting of the full text; and Emily Schuster, our manuscript editor, guided this work through to publication.

Because the term "reconstruction" has great importance in this book, our authors have tried to distinguish between Reconstruction (with a capital letter) in reference to the historical situation in the South after the Civil War and the concept of reconstruction (with a lowercase "r") outside that historical context. Nonetheless, in recognition of Elliott West's significant contribution to our efforts, his term "Greater Reconstruction" retains its double capital letters, as it assumes a direct conceptual linkage to the federal government's program of Reconstruction for the secessionist South.

Introduction

Measuring Reconstruction

Elliott West

If we in the western history guild were told to name the most pressing question we have been asking for the past quarter century or so, my vote would be for this one: how can we bring the West more fully into our national narrative? In historical writing, and certainly in popular culture, the West has most often appeared as a place apart—more than a bit exotic, interesting exactly because of its differentness, peripheral to the major doings of the growing, evolving republic. That impression is at its fullest in the novels, films, and art that provide much of the world's peoples with their only view of the region, but historians, too, have tended often to focus on the West's distance from the main currents and the cultural patterns of national life. In the fine phrase titling a recent book, the West has been pictured as the "American Elsewhere."[1]

In some ways, it should be. Geography alone obviously sets it apart and gives its story some distinctive shape. Its rapid conquest and acquisition and the pace of the changes that followed, including the speedy defeat and dispossession of its Indian peoples, had no parallels in the East. And Lord knows the West has had an exceptional helping of bizarre episodes and characters. The trap here is in allowing its genuine distinctiveness to obscure a point absolutely crucial to understanding the West—namely, that from its acquisition in the 1840s until today, it has reflected and played vitally in shaping the course of American history.

Often it has taken the lead. We cannot possibly trace accurately the contours of national development from 1850 until now without allowing the West to play prominently in the story.

No period had a greater role in shifting the trajectory of our common history than the middle years of the nineteenth century. Among the reasons, besides the obvious suspect, the Civil War, was the explosive expansion to the Pacific in the 1840s—the years, that is, when the West as a region was born. It follows that if we intend to show the West's true significance in our national narrative, we should start there, in that stretch of time from 1845–48, when we expanded our borders by more than a million square miles, to around 1880, when the West as a region had come mostly into focus and when the dislocations and war in the East had settled into patterns that would persist for the next several decades.

Those years included the two topics brought together in the excellent seminar that produced these essays. There was, first, the Mormon crisis in Missouri and Illinois and the exodus and settling of the Saints in the Great Basin and, second, the events we collectively call Reconstruction. The definition of the second topic, Reconstruction, is more than a bit in flux nowadays. Elsewhere I have suggested that we should expand both its temporal and geographical boundaries and think in terms of a Greater Reconstruction that ran from the mid-1840s to 1877 or so and that encompassed the entire expanded nation, coast to coast. Our seminar offered animated discussion about the wisdom and utility of such a notion, but there seemed to be full agreement on its geographical side—that at the least we need to think more about how the recently acquired West fit within the often contentious events between the waning of the Civil War and the traditional stopping place of 1877.

If we start with that—if, that is, the Reconstruction era is made continental— then all sorts of questions, or rather sets of questions, quickly arise. How does the western side of the story generally jibe with the usual—the Southern—side? Who are the prime figures on the western side? In particular, in the points raised in these essays, do those figures include others besides Mormons—Indian peoples and Hispanics, for instance? And if so, how do their stories fit with each other and with others to the East? And finally, getting back to that most pressing issue for us in the guild, how does including the West change and expand our understanding of the Reconstruction era and how it illuminates the course of American history in the generations that followed?

Besides the consensus that we should expand our thinking about these years spatially to include the West, there seemed a clear but implicit agreement on another point: at its core, a unifying theme centered on power. Specifically, a chief concern was redefining federal power in relation to the expanded nation's constituent parts. In the East, that meant most obviously tilting power in the federal relationship toward the central and away from state governments. It meant using that power to open national citizenship to more than four million persons, the South's freed slaves, which meant extending Washington's authority into new areas, notably the right to vote and the birth of new social and economic institutions. The central government took on other expanded powers but then, as Reconstruction waned, pulled back—affecting most tragically the protection and support of those Washington had partially emancipated. In the West, Washington's exercise of power was similar but, if anything, more elemental. Besides overseeing infrastructures of connection and creating new agencies to cope with new challenges and opportunities, it set out, in rough parallel to the South, to set the terms of citizenship for groups, Mormons among them, that in different ways were anomalous within the expanded nation. That in turn had Washington establishing full command over Indian peoples and stretching its authority over social and economic institutions that ranged into the most intimate aspects of people's lives, including their relations with their God and their choice of life mates.

The relative application of federal power, South and West, thus offers us an expanded context for fitting the Reconstruction era into our common story. Brett Dowdle looks through a very wide lens at Washington's efforts to contain western Mormons. When we follow his lead, we find national perceptions of the Saints much entangled with those of other targets of the central government. Just how tangled is suggested by the fascinating letter he quotes from William Tecumseh Sherman in 1874. Comparing Mormons with Indian peoples, he found them both so alien to American values that he doubted whether either would ever be truly part of the national fabric. The chances of Indians ever adopting proper lifeways Sherman found about as likely as "the Leopard changing his spots," and consequently he foresaw an "irrepressible conflict" between the cultures. And so, too, with Mormons. Sherman's phrasing, of course, is redolent of the angry debates that led to the Civil War, mixing slave owners' metaphors about their bondsmen with abolitionists' warnings of slavery's toxic threat to national survival.

Dowdle puts Mormons into this wider context by surveying Washington's campaigns to bring into line what it considered anomalous groups and, by that, to create a truly unified national culture. As Congress worked in the defeated

Confederacy to reshape Southern society, often enough overreaching and falling short, out West it turned its efforts, in Dowdle's phrase, against all who "failed to live up to the requirements of whiteness, Protestantism, and Americanism," including Hispano Roman Catholics in the Southwest, Indians all over the place, Chinese on the Pacific coast—and Mormons in the Great Basin.

While Dowdle gives us the grand view, Brent Rogers tightens the lens to focus on the nearly half century of federal efforts to bring Mormons fully into the national fold. He points out that those efforts began well before the Civil War (as they did, I would add, with the Indians and others) and continued well after 1877, the date traditionally marking Reconstruction's close. He shows us a gradual, step-by-step process that moved not so much by a guiding strategy as circumstantially. It began with the basics, confirming control over the land itself and suppressing what was called open rebellion in 1856–57, and it ended with the church's formal rejection of plural marriage in 1890. The image I had reading Rogers's thorough coverage of the process was of a deep-sea fisherman slowly landing a marlin, heaving back on the line and then reeling in when there is any slack, until finally the fighting fish is subdued. Between Dowdle and Rogers we have both an overview of Washington's Reconstruction campaigns to confirm its power and their particular application to Deseret.

But Mormons were seen as more than simply one group among many whose ways would need to conform to national norms. At least in its rhetoric, the church claimed the right to resist federal authority militarily (while claiming also to be defending the Constitution). It created the Standing Army of Israel. It closed the overland passage where it controlled the trail, thus threatening to sever an essential connection to the gold fields of California. What set the Mormons apart, that is, was their effective claim of an independent institutional right to public, physical power. Patrick Mason's essay puts that claim in a particularly revealing context. He draws on a wider literature to see a monopoly on legitimate violence as an essential prerequisite in defining a modern state. As Janice Thomson has shown, the state's monopolizing of violence itself was a gradual process dating back to early modern Europe.[2] As the United States emerged in the nineteenth century, gaining full control of legitimate violence was critical to its coming of age, and in that process the Mormons, starting with their own bid to be an independent state, posed one of the federal government's great challenges. Mormon violence, "real and perceived," seemed all the more threatening because of prevailing myths about religious fanaticism that linked the church to the more fevered fears around Islam and vaguely to anti-Semitic canards. The Saints, some charged, sacrificed children annually and cannibalized those too old to work.

Mason, then, gives us a helpful angle of vision that again combines West and South in a fuller view of Reconstruction. As differently as the experiences of the Mormon church in the 1850s and the Confederacy in the 1860s played out, both represented challenges to the evolving American state's assertion of exclusive use of power in its most elemental form: public violence. By taking this tack on power and Reconstruction, Mason also redefines the latter. Like Dowdle and Rogers, he sees Washington's efforts as starting back in the 1850s—indeed the "Utah War" of 1856–57 was the critical moment—but because the process that followed involved both the final construction of the national state and the full dismantling of the Mormons' bid for their own, Mason writes that Mormon *re*-construction could truly begin only in the twentieth century, after the Saints' capitulation and the full *de*-construction of the intended Deseret.

Rachel St. John, like Mason, finds the key to the church's place in these years in the realm of state-making. Midcentury witnessed a series of competing efforts to create independent centers of power in what is now the United States. All failed, but how the contested efforts evolved can help us understand results that are largely with us today. She notes two examples. Coast to coast, Washington oversaw the making of a variety of racial hierarchies that kept Anglo Americans at the top and African Americans, Indian peoples, Chinese, and Hispanics beneath them. Those hierarchies in turn corresponded to a variety in types of territorial governance: reservations, delaying statehood in southwestern territories, and more. St. John also argues vigorously that, in studying such processes, we should uncouple western episodes from Reconstruction altogether. Leave its traditional spatial and chronological limits alone, she writes, and treat it as one of several distinct but related stories that together were remaking the nation, East and West.

Institutional violence was the rawest challenge posed by the Mormons as the federal government asserted its power in the West, and so it was the first addressed. The other primary challenge, plural marriage, threatened not outright state control, as in the "Utah War," but rather adherence to cultural ideals that, while centered on the home and family, differed from those of polygamy. Eventually the maturing American state dictated through its legislative powers that its views of home and family would prevail. Christine Talbot once more sets the story of Mormon Reconstruction in the context of South and West, looking in revealing detail at how those famous "twin relics of barbarism" in the newborn Republican Party's 1856 platform, African slavery and Mormon polygamy, were portrayed in the political tracts and popular fiction of the day. She, too, begins the story in the 1840s and 1850s—the comparison was obviously most pressing and vivid before manumission—and adds to our context by reminding us that the nineteenth century was also a crucial time for the evolution of domestic ideals, in particular those concerning marriage and the family. These were years when the model of a patriarchal household was giving way increasingly to one of a companionate marriage based on mutual affection, more equitable, even democratic, authority, and greater respect for women's control over their sexual lives.

For anyone setting out to promote and defend this new ideal, African slavery and Mormon polygamy (or more exactly polygyny, one man with more than one wife) were the perfect foils. Talbot points out helpfully that by the 1850s abolitionists' assaults on slavery shifted their focus from the material wretchedness of bondsmen to the white patriarchy's suffocation of the slave's individuality and fulfillment. Sexual use of slave women was arguably the most grotesque and lurid aspect, and its equation with Mormon polygamy, with goatish slaveholders and LDS patriarchs in common assault on helpless women held in common subordination, was irresistible. Recent work, for instance that of Richard White and Louis Warren, has stressed how the home and its values, often as projected onto the new West through such forums as Buffalo Bill Cody's Wild West shows, held a central place in both federal policies and unifying national visions.[3] Talbot's essay shows us how federal power was implementing that vision from before the war until the end of the century.

Dowdle, Rogers, Mason, and Talbot have this in common: they expand the boundaries of Reconstruction by including Mormons in Washington's wider assertions of power from the 1840s to the turn of the century. Dowdle and Talbot link that assertion to others—Southern slaveholders, Roman Catholics in the Southwest, Chinese, and Indians. It's a necessary expansion, I think, if we are to appreciate fully the remaking of the central government's relationship with the new nation's various parts. Their perspective on power is that of the actor in the story—that is, the central government, as expressed via Congress and the president. In her essay Angela Hudson reminds us that such a perspective is not enough. Any consideration of power and its exercise during these years must include perspectives of both actors and those acted upon. She brings that to a sharp point by juxtaposing the experiences of Mormons with another target of federal power: Indian peoples. Washington muscled both of them during the years of Reconstruction. So, can they both be honestly joined inside one process? Specifically, Mormons were driven first from Missouri to Nauvoo, then from Nauvoo to the Great Basin. By that time roughly a hundred thousand Indians had been removed from the East to lands beyond the Missouri, and in the years ahead tens of thousands more in the West would be removed from their homelands to Indian Territory or to reduced and confined reservations. Weren't these two experiences, the expulsion of the Saints and the removals of Indians, essentially the same thing?

No, answers Hudson. As she puts it in the refreshingly blunt title of her essay, "There Is No Mormon Trail of Tears." Hudson stresses two good points. "Removal" is a dicey term to apply to both experiences. The Saints had only briefly alit in Missouri and Illinois when mobs and militias sent them packing. They had arrived there on a journey starting in New York and pausing in Ohio. However strongly the Mormons claimed deep spiritual roots in the country of the Hill Cumorah in upstate New York and the proclaimed Zion of Jackson County, Missouri, theirs was a history of westering scarcely a quarter century old. Indian peoples from New York and Alabama to Oregon and Nevada by contrast were uprooted from homelands they had inhabited often for unimaginable stretches of time, places to which they were bound so intimately that leaving was a severing of identity itself. Forced to leave such places: now *that* was a trail of tears. And in fact, Hudson points out, the Mormons themselves were complicit in the conquest and dispossession of Indians. They might claim them as spiritual kin, the Lamanites of old, but Mormons also saw themselves as Christians on a civilizing mission, which necessarily required Indians to surrender their cultures and most often their lands. Thus, Mormons were not victims in a more widely defined trail of tears. They were, rather, among the perpetrators of it.

This is a crucial point, one that Mason also makes in his essay on the federal state's steady monopolizing of legitimate violence. Washington sent troops against Deseret when Mormon leaders defied federal authority, he points out, but it was perfectly fine with Mormon leaders using their independent power to suppress and remove Indian peoples when they were in the way. But Hudson's good point in turn, by focusing on fundamental differences among those acted upon, should not obscure their similarities—indeed their equation—from the perspective of those doing the acting, the shapers and executors of federal power. She takes aim in particular at my own partnering of Indians, freed peoples, Hispanics, and others under a Greater Reconstruction. My partnering was of those groups as objects of essentially the same federal intent. But I make clear as well that the essential natures and histories of those groups, and certainly the consequences of Washington's policies toward them, were greatly different, and the differences of Indian peoples were of another order from the rest. One key to fitting all their stories within a single national narrative is to hold in tension, on the one hand, Washington's determination to see them as much the same and, on the other hand, the widely varied realities among the groups and their stories. Such a stereo optical view is our best bet to give those events the sense of depth they need.

It is a point that might be applied as well to the three remaining essays by Clyde Milner, Eric Eliason, and Jared Farmer. The parallel in question here involves not the American Indian Trail of Tears but the Lost Cause, the romanticized recreation of the Confederacy as a nation of benighted victims. Milner's, Eliason's, and Farmer's focus is less on dissecting and analyzing actual events of the day than on looking back on them—or, rather, looking back on how Mormons and Southerners looked back. The issue here involves not power but historical identity. As with the Trail of Tears, the basic question is, if there is a reasonable parallel between the central government's policies toward the two groups during Reconstruction, in this case Mormons and Confederates, does the parallel extend further? In shaping their collective identities around these years, did both groups develop a mythic vision of martyred defeat, a Lost Cause that continues to inspire an ennobling resentment toward Washington? For anyone looking even briefly at the question, the answer comes quickly: no. That just as quickly brings a second question: why not?

In Eliason's spirited (and often very funny) essay, he lays out several answers, starting with his own question: if there was a Lost Cause, just what did the Mormons lose? The only measurable physical confrontation with Washington was the "Utah War" of 1856–57. Its causes, if exaggerated at the time, were genuine—Eliason's defense ("We didn't start anything") overreaches a bit—but as wars go, despite Deseret's overheated rhetoric, this one was pretty thin beer. There were casualties, but, setting aside the Mountain Meadows Massacre, they were few, certainly in contrast to the war triggered by the South's challenge to Washington's authority. Federal control was effectively shared with LDS leadership from that point on, with nothing remotely resembling the occupation of the defeated Confederacy. In the end, Eliason writes, Mormons "trimmed only polygamy and theo-democracy." Some would say (and I would agree) that surrendering "only" that, especially the latter, came close to abandoning a critical part of the Mormon church's avowed divine purpose, and that, at least, seems pretty close to a cause that was lost. Mormons did, however, retain much of their domination of their region, and their leaders have continued to act with a powerful hand in secular affairs. Far from hanging on to a persistent defiance in the face of defeat, they have labored in much of the twentieth century to portray themselves as firmly in the American mainstream—and this in the face of grotesque popular depictions of them.

Milner pays particular attention to that last intriguing point. As defiant Southerners were establishing their separateness by monumentalizing their heroic defeat, Northerners were buying that narrative in the name of national reconciliation. Meanwhile, as Mormons were doing their all for their own reconciliation, embracing fully a national identity, they were being portrayed in popular culture, through fictional potboilers and more than forty films, as a corrupt and subversive people apart. Obviously, the nation had more at stake in reconciling with the South than with a small religious minority in the desert West, but the juxtaposition is striking and emphasizes if nothing else the crosscurrents always there within efforts to find a national cultural unity. In any case, Milner focuses on the evolving celebration of Pioneer Day to track Mormons' rewriting of their narrative of identity. It no longer told of a people put-upon and expelled. The Saints now had come to the shores of the Great Salt Lake not in an exodus from oppression but as actors in an epic of expansion, partnered now with the other mythic stories of heroic westering. Their cause was now the nation's, and so it was not lost but won.

Farmer's smart essay reiterates and adds to these points. Even when the migration narrative's focus is kept on founding Deseret, its pioneering overtones jibe nicely with, to use the current academic term, settler colonialism. It has a "kernel of Americanness" that allowed the Mormon church to ease a story of religious mission with little grinding of gears into one of national destiny. Still, Farmer adds, there are echoes of the former among today's Mormons. Fundamentalists openly practicing "the Principle" of plural marriage, the movement to shift public lands from Washington's control to Utah's, and recent public reminders, in the face of Muslim-bashing, of earlier federal assaults on the Saints and their practices—these have their resemblance, however tepid, to the far more vigorous and apparently deathless hostility toward Washington in the former Confederacy.

Farmer also stresses a theme present but largely subdued in the other essays: race. A key reason Mormons were able so easily to position themselves as heroic pioneers was demographic. They were overwhelmingly white. As the images of an autocratic and treasonous Mormon society faded, Farmer reminds us, mainstream America could hail its success and prosperity as a "triumphal and implicitly racist story" that fit comfortably within that of the nation at large.

His reminder is vital to situating LDS history inside those crucial years of the mid-nineteenth century. Whatever happened—however the federal government applied its power to this or that region or group—the consequences unfolded inside a racial order that bent those consequences in different directions.

Late in the seminar John Mack Faragher made the point succinctly. We had discussed Washington's policies toward Mormons, freed peoples, Indians, and Hispanics. If we should consider all those policies as part of Reconstruction (and Faragher had serious doubts whether we should), and if the general goal of them all had been to integrate those groups with reasonable comfort into the national family, where was the success? Freed people were soon relegated to the bottom of the Southern economic and social order; Indian peoples scraped barely by on bleak reservations; Hispanics were marginalized and, like freed people and Indians, demeaned and dismissed in popular culture. The results are with us today. Go a-Googling to find the poorest counties in the nation, and you will see that most in the top ten are dominated by those three groups. Only the Mormons prospered. That was partly, it can be argued, because they retained far greater autonomy than the others—the former slaves abandoned to the strictures of Southern power, Indians saddled under an incompetent and corrupt bureaucracy, and Hispanics denied the land and resources of their immediate world. But another difference is obvious. Mormons were white. Especially after they abandoned polygamy and as the canards about them fell away, they found the avenues toward economic, social, and political power far wider and more accessible than for the others.

The Mormon experience thus reminds us of the considerable differences among the various groups, South and West, playing roles in the remaking of the nation in the middle of the nineteenth century. It is a useful exercise to look for themes that might tie together their experiences into a single satisfying story. Whether an expanded version of the traditional Reconstruction narrative can serve as that story inspired some spirited give-and-take in our seminar. If we stretch its boundaries too far, as Rachel St. John suggests in her essay, its lessons can lose their shape and sharpness. Reconstruction might begin to look less like a historical era and more like a pair of Spandex shorts. I find the idea of a Greater Reconstruction both accommodating and illuminating for events during the thirty years or so after our expansion to the Pacific. And, if nothing else, the seminar producing these essays ended with unanimous agreement that however we might label that crucial period and its shifting of the national narrative, its perspective must be truly continental. That is, however we choose to tell the story, the American West must have a prominent place in it. Only when it does will we have a chance to chart the trajectory of those changes and to gauge how they shaped American life from then until now.

Notes

1. Jimmy L. Bryan Jr., *The American Elsewhere: Adventures and Manliness in the Age of Expansion* (Lawrence: University Press of Kansas, 2017).

2. Janice E. Thomson, *Mercenaries, Pirates, and Sovereigns: State-building and Extraterritorial Violence in Early Modern Europe* (Princeton, N.J.: Princeton University Press, 1996).

3. Richard White, *The Republic for Which It Stands: The United States during Reconstruction and the Gilded Age, 1865–1896* (New York: Oxford University Press, 2017); Louis S. Warren, *Buffalo Bill's America: William Cody and the Wild West Show* (New York: Vintage, 2006).

PART I
Background Issues

Interlude 1

Wrestling Practice

Anne Hyde

In 1830, 1850, and 1870, the United States didn't know what it wanted to be when it grew up. By 1890 it did. Such maturity came out of practice. Everyone drilled to preserve their own vision of a fully imagined United States: indigenous nations, squatters, private adventurers, international companies, religious sects, and federal troops. All the decisions about what nationhood and citizenship meant, who could participate, what the benefits and responsibilities of citizenship might be, and who would enforce those rules and how, were hammered out by bitter experience in the nineteenth-century West.

Few observers would have predicted what emerged on the far end of that process. Mormons are a case in point. After being driven out of Missouri and Illinois, despised as an aberration and the moral equivalent of enslavers, and marched upon by the U.S. Army, by the 1890s they found an uneasy place in the United States. The bar of citizenship, tempered over decades, could now be stepped over by Mormons. Reconstruction, usually viewed as the first episode of federal power grandly deployed, and specific to the rebellious states of the South, is actually a much larger and longer endeavor.

The United States, ever expanding in population and landmass from the 1790s to the 1850s, bumped up against both weak and powerful New World and European empires, but also against new communities born and bred in its own republican womb. Buoyant religious sects, obstreperous squatters, and confident filibusters created chaos everywhere state, national, local, or cultural borders dared appear. Expansion, because it was never into empty space, created resistance of all kinds. Both rebels and defiant scofflaws presented difficult and expensive political challenges for a nation trying to enforce laws and borders. Sometimes stopping these people from breaking laws required sending out the army or other federal enforcers. Those moments turned what government officials and theorists might have imagined would have been a century of nationhood and orderly development into a century of war.[1]

The chasm between what government aspired to do and what it could actually do, especially in the West, became grimly obvious. Managing opposition from indigenous nations, imperial armies, filibusters, border jumpers, and Mormons required state administrative and military capacity that cost money. The era of most rapid expansion spawned an equally vigorous era of rebellion and challenge that the federal government couldn't control. As Elliott West and our authors here point out, nothing about this was exceptional. New republics, like the United States in the early nineteenth century, produced newly confident citizens, including groups like the Mormons or evangelical abolitionists who consistently defied authority.

Three important fights in the 1850s strengthened both sides: sectional violence in Kansas, Indian War from the Pacific coast to Texas and Minnesota, and Mormon intransigence and then war in Utah. The tactics involved legal strategies, military force, and cultural warfare. But the context here was the infantilizing position of being territories and not states. Territories were weak. The federal government appointed governors, judges, and a range of officials and decided how and when a state conducted business. Whether in Kansas, Wisconsin, Minnesota, Indian Territory, or Utah, federal supervision and inept outsiders appointed to run things made residents resentful and sometimes defiant.

None of these wrestling matches between federal entities and the rebellious groups who pushed back were the same. Angela Pulley Hudson's essay makes clear the differences between Mormon exodus and Indian removal. Both means and ends diverged. Mobs, aided and abetted by the governor of Missouri, drove Mormon communities out of their homes in Missouri and Illinois in an era of common mob violence. Indian removal, however, was always government policy: sober decisions to use decades of military force, to ink acres of paper with treaties, and to build an entire arm of the federal government in the effort to destroy Native nations. That is different than the governor of Missouri enabling traditional extralegal violence and vigilante justice to do vicious work against innocent Mormons.

Both were heinous, but as Hudson notes, the end result placed Mormons "inside the bounds of Christian Anglo-American civilization, not outside of them, as Indians were presumed to be." And Brigham Young's brinkmanship in 1857, when he resolutely defied President James Buchanan's orders even when delivered by a U.S. Army on the march, succeeded. He didn't lose control of Deseret or Utah Territory. Compare that to Cherokee or Navajo leaders who took resolute stands in North Carolina in 1837 or New Mexico in 1862: their people ended up stateless, starving, or dead.

The federal government lost a lot of these battles in the 1850s. Whether this was lack of will or might is hard to tell. For example, after the U.S. war against Mexico and its huge cession of land, the U.S. government wanted to build a railroad despite a host of newly troublesome rebels like Comanche warriors, former Mexican Army soldiers, Texas and New Mexico homesteaders, and slaveholders. Choosing to bring troops in and, after gold rushes in California and Colorado, to bring precious metal out, the army and powerful financial interests agreed on the strategic value of a railroad connecting East and West. Even so, because of implacable and skilled foes in Native armies and the U.S. Congress, no railroad could be built. Similarly the U.S. Army couldn't stop powerful Indian nations on the northern and southern plains or in the Pacific Northwest from killing anyone who marched into their homelands.

However, constant struggle taught lessons about legal, military, and cultural tactics. And as in wrestling, even if one side won, the other side got a little stronger with each pushback. Both winners and losers came out of these contests meaner, leaner, and less likely to submit. When the California gold rush and its hundreds of thousands of migrants brought another dose of disorder to the situation and brought the Mormon State of Deseret and then Utah Territory squarely into national view, both the Mormons and the federal government had practiced. The federal government had to do something, even if James Buchanan really didn't want to, fearing the message that federal action around the Mormons might send to slaveholders in the South. Slowly and carefully, U.S. troops marched toward Utah's more than forty thousand Mormons in that winter of 1857. Slowly and carefully, both sides negotiated new rules of citizenship. The Mormons had fled Missouri and Illinois, but now they prepared to stand and protect Utah. In the end, they didn't have to battle an army.

The Mormons' biggest challenge, however, came from a different direction. Another part of the shifting moment, as the authors in this volume point out vividly, emerged at the cultural level. Ideas about marriage and family leapt into the antebellum era's wrestling ring. A different rebellion, this time a social one, saw large families grounded by patriarchal control replaced, in the ideal, by smaller companionate marriages. Affection, not power, was supposed to be at their hearts. Families that operated as large corporate working units, such as polygamous families, now seemed like relics. In fact, as Christine Talbot points out, such families became one of the "twin relics of barbarism": polygamy and slavery united as entwined threats to a modern republic.

None of this was peripheral. Mormon rebellion, both on the political and familial front, stabbed at the heart of nation-building, and everyone knew it. Patrick Mason makes a crucial point in his essay that the Mormon case illustrates evolving notions of who should enforce the law or cultural norms: local communities or a central state. In the 1850s that question wasn't settled. But clearly by the 1890s when Mormon men redefined themselves as republican men by acting like citizens—taking Indian land and denouncing polygamy—their episodes of extralegal violence became tolerable. Violence evolved from a community and individual undertaking to the central role of a legitimate state.

After long practice in the territories of Kansas, Nebraska, New Mexico, and especially Utah, and then in the halls of Congress during the Civil War, a new form of federal power and willingness to use it—Reconstruction—arrived. Rachel St. John argues that Reconstruction was quite different from the chaotic era of the early Republic when everyone challenged what the state could do. After Reconstruction and the long legal fight with Mormons, the job of the federal government and what would not be tolerated from citizens was clearer. Seceding from the United States or making separate laws in defiance of the Constitution was beyond the pale of citizenship.

Nonetheless, Americans of all sorts, their rebellious muscles strong and practiced, would continue to challenge that clarity: lynching, marching, suing, squatting, and killing each other, but no longer declaring and fighting wars on behalf of their own states.

Note

1. Paul Frymer, *Building An American Empire: The Era of Territorial and Political Expansion* (Princeton, N.J.: Princeton University Press, 2017); and Steven Hahn, *A Nation without Borders: The United States and Its World in an Age of Civil Wars, 1830–1910* (New York: Viking, 2016) present entirely different views of nation-building, but they are both useful for thinking about expansion, power, and Mormons.

= 1 =

There Is No Mormon Trail of Tears

Roots, Removals, and Reconstructions

Angela Pulley Hudson

In the winter of 1838, nearly twelve thousand Missouri Mormons endured a forced migration into western Illinois, crossing the Mississippi River in wretched and withering conditions. The Cherokee Trail of Tears took place that same bitter winter, as some sixteen thousand Cherokee men, women, and children were marched from their homelands in the East to territory on the western side of the Mississippi, many on foot and bereft of winter clothing.[1] Both groups had endured military occupation and suffered plunder, beatings, and rape at the hands of angry mobs and opportunistic individuals. Both the Mormons and the Cherokees were accused of political presumption. Both saw their leaders unjustly jailed and had their printing presses destroyed. Both unsuccessfully petitioned federal leaders to intervene on their behalf. The similarities between the two episodes and the very fact of their coincidence in time and place suggests a striking convergence of experience. As I and others have noted elsewhere, Mormons and their opponents frequently mobilized rhetoric linking church members to Native peoples. But there were vast and significant differences between the two phenomena. Similarity is not equivalency, and all persecution is not the same.

Nevertheless there was a persistent tendency, particularly among antebellum anti-Mormons, to compare Mormons and Indians. The logic deployed to justify removing both groups reveals some parallels on both local and federal levels and the resemblance often appears in bold relief. As Paul Reeve notes in his study of the racialization of nineteenth-century Mormons, "Like their Native American counterparts, Mormons were confronted with treaties of removal, forced from their homes, faced an extermination order, endured additional extermination rhetoric, were dehumanized as nits that make lice, and relegated to a diminishing land base."[2] Both groups were considered American "problems." And it could be argued, as Elliott West does in the introduction to this volume, that Mormons and American Indians (among others) were subjected to disciplinary state policies that bring to mind Reconstruction. However, the Mormon faith emerged from the very "heart of Anglo-American culture," a culture itself incubated in colonialism. Like other Americans, Mormons were perpetrators and beneficiaries of settler violence, both banal and extraordinary, against indigenous people.[3] Considering the apparent resemblances between anti-Mormon and anti-Indian rhetoric and policies can illuminate questions of state power, Americanization, and intolerance during the nineteenth century. But acknowledging that the history of the United States is a history of colonialism in which Mormons have been enthusiastic, if not always welcome, participants complicates the implied commensurability of Mormon and Indian removal experiences.

This essay argues that, despite some resemblance in the particularities of Mormon removal and Indian removal, comparing the two and labeling both part of what West calls a "Greater Reconstruction" elides both "Mormon complicity in Indian dispossession" and the very nature of settler colonialism.[4] I contend that there is no Mormon "Trail of Tears" and further assert that American Indians were not "reconstructed" in either greater or lesser terms. Although West's formulation of an expanded and expansive era of Reconstruction is a productive model to think with, and while several essays in this collection make compelling claims linking state-formation to the "reconstruction" of Mormons and other populations, indigenous people occupy a unique position as original possessors of the continent. Omitting that fact by lumping them together with other "others" is itself part of the settler colonial apparatus. As Jodi A. Byrd has argued, "Transforming American Indians into a minority within a country of minorities is the fait accompli of the colonial project that disappears [Native] sovereignty, land rights, and self-governance."[5]

This chapter first considers the founding of the Mormon religion, early Mormon attitudes toward Native North Americans, and the roots of Mormon removal. It briefly addresses the origins of Indian removal and compares key tropes and images in both episodes that demonstrate their apparent resonance.

The essay considers Mormon attitudes toward Native peoples and their forced emigration, and highlights the important differences between Indian removal and Mormon removal. These differences—and their consequences—are reducible to one key, and perhaps quite obvious, point: Mormons were not forced *from* ancestral homelands, but rather embarked on (and celebrated) their migration *to* a new homeland. Moreover, the "zionward" journeys of Mormon pioneers required both the ideological and physical displacement of indigenous peoples. The essay concludes with a discussion of why Indian removal and subsequent federal policies toward Native people do not fit within the concept of a "Greater Reconstruction," despite its utility within other analyses in this volume.

———

In the fall of 1830, shortly after Choctaw leaders signed the first treaty of the removal era, a handful of hopeful missionaries set off from central New York to visit the western Indians. The men intended to spread word of a new religion that would come to be known as Mormonism. Traveling west through Buffalo, they stopped briefly to preach to the Seneca Nation at Cattaraugus and then continued along the southern shore of Lake Erie, stopping next in Ohio, in an area known as the Western Reserve.[6] Americans in the vicinity were engaged in the business of progress, building canals, advancing steamboat navigation, and rapidly expelling the remainder of the region's Native inhabitants; between 1817 and 1825, twenty-five treaties separated tribes from their lands, including those belonging to the Shawnees, Wyandottes, Potawatomis, Ottawas, Ojibwas (Anishinaabes), Senecas, and Delawares. The missionary band that arrived in Ohio in 1830 was motivated by the religious prophet Joseph Smith Jr., who told of mysterious buried golden plates containing an ancient history of North America, and their hope of bringing this new religion to the Indians then receding into the West. They carried the text Smith had translated, called the Book of Mormon, and urgently sought converts to help them proselytize American Indians, a people they called the Lamanites.[7]

According to the Book of Mormon, diasporic peoples had arrived in the Americas from the ancient Middle East after the fall of Babel. Most prominent were the fratricidal factions of Nephi and Laman, named for two sons of Lehi, whose family had fled Jerusalem around 600 B.C.E. A millennium later, the Lamanites managed to destroy the Nephites, only to have their own civilization fall to ruin. According to the Book of Mormon, those Lamanites who survived were among the ancestors of American Indians. Although they were a degraded race, their skin darkened by their transgressions, the Lamanites held a special place in the prophetic vision offered by the Mormon testament. A prophecy held that they would one day have the "scales fall from their eyes," and by acknowledging the truth of Christianity would become lighter and "delightsome" (2 Nephi 30:6).[8] One modern scholar has gone so far as to describe the Book of Mormon as not merely a "record of the 'Lamanite' or Native American people," but a "manifesto of their destiny."[9]

As such, Smith's keenest interest was for the Mormons to settle to the west, alongside or among the Lamanites whose fate was intertwined with that of the church.[10] And so, within a year of the faith's founding, the people who would be known as the Latter-day Saints (LDS) began to migrate to Missouri, where they would establish their Zion "on the borders by the Lamanites" (Doctrine and Covenants 28:9). Sudden and violent anti-Mormon sentiment soon emerged among Missourians who feared that their new neighbors harbored abolitionist sentiments, an intention to unite with the Indians, and a plan for political control. To make matters worse, the radical new settlers declared their intention to righteously overspread the land they believed God had provided for them, and they did little to conceal their belief that Independence, Missouri, was the New Jerusalem.

By mid-1833, anti-Mormonism, once limited to scurrilous editorials and obscure pamphlets, exploded into full-blown vigilante violence. Newly settled Mormon families in Missouri were targeted in the ensuing attacks. Recognizing the need to either insulate or isolate the Mormons from their opponents in the state, the Missouri legislature organized an "Indian-style reservation," where the offending Saints could live "safe from intrusion and molestation," but under the watchful eye of a government superintendent.[11] The borders of the reserved lands proved entirely inadequate to protect the Mormons and anti-Mormons from one another, however, and by 1838, angry mobs were driving the Saints from the state.[12] Among other charges, non-Mormon Missourians contended that the "sect of 'pretended Christians' had a corrupting influence on slaves, offered free blacks a share in their Zion, and boasted of their imminent possession of the county," and accused them repeatedly of "Indian tampering."[13]

While anti-Mormons largely misunderstood Mormon intentions with regard to American Indians, it is perhaps unsurprising that Mormonism, the most successful homegrown religious tradition in the United States—a nation that has used "Indianness" to express everything from anti-tax revolt to modern environmentalism—is deeply invested in indigeneity. As suggested above, the church's early attention to American Indians stemmed from several sources. The impulse to evangelize the Indians, although shared among many Protestant denominations, took on a distinct connotation for early Mormons because Native peoples of the Americas were seen as an essential part of the faith's millenarian promise. Both the Book of Mormon (e.g., "impart the word of God to their brethren, the Lamanites," Mosiah 28:1) and Joseph Smith's early revelations (e.g., "And now, behold, I say unto you that you shall go unto the Lamanites and preach my gospel unto them," Doctrine and Covenants 28:8) communicated the missionary imperative that inspired the new religion's followers to proselytize "the Lamanites, residing in the west."[14] Converts carried this directive with them as they moved westward, trying and often failing to bring the modern descendants of the ancient Lamanites into the fold.

Owing to the special place accorded Lamanites and their descendants within LDS theology, American Indians were considered a sort of "spiritual kin" by some early Mormons, who likewise came to think of themselves as diasporic and persecuted.[15] This was one of many ways that nineteenth-century Mormon believers "defined themselves as a people[,] by stressing their distinctiveness from the Gentiles" and aligning their circumstances with those of American Indians.[16] Explaining this affinity, Joy Porter argues that Native people held a special place in Smith's "spiritual imagination" and that he was heavily influenced by widespread antebellum discussions about Indian origins (in relationship to the biblical account of Genesis).[17] Smith's personal fascination with Indians, combined with the broader national romance of the noble savage, provided early converts a steady dose of myth that "mixed the themes of the last days, the destiny of the Native American, and the promised New Jerusalem."[18] A key component of Smith's pronouncements was that American Indians were integral to the "gathering" of peoples that formed the necessary precondition for the founding of Zion and the second coming of Christ. Proclaiming the intertwined fates of Mormons and Indians might have signaled the Saints' interest in and sympathy for the plight of Native peoples, but it also worked to obscure the participation of converts in displacing those very people from their homelands, in part by claiming that Mormons and Indians were "fellow lost Israelites."[19]

Although the Book of Mormon does not posit that Native North Americans descend from a Lost Tribe of Israel, it was nevertheless regarded as a true account of their origins, their own tribal creation stories notwithstanding. And it shares with the Lost Tribes thesis a belief in the essential foreignness of American Indians—that they were not original to this land but arrived from elsewhere, much like the Europeans who would arrive later. This belief has a long history that preceded the establishment of the Mormon faith. But it gained momentum during the antebellum period and particularly during the era of Indian removal in part because it answered both the theological question of why the Bible had not accounted for this unique and isolated population and the ideological question of whether or not American Indians were truly indigenous to the continent and thus had a prior right to the soil that settlers coveted. As one scholar helpfully concludes, the theory of Hebraic origins reassured early Mormons that their beliefs did not contravene the biblical account of a single divine creation, while also distancing them from complicity in the displacement of American Indians, who were, after all, the progeny of a diasporic tribe themselves.[20]

In a more insidious vein, the notion that Native North Americans were not the rightful possessors of their territories often hinged on rhetoric that depicted them as "wandering savages." During the early national and antebellum periods, populous and long-settled indigenous nations in the eastern part of the United States, including the Cherokees, whose experience of forced relocation has come to stand in for Indian removal more broadly, were increasingly characterized as "nomadic" and "roaming." Mormons were not immune to this thinking. Jacob Hamblin, who helped shape LDS Indian policy in the West and who has long been lauded as an example of Mormon magnanimity toward Native peoples, described the lands of his youth as an "unsettled wilderness inhabited only by a few Indians or Lamanites."[21]

Indeed, depicting Native peoples as "unsettled" and incapable or unwilling to "improve" the land was an essential part of the colonial mindset, providing ideological justification for dispossessing and ultimately relocating them to a territory west of the Mississippi River.[22] Michigan territorial governor Lewis Cass distilled the rationale in a January 1830 issue of the *North American Review*. "A tribe of wandering hunters," Cass proclaimed, "depending upon the chase for support, and deriving it from the forests, and rivers, and lakes, of an immense continent, have a very imperfect possession of the country over which they roam." When colonists first arrived in Native North America, Cass maintained, they "found it in a state of nature, *traversed, but not occupied*, by wandering hordes" [emphasis added].[23] This perspective was encoded in the Indian removal act itself and emphasized by President Andrew Jackson in his subsequent message to Congress lauding the effects of the legislation: "What good man would prefer a country covered with forests and ranged by a few thousand savages, to our extensive republic, studded with cities, towns, and prosperous farms[?]"[24]

No principle was mobilized more frequently in discussions of "the Indian problem" than that of civilization—or Native peoples' lack thereof. The idea of removing American Indians to the West existed at the founding of the nation, informed federal policies that were (and sometimes still are) seen as humane and charitable, and resulted in a series of Supreme Court cases that forever altered federal Indian affairs and the course of national history. The "civilization" plan or program was a hallmark of early federal Indian policy and is most closely associated with Thomas Jefferson, who championed it enthusiastically. Jefferson argued that Indian men could be taught to plant small farms, while Indian women should become spinners and weavers, emulating Anglo-American women. A belief that the self-sufficient yeoman farmer was the epitome of American manhood underlay this policy and later undergirded Mormon "pioneering," but it was also quite blatantly tied to the acquisition of Native peoples' lands.

The ideology of "improvement" unequivocally required Indians to surrender their territory. Abandoning the hunt (which requires vast territory on which to follow game seasonally) and becoming small-scale farmers meant American Indians would need less land. Jefferson described the civilization plan thus: "When they withdraw themselves to the culture of a small piece of land, they will perceive how useless to them are their extensive forests, and will be willing to pare them off from time to time in exchange for necessaries for their farms and families." Even as he proposed reforming Native ways of life to more closely resemble those of Anglo-Americans, Jefferson was busy developing concrete mechanisms for effecting their dispossession. To accelerate the process, he explained that trading houses (known as "factories") would be established in their territories, and "we shall push our trading uses, and be glad to see the good and influential individuals among them run in debt, because we observe that when these debts get beyond what the individuals can pay, they become willing to lop them off by a cession of lands."[25] Over the first two decades of the nineteenth century, the federal government continued to promote the civilization program, sending agents into indigenous communities and encouraging missionaries to spread the campaign. The Mormons wanted to be a part of this effort, but were continually rebuffed by federal agents who feared a "threatened association" of Mormons and Indians and worried that the Saints would not be effective civilizers.[26]

To a greater extent than any other Indian nation or tribe in North America, the Cherokees fulfilled many of the most extravagant expectations of the "civilization" program.[27] During the first quarter of the nineteenth century, the Cherokee Nation essentially remade itself in the image of the United States. Great numbers of Cherokee people became small-scale farmers and some developed plantations, complete with African-descended slaves, like their elite white neighbors; they built roads, established a newspaper, created a bicameral form of government, adopted written laws, and ratified a constitution, and many converted to Christianity. Their leaders heeded the secretary of war's advice when he told them, "You see that the Great Spirit has made our form of Society stronger than yours, and you must submit to adopt ours, if you wish to be happy . . . Without this, you will find you will have to emigrate or become extinct as a people." But, in fact, no amount of acculturation would be enough, because the Cherokees and their Indian neighbors were situated on some of the most resource-rich lands in the South. As the 1820s wore on, the patience of states bordering the Indian nations wore thin.

When, as part of their civilized reforms, the Cherokees ratified their new constitution in 1828, asserting themselves to be a sovereign and independent nation with complete jurisdiction over their own territory and affairs, it raised the hackles of neighboring state Georgia, whose leaders believed their state had jurisdiction over Cherokee territory. Georgia statesmen had long argued that the federal government had been negligent in fulfilling the Compact of 1802, an accord signed during Jefferson's presidency as a final effort to settle the western claims of the original thirteen states. In exchange for the western land Georgia relinquished, the federal government had promised to terminate Indian title to lands within the remaining boundaries of the state "as soon as it can be done peaceably and on reasonable conditions."[28] The election of Andrew Jackson, which coincided with both the ratification of the Cherokee constitution and the discovery of gold on Cherokee land, brought the issue into further relief.

Importantly, as I and others have written elsewhere, the removal of southern Indians was inextricably bound up with the expansion of chattel slavery. The Native nations of the South were problematic not merely because they asserted a sovereignty inconsistent with state and federal claims, but also because they remained in possession of the fertile lands of the cotton belt that white Americans aspired to develop using the forced labor of African-descended slaves. As Joel W. Martin observes, "The antebellum white South, devoted to slavery at all costs, was expanded, empowered, and consolidated by Indian Removal."[29] Civilization rhetoric aside, removal enabled the spread of chattel slavery, which enabled the growth of domestic and international commerce, emboldening the nation to further expand its borders and contributing to sectional debates that culminated in the Civil War.

Indian removal did not spring fully formed from the head of Andrew Jackson, however, nor did it suddenly become tenable in the 1830s. Nearly all treaties signed between 1815 and 1830 had included clauses incentivizing the voluntary relocation of eastern Indians to western lands, and the combination of predatory lending practices, "civilization" programs, and outright theft pressured some individuals and communities to acquiesce. But Indian removal didn't become official policy until 1830. In May of that year, Congress passed the Indian removal bill, authorizing the president to negotiate treaties to permanently relocate eastern American Indians beyond the Mississippi River. In Jackson's address to Congress, he argued that removal was not only in the best interests of the United States, but also of the Indians themselves. And, referencing both the Compact of 1802 and similar controversies with other states, he asserted that a wholesale relocation of eastern Indians would "put an end" to conflicts between the states and the federal government, signaling the importance of Indian affairs to states' rights debates of the era.[30]

While the call for relocating eastern Indian peoples reached fever pitch, Joseph Smith was busily translating and disseminating a "manifesto of their destiny." Thus, at the very moment that a final solution to the Indian problem was emerging from federal and local authorities, a narrative of Indian dispersal was sinking into the minds of early Mormon converts. Predictably, these converts were not opposed to Indian removal. On the contrary, many saw the displacement of eastern Native groups as the fulfillment of prophecies regarding the gathering of peoples in preparation for the end of days. The first periodical of the church, the *Evening and Morning Star*, suggested that federal Indian relocation policies were evidence of the nations of Israel being brought back together by the hand of God. Far from lamenting the forced relocation of indigenous peoples from their ancestral homelands, the Mormon faithful celebrated Indian removal.

For members of the early church, the forced emigration of Native people was the key to the creation of a New Jerusalem, a boundless Zion where red and white believers would ultimately flourish together.[31] For instance, the *Evening and Morning Star* declared in 1832 that news of the arrival of displaced Kickapoos, a group that rivaled the Delawares for the unfathomable number of removals they endured, was surely "glad tidings."[32] During the same years, Cherokee memorialists protested their "oppression," vigorously resisted the "robbery" of their homelands, and decried their anticipated "forcible expulsion . . . from the land of their nativity," while Mormon worshippers heralded Indian removal as "the great doings of the Lord" and proclaimed that "it affords us great joy to see the work of the gathering go on so rapidly."[33]

Despite the tendency of persecuted Mormon faithful to proclaim their kinship to and celebrate the "gathering" of American Indians, they nevertheless often regarded the concrete presence of Native people in their midst as an annoyance, burden, or direct threat. Shortly after the first group of converts migrated to Missouri, elders wrote back to Mormons in Ohio and cautioned that although the gathering of the Israelites was cause for celebration, "the disadvantages of settling in a new country, you know, are many and great" and advised congregants to refrain from flocking to Zion until preparations had been made to raise sufficient crops. Chief among the problems of subsistence in the region was that the U.S. government was relocating Indians "or remnants of Joseph" to the vicinity and special status or not, "they must be fed."[34] The gathering of the Lamanites was turning out to be terribly inconvenient.

Over the succeeding decades, fantasies about Lamanite redemption continued to clash with the very real and often troublesome needs and desires of *actual* American Indian peoples who competed with and resisted the Mormons. Some encounters were merely irksome, like when a pair of Mormon migrant children had their carefully picked and cleaned currants confiscated by a laughing Indian.[35] In other cases, diarists wrote of lurking Indians in more menacing terms, particularly near Winter Quarters, the temporary encampment to which persecuted Saints had fled following their expulsion from Illinois.[36] At the time, the Mormons were squatting on Omaha land, so their complaints about the trespasses of local Native people appear hypocritical at best. And it seems the Omahas regarded the Mormons encamped in their territory on much the same terms. Despite concrete promises to help deflect Lakota attacks and abstract notions of Lamanite redemption, Mormon-Indian relations at Winter Quarters mostly revolved around the theft of resources.[37] Mormons took Indian land and timber; Indians took Mormon livestock and food.

Prior to these encounters, Mormon thinkers had already demonstrated that they were influenced by literary and political discourses on the "Indian character," many of which reflected a belief in Native peoples' inherent barbarity. For example, the uncommon religious expressions of early converts in Ohio revealed a rather common Anglo-American vision of Indians as savage, unruly, and bloodthirsty. While professing an earnest desire to proselytize to the Lamanites in the West, some adherents represented Native peoples according to stereotypical images found in popular fiction and sensationalistic journalism. In various episodes of "playing Lamanite," they pretended to "tomahawk and scalp each other, and rip open the bowels and tear out the entrails."[38] And, of course, the very impulse to convert American Indians to the Mormon faith (or any religion other than their own) was itself rooted in a pervasive western ideology that found indigenous cultures wanting and Native peoples inherently lacking.[39] Indeed, as Jared Farmer has put it, "While Mormons inherited from Joseph Smith an unusual racialist perspective on Native Americans," namely that they were descendants of the Lamanites and destined for redemption, "they also inherited a normative racist perspective from Euro-American culture."[40]

The jarring reality of Native people as complex, unpredictable *people* instead of romanticized, idealized future brethren shook Mormon resolve and further distanced them from the Indians with whom they were so frequently linked. Such moments highlighted the "tension in Mormon thought between Indian-as-brother and Indian-as-other; between sympathy and contempt, belief and doubt."[41] That these disjunctures often emerged from differential understandings of land should give us pause. In fact, while many Saints may have held fast to the fantasy of Lamanite conversion and redemption, they had few illusions about how to deal with pesky Indian land claims. For instance, Brigham Young, the new church president following Smith's death in 1844, imitated his Anglo-American forebears, negotiating fraudulent treaties and ultimately seeking government approval for preemptive settlement, a process of extralegal colonization followed by retroactive legitimation that had characterized American expansion from New York to Georgia since independence.

Still, both Mormons and their opponents described the persecution of the LDS converts in terms reminiscent of the rhetoric employed in Indian removal. The synchrony of the two episodes is not enough to explain the concordance. Anne Hyde suggests that both American Indians and Mormons troubled notions of "how settlement should occur and who should benefit from it."[42] Sarah Barringer Gordon asserts that both groups threatened the civilized institutions of American life with their apparent "barbarisms."[43] And Paul Reeve argues that construction of "Mormons as Indians" by their opponents was itself "a motivating factor" in their expulsion.[44] Despite the fact that Mormons were both agents and beneficiaries of Native dispossession, antebellum accounts of Mormon persecution, first in Missouri and then in Illinois, bear a remarkable resemblance to the rhetoric and testimonies surrounding Indian removal, underscoring scholarly and lay characterizations of the two situations as congruent. A few examples will demonstrate the point.

When the citizens of Missouri united to drive Mormons from the state, they warned that if the Saints resisted, they were prepared "to use such means as may be sufficient to remove them."[45] Governor Lilburn Boggs's October 1838 "extermination order" likewise declared that the Mormons should be "treated as enemies, and . . . be exterminated or driven from the state."[46] Meanwhile,

General Winfield Scott, who oversaw the forced removal of the Cherokees, asked them ominously, "Will you . . . by resistance, compel us to resort to arms? . . . Or will you, by flight, seek to hide yourselves in mountains and forests, and thus oblige us to hunt you down?"[47] A few years earlier, the official responsible for the violent expulsion of Sauk and Fox people from their homelands had warned the tribe, "My business is to remove you, peaceably if I can, but *forcibly* if I must!"[48]

Local newspapers and citizen groups could be even more unrestrained in their respective determination to dislodge the Mormons or the Indians in their midst. Consider the declaration of an Illinois newspaper editor who advised his readers, "This is sufficient! War and extermination is inevitable! . . . We have no time for comment, every man will make his own. LET IT BE MADE WITH POWDER AND BALL!!!" A citizens' council echoed the inflammatory tone, declaring, their "readiness to co-operate . . . to exterminate, utterly exterminate" the Mormons whom they believed guilty of threatening their livelihoods if not their lives.[49] What's more, Mormon adversaries explicitly linked their fears of the Saints to concerns about "bloody disasters" in the effort to remove southern Indians and admitted that their "panic" stemmed in part from fear of a Mormon attack in the "Indian style."[50]

The surviving eyewitness narratives of the two concurrent episodes also resonate with each other. Just a few months before the Cherokee removal was to begin in earnest, Elias Hutchings described the rise of anti-Mormon violence in Missouri. Mobs began to roam the settlements of church members first with the intent to "rob and plunder and to destroy property," and later, he alleged, "marching in companies falling upon the brethren and killing in most inhuman maner [sic]." He summarized Gentile persecution of the Mormons like this: "Trule the seens to those who witnessed what my eyes have beheld was heart rending how we left this state being forced amediately away and not all having teams at their comand and the few teams that was with us was very busy carrying families perhaps one days journey . . . Thus were the saints exposed to the cold rain, and the inclemency of the weather."[51] Similarly, Apostle Parley Pratt narrated his bondage at the hands of anti-Mormon foes, recounting that they "banished his wife and two little infant children from their homes, robbed of their all, to wander in a land of strangers."[52]

Eyewitness accounts of the prolonged effort to remove the Cherokees from the East echo the Mormon descriptions. Eliza Whitmire, formerly enslaved among the Cherokees, recalled the experience of removal saying, "The women and children were driven from their homes, sometimes with blows and close on the heels of the retreating Indians came greedy whites to pillage the Indian's homes, drive off their cattle, horses, and pigs."[53] Cherokees and other Indian southerners were frequently made to travel on foot, leaving traces of their blood in the snow. The lasting image of people forced from their homes and made to march until they bled is one of the most frequently cited recollections of Indian removal and has been passed down in families for generations.[54] Mormons, too, told of their people driven into the harsh winter weather and drew upon the very same image. A petition to Congress, praying for federal intervention, told of Mormons who "fled in every direction, women & children through the dead of Winter marked their footsteps with blood."[55] One Mormon writer vividly committed the image to verse, saying his people were made to "wander forth unfriended by the world . . . / Their children barefoot treat the frozen ground, / And leave their footsteps red with infant blood."[56]

Several years later, after the Mormons had reconstituted themselves on both sides of the Mississippi River and built their new capital at Nauvoo, they again faced local antagonism that ultimately resulted in their expulsion and temporary settlement at Winter Quarters. An observer in Illinois suggested that while "the removal of the Mormons" was supposed to proceed "peaceably, and with all possible dispatch," they were instead subjected to "wanton" acts by those with a "desire to shed blood, or to plunder."[57] Compare this with the testimony of Evan Jones, a missionary who witnessed the forced removal of the Cherokees from their eastern homelands: "The Cherokees are nearly all prisoners. They have been dragged from their houses . . . [which are] left a prey to plunderers, who, like hungry wolves, follow in the train of the captors."[58] Likewise, one account of anti-Mormon violence in Illinois described "a man of near sixty years of age . . . [who] was taken from his house . . . stripped of his clothing, and his back cut to pieces with a whip, for no other reason than because he was a Mormon."[59] Meanwhile, Major Ridge and his son John Ridge, both of whom had reluctantly signed the Treaty of New Echota (1835) agreeing to Cherokee removal west of the Mississippi, lamented the horrific treatment of their people by both citizens and lawmen in Georgia, saying, "The lowest classes of the white people are flogging the Cherokees with cowhides, hickories, and clubs. We are not safe in our houses—our people are assailed by day and night . . . without law or mercy." Despite the fact that the emigration of Native peoples from Georgia was supposed to have occurred "peaceably and on reasonable conditions,"[60] the Ridges grieved, "We shall carry nothing but the scars of the lash on our backs."[61]

These comparisons are not meant to suggest that either Mormons or Native peoples borrowed from one another's description of events. Indeed, one could probably scour narratives of ethnic or religious cleansing from around the world and turn up nearly identical accounts. But these eyewitness and participant testimonies do reflect some key elements that were shared across both expulsions, namely, the unvarnished exercise of state power (in the form of legislation, executive orders, and military mobilization) combined with the equally unvarnished display of avarice and brutality on the part of non-state actors determined to benefit from the removal of the "problem" population. The tendency of Mormon and Native writers to highlight the suffering of women, children, the elderly, and the infirm likewise mirrors rhetorical strategies used worldwide to signal injustices perpetrated by the powerful against the weak, but it also emphasizes in gut-wrenching detail the human cost of state-sanctioned violence.

Ironically, although accounts of Mormon removal and Indian removal resemble one another and despite the fact that the former was partially justified by allegations of "Indian tampering," Mormons and their allies likened the actions of anti-Mormon forces to the inhumane practices of "savage" Indians. When Hutchings confronted a mob in Missouri, he compared them to "uncivilized Indians who are barbarous in their many acts" and chastised them, asking, "And now shall we descend to the savage principles of the savage tribes of the West?"[62] A witness declared that the most violent of the anti-Mormons in Illinois displayed conduct that "would disgrace a horde of savages." Describing the duplicitous agreements Mormons were made to sign as they fled the state, he asked, "Is there a barbarous nation on earth, capable of imposing on an unoffending opponent a more cruel set of terms than is exhibited in these treaties[?]" before concluding, "The Indian Warrior of North America, to the conquered and subdued hero, who had but just wreaked his hands fresh in his brother's blood, for revenge, might equal them."[63] In the same breath that Joseph Smith decried his people's treatment as though they had been "some savage tribe," he drew attention to the barbarity of anti-Mormon forces who attacked the Saints with their "faces painted like Indian warriors . . . committing murder, robbery, and house burning."[64] Despite the seemingly parallel experiences of removed Indians and persecuted Mormons, the special place of Lamanites in LDS theology, and even the report that a Native woman had provided food and shelter to a group of persecuted Saints, the impulse to characterize the "uncivilized" behavior of their foes in terms of Native stereotypes was irresistible.[65] It clearly defines the Mormons as inside the bounds of Christian Anglo-American civilization, not outside of them, as Indians were presumed (by both the Saints and their enemies) to be.

Indeed, nineteenth-century Mormons were not so different from other Americans in their views on Indians as they might have believed or as some of their descendants may wish to believe today. Their proscriptions for Native peoples more closely resembled American ideologies of "civilization" and the paternalism of federal Indian policies than they diverged from them. They cast Indians in savage terms, squatted on tribal land, and concocted schemes to build roads and later railroads through Indian territories.[66] They provoked the Indians and then punished them for reacting. They spoke of themselves as "civilized" and heralded the many "improvements" they made to the lands they settled, while depicting Native people as "filthy, degraded, miserable human beings" undeserving of the continent's bounty, which they squandered through their indolence and stupidity.[67] They dug up Indian graves and put the bones to their own purposes.[68]

For all the "prejudice and persecution" they endured, the Mormons held their own prejudices against the Indians, consistently representing them, in both LDS theology and "pioneer" behavior, as lacking. This "description by deficiency" was a hallmark of colonial ideology from the earliest meetings between Europeans and Native North Americans and characterized even the most sympathetic and doctrinal Mormon views of the Lamanites.[69] Although removal of targeted eastern Indian nations to western territories was largely complete by the end of the 1840s (with the notable exception of the Florida Seminoles), Orson Pratt was right on key with the national project of reforming the Indians when he summarized their position in the fulfillment of prophecy stating that, in time, "many of the Indian nations will become a civilized and Christian people." What was not stated was that Mormon migrants, not only in Utah, but also in Ohio, Missouri, Illinois, Nebraska, and Iowa, were "gathering" on (or colonizing) Indian lands. Both principles (civilization and dispossession) were also at the heart of an evolving federal Indian policy exemplified in treaty language from the 1850s through 1871, which was primarily aimed at creating and enforcing the boundaries of reservations, but also promised that government support would "improve the moral and social condition" of Indian signatories.[70] The reservation movement of the succeeding decades would be cast as "pacification" and official pronouncements would continually promise to "civilize" the Indians of the far West. But like the Jeffersonian policies of the early nineteenth century, the ultimate goal was dispossession and the ultimate fate of the Indians was presumed to be disappearance. Within this context, Mormon migrants committed and benefitted from the "ordinary and systematic violence of colonization."[71]

Laying bare these rather ordinary anti-Indian beliefs and practices—what Mark Rifkin has called "settler common sense"—does not, however, sufficiently put to rest the parallelism seemingly evident in anti-Mormonism and Indian removal or address their relative positions within West's temporally and geographically expanded "Greater Reconstruction."[72] To do that, we need to consider two other interrelated components of the question: namely, that Native peoples, despite Mormon claims to the contrary, *did not* celebrate their forced relocation as a prophetic gathering and that nineteenth-century Mormons *did*.

As noted above, Mormon migration away from the violence of anti-Mormons, although terrifying and painful for those who endured it, was also regarded as the fulfillment of prophecies regarding the gathering of nations. By contrast, indigenous peoples forced to leave their homelands understood their expulsion in the starkest terms as destructive of their communities, their histories, and their very identities. This rather obvious point of distinction can be underscored by attention to the ways in which Native North Americans have historically understood and related to their homelands.

There are myriad sources that we can turn to for evidence of Mormon optimism regarding their migrations from the East to the West, but a few examples will suffice. Speaking of the expulsion from Illinois that sent the Saints into the unorganized territories across the Mississippi, Ann Young recalled, "Notwithstanding the facts of the enforced emigration, the uncertainty of their future, and sacrifices they had been compelled to make, the migrating Mormons were not a uniformly unhappy party, and they managed to make their stay in Winter-Quarters lively, if not merry."[73] Young's reflection appears in an exposé about polygamy that was deeply critical of both Brigham Young (her former husband) and the church in general, but it is her memories of the migration that are most pertinent here. Contrary to her otherwise virulent anti-Mormonism, Young's recollections of the exodus were overwhelmingly positive, even joyful, despite the persecution that necessitated the Saints' relocation and the hardships suffered as a consequence.[74]

Other Mormon migrants recalled their forced flight with greater despair, but nevertheless echoed Young's retrospective claim that they were generally hopeful about what awaited them in the West. Many had lost their homes and possessions and were suffering from illness and exposure as they journeyed from Nauvoo to Winter Quarters and then westward across the interior of the continent. Yet James Little, whose brother died on the trip, remembered, "In the midst of suffering there was comfort and consolation to these people in the thought that they were leaving their enemies. All were cheerful and happy in anticipation of finding a resting place from persecution somewhere in the solitudes of the Rocky Mountains." Looking back brought only pain, but looking forward (meaning westward) was "pleasant." Little concluded, "Yes, it was deliverance from bondage. Better, far, the freedom of the wilderness than the chances of suffering and death from a vindictive populace."[75]

Among the memories the LDS migrants recalled were the traveling songs they sang as they proceeded further and further away from the Gentile menace. Despite or perhaps because of the hardships they endured during the travails that would later be memorialized and heroicized as "pioneering," they raised their voices to celebrate the lands to which they were headed. "The Saints can be supported there," went one song heralding a possible destination beyond the great western mountains, "And taste the sweets of liberty, / In Upper California—O, that's the land for me!" They serenaded each other with fantasies of colonial possession: "We'll go and lift our standard, we'll go there and be free, / We'll go to California, and have our jubilee; / A land that blooms with endless spring, / A land of life and liberty, / With flocks and herds abounding—O, that's the land for me!"[76] As one scholar put it, "Pioneering was the least bizarre aspect of Mormon history."[77] It reflected that great western dream that gripped the nation during the nineteenth century and would sooner rather than later confront the recently removed Indians in their new homes across the Mississippi.

Apart from the spiritual jubilation generated by comparing their exodus to that of Old Testament exiles, it is clear that Mormons understood themselves to be actors in the American drama of progress through westering. In an 1839 petition to Congress, decrying their mistreatment at the hands of Missouri mobs, Joseph Smith and other leaders stated, "Through [sic] they had wandered far from the homes of their childhood, still they had been taught to believe that a Citizen ~~of~~ <born in any> one state, in this great Republic, might remove to another and enjoy all the rights & immunities of Citizens of the State of his adoption." Reflecting a deeply held and oft-repeated colonial vision of the continent, they said they had found the land "wild and uncultivated" but left it "well improved and stocked."[78] They claimed their birthright as "true Americans" and "free born sons of Columbia," determined to settle and possess the land.[79] And in so doing, they embodied the very principles that empowered and justified Indian removal.

By contrast—and it's one worth really considering—for many if not most eastern American Indians, the forced migration to western lands was nothing short of spiritual death. Not only did thousands of men, women, and children perish during the removal, but for a number of their societies, the lands to the west were cosmologically defined as a place of darkness, despair, and peril. Like the Mormons, they too sang songs of their experiences but theirs were dirges and lamentations. One English-speaking Creek man sang of the removal thus, "Their children—look! By power oppressed,/ Beyond the mountains of the west,/ Their children go—to die,/ By foes alone their death song must be sung."[80] As their testimonies show, most eastern Native people did not feel that leaving their ancestral homelands was a viable option, despite the increasing violence they faced there, and they did so only out of intense desperation. Indeed, in one petition to the secretary of war, a group of headmen explained of their people's despair: "They view a removal as the worst evil that can befall them."[81]

Many nineteenth-century indigenous people described emigration as the unthinkable act of abandoning the bones of their ancestors. The "aged fathers and mothers" of the Creek nation beseeched their leaders to help them "remain upon the land that gave [them] birth, where the bones of their kindred are buried, so that when they die they may mingle their ashes together."[82] This oft-repeated sentiment referred to the actual burial sites of generations past and highlights the "power of ancestral bones to mobilize emotions," both among the speakers of such sentiments and their listeners.[83] But it was also a way that eastern Native people tried to convey a complex worldview through which they conceived of the land, rocks, and waters of their home, as well as what European-descended peoples would call the flora and fauna, as their relatives. Separation from their homelands meant the loss of not only territory and community (and often, by extension, sovereignty), but also foodways, medicine, language, and even time itself.

American Indian communities facing removal did not see new opportunities in their future; they saw utter devastation. On the eve of their expulsion from lands the Mormons had recently claimed as their own, Omaha leader White Horse confessed, "Now the face of all the land is changed and sad. The living creatures are gone. I see the land desolate, and I suffer unspeakable sadness. Sometimes I wake in the night and feel as though I should suffocate from the pressure of this awful feeling of loneliness." As James Taylor Carson explains, "While the disruptions to their economies, cultures, and lives were profound, removal triggered above all a crisis of cosmology because it upset the spiritual systems of ritual and power that Native Americans had written into the landscape."[84] Being ripped from their homelands and forced to live elsewhere wasn't a simple matter of exchanging one habitation for another. It was a complete unraveling of their social fabric.

Understanding this unparalleled pain requires an acknowledgement that historic American Indian ways of thinking about identity and history hinge less on time (and thus even less on notions of "progress") and more on place. Many scholars have addressed the complex role that place and place-making have held for human societies and for indigenous North American societies in particular.[85] Anthropologist Keith Basso puts it eloquently: "If place-making is a way of constructing the past, a venerable means of *doing* human history, it is also a way of constructing social traditions and, in the process, personal and social identities. We *are*, in a sense, the place-worlds we imagine."[86] Vine Deloria Jr. was one of the first writers to articulate the distinctions between western and indigenous approaches to place. In *God is Red*, he also alluded to their implications for removed nations.

> The vast majority of Indian tribal religions . . . have a sacred center at a particular place, be it a river, a mountain, a plateau, valley, or other natural feature. This center enables the people to look out along the four dimensions and locate their lands, to relate all historical events within the confines of this particular land, and to accept responsibility for it. Regardless of what subsequently happens to the people, the sacred lands remain as permanent fixtures in their cultural or religious understanding. Thus, many tribes now living in Oklahoma, but formerly from the eastern United States, still hold in their hearts the sacred locations of their history.[87]

The sacredness of places *must* be held in the hearts of those forced from their lands because it can no longer be experienced as an external reality, he implies. Similarly, Cherokee scholar Robert K. Thomas observed that ethnic minorities in many places around the world owed their continued existence to the persistence of memory-places that were both visible and "visitable," something that tribes removed in the nineteenth century lost and, at the time, believed they had lost forever.[88]

Homelands, constructed over hundreds and thousands of years through the processes of place-making and identity-building, were the spaces where indigenous realities "took place." As Carson, Basso, Deloria, Thomas, and others suggest, places provided the anchors that keep Native identities from becoming unmoored, providing material reminders (sometimes literally working as terrestrial mnemonic devices) of a peoples' past, their beliefs about the sacred, and their responsibilities toward one another and the world around them. This is not to say that Native peoples' relationship to places was or is static. Nor should the role of land in indigenous epistemologies be reduced to "simply some material object of profound importance... (although it is this too)."[89] Better to think of it as an integral strand in a web of relations and meaning, which forced removal swiftly frayed.

American observers were not unaware of Native peoples' perspectives on their dispossession and relocation, though they probably could not fathom its cultural roots or meanings. After all, as Basso puts it, place-making is both an imaginative and a cultural activity and cannot be understood except "in relation to the ideas and practices with which it is accomplished," which were (and still are) largely unavailable to outsiders.[90] Nevertheless, some nineteenth-century commentators incorporated what they understood of Native peoples' attachment to their homelands in their statements of opposition to or support for Indian removal. One uncharacteristically sympathetic southern writer said of the Creeks, "They were attached, by the strongest ties, to the land of their ancestors; they had there drawn the breath of infancy, and they there wished to repose their bones, when the winter of life should sweep over them, and summons them to the tombs of their fathers."[91] Even staunch pro-removal advocate Lewis Cass admitted that colonization struck at the very fact of indigenous existence, embedding the destruction of their communities in the language of progress and improvement, saying, "We have ploughed up the bones of their fathers."[92] In the midst of Sauk and Fox removal, a group of militia men in Illinois turned image into action, digging up tribal graves and mutilating the bodies, some freshly buried, in an apparent attempt to heap cultural insult onto the literal injury of attack and dispossession.[93]

Others were less shockingly malicious, but nevertheless openly mocked Native attachment to their homelands. A particularly vicious Georgia jurist accused Indian leaders of "mouthing a great deal about... their dripping blood and the graves and bones of their fathers and all that pathetic nonsense."[94] And Andrew Jackson derided the idea that removal would have a destructive effect on Native communities, stating, "Doubtless it will be painful to leave the graves of their fathers; but what do they more than our ancestors did or than our children are now doing?... Our children by thousands yearly leave the land of their birth to seek new homes in distant regions. Does Humanity weep at these painful separations from everything, animate and inanimate, with which the young heart has become entwined?" No, Jackson concluded, like the Mormons heading for the far West, migration was "rather a source of joy," emblematic of American mobility, opportunity, and progress. Trotting out the shibboleth of Indian vagrancy, he asked, "Is it supposed that the wandering savage has a stronger attachment to his home than the settled, civilized Christian? Is it more afflicting to him to leave the graves of his fathers than it is to our brothers and children?"[95]

This willful recasting of Indian dispossession and exile in the terms of American westering lays bare one of the essential problems with comparing Mormon removal to Indian removal. The Mormons heading "zionward," whether migrating to Missouri, to Illinois, to Winter Quarters, or further west, saw themselves not as "wandering savages" but as "settled, civilized Christians." Their peregrinations were temporary hegiras, a passing but necessary phase in their journey to becoming Mormon. As West has contended, "The outward events of the conversion, the gathering and the exodus," the Mormon origin story if you will, "show a religion and a community taking shape." The "tearing down" of Mormonism during their persecution was also the foundation of their "building up," and painful though it was, the stories of their travails on the migration to the West worked to consolidate their shared identity.[96]

Native peoples forced from their homelands drew no such solace from their stories of removal—indeed, they had been deprived of the very tools with which to do so. Tiya Miles distills the impact of Cherokee removal, explaining, "Indian Removal disrupted the relationship between Cherokees, their homeland, and the stories that lived there. As a result, the cultural values embedded in those stories could no longer be reinforced through the visible markers of place."[97] While later generations would come to solemnly memorialize the Trail of Tears and the analogous experiences of other eastern nations forced into western territories, and despite the fact that the Cherokees and their neighbors were remarkably successful in reestablishing their social institutions out west, the legacy of removal remains a deep wound in their collective psyche—a dramatic break, a vast hiatus that some have likened to the middle passage rather than a rite of passage, as West and others contend it was for Mormons. In fact, the lasting scars of removal have recently been linked to what psychologists call "historical trauma," a scaffolded set of symptoms stemming from painful experiences passed down through generations that continue to take a toll on the mental and physical health of Native communities.[98]

By contrast, the removal of the Mormons stands as a key pillar in their shared identity. Expulsion from the East formed an essential part of the Mormon experience. Those who lived it romanticized it later. And those who only vaguely grasped it embellished it according to their own needs and desires. The migration, memorialized as an Old Testament-style exodus, combined with the subsequent and quite deliberate efforts to collect and recollect the experience, also informed the Mormon view of the lands they colonized in the Intermountain West. Engaging in their own process of place-making, the Mormons created a "homeland" with its own "endemic spiritual geography."[99] But doing so depended on the literal and metaphorical erasure of indigenous peoples and their own place-based identity claims.

Although I've primarily used the Cherokee Trail of Tears to demonstrate the superficial similarities between Indian removal and the expulsion of the Mormons from Missouri and Illinois, it's worth pausing here to remember that Indian removal was not, in fact, a single episode. Indeed, we may err in even calling it an event. Considering the forced migration of the eastern Cherokees in the context of other nineteenth-century policies of Indian removal certainly helps place the 1838–39 Trail of Tears in a broader, national perspective. But in setting Indian removal apart from anti-Mormonism, we should also heed Patrick Wolfe's reminder: "For all its concentrated horror . . . the Trail of Tears was not an isolated event . . . it brought together key components of an eliminatory process" we know as settler colonialism. We can then ask ourselves whether federal and local assaults on the Mormon church and individual Mormon believers truly constitute "a historical relationship of inequality" parallel to that inflicted upon indigenous North Americans.[100] However similar the national effort to "reconstruct" the Mormons may appear in comparison to policies toward American Indians, the latter relied upon the unshakeable belief that Indians were, one way or another, going to "melt away." In this sense then, reconstruction—tearing down and building back up in proper order—was never the end goal of the federal policies directed toward Native peoples, despite rhetoric to the contrary. The assumption (and at times, the stated goal) was that American Indians would be eliminated. Other policies of reconstruction in the United States sought to discipline but also to *reconcile* wayward populations. Indeed, West casts the reconstruction of Mormons as the "outward reconciliation of the Saints and American society."[101] On the contrary, as critical Indigenous Studies scholar Sandy Grande puts it, "the very nature of settler colonialism precludes reconciliation" because it requires the elimination of the Native, either through annihilation or assimilation predicated on complete cultural erasure.[102]

Although Mormons were held apart from American progress and democracy, seen as enemies of the state, and often regarded as fundamentally different from non-Mormon white Americans, they were never in danger of disappearing. On the contrary, Mormons proved incredibly prolific, much to the chagrin of their enemies. Just as there was no Mormon Trail of Tears, there was no viable "vanishing Mormon" narrative to deploy as a weapon against their very existence. This is in part because they were already engaged in the settler colonial enterprise of reproducing themselves by disappearing indigenous others. Plus, their numbers were ever increasing, again to the horror of their opponents, through their immensely successful foreign missionary efforts.[103] But it was also because however savage anti-Mormons thought the Saints were, however tyrannical they found their leaders, however unsettling were their theological, political, financial, and marital practices, they did not see them as weak, dependent children who not only stood in the way of progress but lacked the very ability to progress. It is hard to imagine an anti-Mormon equivalent of Secretary of War Thomas McKenney's summation of Indian removal: "No human agency can reform them as a people . . . Humanity and justice unite in calling loudly upon the government as a parent promptly to interfere and save them."[104] Of course, "saving" the Indians in McKenney's estimation, as was true of most mid-century observers of the "Indian problem," was only a temporary move, since it was only a matter of time before the American Indian succumbed to the "destruction which awaits his race."[105]

Despite localized and admittedly vivid rhetoric like that uncovered by Paul Reeve and Spencer Fluhman in their recent studies on anti-Mormonism, there is simply no legitimate—and *lasting*—parallel to the totalizing logic of settler colonialism that underlay federal policies toward American Indians from the era of Jefferson well into the twenty-first century. While travelogues, moralizing tracts, local mobs, and disaffected apostates railed against the Mormons and their practices from the founding of the church forward, and although they were sometimes seen as racially degraded, placed alongside Indians, African Americans, and Chinese immigrants, Mormons could (and many did) leave the church and melt back into white society. Framing people in the language of oppression is not the same thing as oppressing them. Mormons and anti-Mormons both stood on the same ground, looking in the same direction—to the West, believing (though on somewhat different authorities) that they were entitled to what lay before them.

Too closely aligning the experiences of persecuted Mormons with removed Indians runs the risk of masking the structures of inequality that enabled the latter's persecution and from which the former profited. As John Mack Faragher has helpfully explained, "The American settler state was founded on the promise of westward expansion, and the colonization of vast areas of the continent intensified as settlers moved across the Appalachians into the great Mississippi Valley, waged wars of extirpation against indigenous peoples, and pushed the national state to enact a comprehensive policy of Indian Removal."[106] In other words, both Indian removal and the exercises of state power discussed in this volume by Christine Talbot, Patrick Q. Mason, Brent Rogers, and Brett Dowdle existed within and were enabled by the larger structure of settler colonialism, which is predicated on the disappearance (through extermination, forced migration, and/or cultural modification) of the indigenes.

In West's "Greater Reconstruction," the concern was "as much about control as liberation, as much about unity and power as about equality."[107] The seductive but ultimately unsound comparison between Mormon removal and Indian removal lays bare a fundamental flaw in applying this formulation to a colonized population. With respect to American Indians, the question of control was not only about bodies whose behavior needed to be disciplined or reformed by an ever-growing federal power. At its core, settler colonialism in the American grain presumes settler and state control of the land and its resources. The primary thing it requires of indigenous people is their disappearance, one way or another. Westering nineteenth-century Mormons were no more outside this structure than were African American exodusters, settling in Indian Territory after the end of Reconstruction, or Southern Confederates remaking themselves as New South agrarians whose Indian-less lands enabled remembrances of a fabled "Old South" identity.

Indian removal was not an effort to reform or "reconstruct" Native peoples and neither were the policies that followed. Despite the increasing rhetoric of assimilation that characterized federal Indian policy from the 1850s–1880s and the creation of institutions like boarding schools that seem aimed at incorporating Native peoples into the body politic, the promise of citizenship was always a losing proposition in terms of Indian land. To "kill the Indian and save the man," as Richard Henry Pratt famously put it, appears on its surface to represent an assimilationist impulse akin to that which undergirded the Thirteenth, Fourteenth, and Fifteenth Amendments, Reconstruction policies in the South, and the incorporation of Utah as the forty-fifth state. One might productively substitute "slave," "rebel," or "polygamist" in place of "Indian" in Pratt's phrase. But it is important to remember that killing the Indians—literally, culturally, and politically—achieved a singular goal that links us back to the history of the United States as a settler colonial state: it "liberated" the land from Native control. Federal policies had been moving in this direction from the founding of the nation and only accelerated as the nineteenth century progressed: removal, the reservations, the end to treaty-making, allotment, and cultural modification, not to mention violence at the hands of state and non-state actors—including Mormons—all worked to wrest Indian land from Indian hands. If there are no Indians, there is no Indian title. One might go a step further, in fact, and suggest that without the eradication of Indian title, none of the "Greater Reconstruction" debated in this volume, including that of the Mormons, could have taken place.

―――

While this essay has largely been focused on antebellum roots and removals, a post–Civil War coda is perhaps in order given our collective interest in "Reconstruction" within this volume. Near the end of the nineteenth century, at the same time that allotment was destroying the last vestiges of Indian landholding and Mormons were debating their incorporation into the body politic at home, the United States was deploying "weaponized stories" (to borrow a phrase from Jared Farmer's essay) of its own superiority to realize its imperial ambitions abroad. On the plains and in the Pacific, the seizure of indigenous lands and the destruction of indigenous sovereignty accompanied American troops and businessmen. The "pulverizing machine" ran on a potent mixture of state power, capitalist greed, and biopolitics. And as with their enthusiastic westering on the American continent, Mormons demonstrated their suitability for citizenship by becoming agents of empire.

Although motivated by missionary impulses, Mormons nevertheless participated in the colonization of Pacific homelands like Hawaii and actively dispossessed indigenous people of their lands and, for those who converted, their history, offering an interesting analogue to the destiny manifesting itself for Lamanites back home. Polynesians, Hokulani K. Aikau observes, are understood in Mormon theology as "cousins" to American Indians and, though not exactly Lamanites, they likewise stand apart from a genealogy of whiteness that "whether literal or metaphoric ... persists as a privileged state of being" within the church. And yet, because of both the scriptural and doctrinal centrality of Native peoples to the church and the attendant opportunities offered by such validation, she argues, the appropriative practices that characterize LDS history have not entirely foreclosed the space in which indigenous identities can be reclaimed. In her deeply personal history of Mormon "Hawaiianness," *A Chosen People, A Promised Land: Mormonism and Race in Hawai'i*, Aikau sets out to understand "how it is that colonial religious traditions such as Mormonism can be lived and inhabited as sites and sources of indigenous cultural vitality."[108] She confesses that, given its deep historical investment in settler colonial projects,

Mormonism appears to be "wholly incompatible" with indigenous survival, much less revitalization.

Aikau's candid observations strike right at the heart of the paradoxical Mormon promise to indigenous peoples, one in which Native folks were "cursed to be inferior yet promised to be superior . . . destined to save the world," but incapable of saving themselves.[109] On the one hand, indigenous people are told they are chosen and, although fallen and degraded, are destined for redemption and salvation. On the other, they have historically been expected to surrender their land, resources, and often their identities to the church's mission. This fundamental contradiction underlies many debates about the place of Native peoples within Mormonism, provides the key to understanding why comparisons of Mormon removal and Indian removal are ultimately untenable, and illuminates the cultural "work" that such comparisons have performed and continue to perform, namely the elision of Mormon complicity in the crimes of settler colonialism.

In her conclusion, Aikau asserts that some indigenous people in Mormon-American contexts have been able to regenerate themselves and revitalize their communities, despite the intended and unintended consequences of colonization by the state and the church. They have been able, in at least some cases, to "inhabit" the faith and make it a site for renewal and reappropriation of their own identities. In closing, I want to suggest that these efforts at restoration and recovery, or what Melanie Benson Taylor refers to in a related context as "reconstitution," are the most important forms of *reconstruction* to which we can turn our attention.[110] These complicated but creative acts of persistence, like those of former slaves who embraced a deeply flawed but still hopeful Reconstruction, are those most deserving of consideration.

Notes

1. On the number of Mormons forced from Missouri, I base my estimate on Max H. Parkin, "Missouri Conflict," in *Encyclopedia of Mormonism*, vol. 1, ed. Daniel H. Ludlow (New York: Macmillan, 1992), 931. On the number of Cherokees expelled from their homelands, I use the estimate of Russell Thornton in "Cherokee Population Losses during the Trail of Tears: A New Perspective and a New Estimate," *Ethnohistory* 31, no. 4 (Autumn 1984): 292–93. Somewhere between 4,000 and 8,000 Cherokees are estimated to have died during the Trail of Tears. By contrast, it is estimated that about 40 Mormons died during the Missouri war and another 2,000 died during their extended stay at Winter Quarters.

2. Paul Reeve, *Religion of a Different Color: Race and the Mormon Struggle for Whiteness* (New York: Oxford University Press, 2015), 74.

3. Anne Hyde, *Empires, Nations, and Families: A New History of the North American West, 1800–1860* (New York: Harper Collins, 2011), 358.

4. Elliott West, "Reconstructing Race," *The Essential West: Collected Essays* (Norman: University of Oklahoma Press, 2012), 119; Amanda Hendrix-Komoto, "'Do They See Me?': Race and Mormon History," *Reviews in American History* 44, no. 3 (2016): 454.

5. Jodi A. Byrd, *Transit of Empire: Indigenous Critiques of Colonialism* (Minneapolis: University of Minnesota Press, 2011), 137.

6. Mark Lyman Staker, *"Hearken, O Ye People": The Historical Setting of Joseph Smith's Ohio Revelations* (Salt Lake City: Greg Kofford Books, 2009), 49–52.

7. Richard Bushman, *Joseph Smith: Rough Stone Rolling* (New York: Knopf, 2005), 64, 82–83, 93; Paul C. Gutjahr, *The Book of Mormon: A Biography* (Princeton, N.J.: Princeton University Press, 2012), 5.

8. The original passage was "white and delightsome," appeared sometimes as "light and delightsome," and now reads "pure and delightsome." Both the logic of the original wording and the subsequent changes are a matter of considerable discussion and debate. For a comprehensive, though not unbiased, history of the phrase over many editions, see Douglas Campbell, "'White' or 'Pure': Five Vignettes," *Dialogue: A Journal of Mormon Thought* 29, no. 4 (1996), 19–35.

9. Ronald W. Walker, "Seeking the 'Remnant': The Native American during the Joseph Smith Period," *Journal of Mormon History* 19, no. 1 (1993), 3.

10. Walker, "Seeking the 'Remnant,'" 12–13.

11. Reeve, *Religion of a Different Color*, 72–74.

12. Walker, "Seeking the 'Remnant,'" 15–16; Kenneth H. Winn, "The Missouri Context of Antebellum Mormonism and Its Legacy of Violence," in *The Missouri Mormon Experience*, ed. Thomas M. Spencer III (Columbia, Mo.: University of Missouri Press, 2010), 23; Claudia Lauper Bushman and Richard Lyman Bushman, *Building the Kingdom: A History of Mormons in America* (New York: Oxford University Press, 1999), 26.

13. On accusations of interfering with slaves, see, among others, J. Spencer Fluhman, *"A Peculiar People": Anti-Mormonism and the Making of Religion in Nineteenth-Century America* (Chapel Hill: University of North Carolina Press, 2012), 53; on "Indian tampering," see Walker, "Seeking the 'Remnant,'" 15; Reeve, *Religion of a Different Color*, 64–72. Parley P. Pratt offered a refutation of the charges against the Mormons. Parley P. Pratt, *Late Persecution of the Church of Jesus Christ, of Latter Day Saints*, 2nd ed. (New York: J. W. Harrison, 1840), 6–7.

14. *History of the Church*, 1:118, quoted in Staker, *"Hearken, O Ye People,"* 49.

15. Jared Farmer, *On Zion's Mount: Mormons, Indians, and the American Landscape* (Cambridge: Harvard University Press, 2010), 16, 57. See also Christopher C. Smith, "Playing Lamanite: Ecstatic Performance of American Indian Roles in Early Mormon Ohio," *Journal of Mormon History* 40, no. 3 (2015), 131–66.

16. Charles L. Cohen, "The Construction of the Mormon People," *Journal of Mormon History* 32, no. 1 (2006): 45.

17. Joy Porter, *Native American Freemasonry: Associationalism and Performance in America* (Lincoln: University of Nebraska Press, 2011), 96–97.

18. Walker, "Seeking the 'Remnant,'" 5.

19. Reeve, *Religion of a Different Color*, 56.

20. On this point, I am especially indebted to Porter's clear articulation of what is at stake in the Lost Tribes thesis. Porter, *Native American Freemasonry*, 99–101.

21. Hamblin, quoted in Cohen, "The Construction of the Mormon People," 50. On Hamblin's complicated legacy, see Todd M. Compton, *A Frontier Life: Jacob Hamblin, Explorer and Indian Missionary* (Salt Lake City: University of Utah Press, 2013).

22. Many scholars have analyzed the rhetoric of "improvement" that was used to rationalize the theft of indigenous lands, with a particular emphasis on the Judeo-Christian foundation of such views (rooted in Genesis) and its enshrinement in English and later Anglo-American legal traditions. One of the most convincing and influential of these analyses is William Cronon, *Changes in the Land: Indians, Colonists, and the Ecology of New England* (New York: Hill and Wang, 1983).

23. Lewis Cass, "Removal of the Indians," *North American Review* 30, no. 66 (January 1830): 77.

24. Andrew Jackson, "Second Annual Message," December 6, 1830.

25. Thomas Jefferson, Letter to William Henry Harrison, Governor of the Indiana Territory, February 27, 1803.

26. Fluhman, *"A Peculiar People,"* 87; Farmer, *On Zion's Mount*, 58.

27. It should be noted here that Cherokee leaders like John Ridge, as well as their Euro-American supporters like William Wirt, tended to overstate the degree to which Cherokee citizens adopted the ways of their white neighbors. But, more so than other Indian nations of the era, Cherokee leadership launched a full-throated defense of their sovereignty that highlighted such accommodation and thus we have a stronger and more accessible record of these changes in the Cherokee Nation than elsewhere.

28. U.S. Congress, *Articles of Agreement and Cession*, April 24, 1802.

29. Joel W. Martin, "'My Grandmother Was a Cherokee Princess': Representations of Indians in Southern History," in *Dressing in Feathers: The Construction of the Indian in American Popular Culture*, ed. S. Elizabeth Bird (Boulder, Colo.: Westview Press, 1996), 134. I also address this point in *Creek Paths and Federal Roads: Indians, Settlers, and Slaves and the Making of the American South* (Chapel Hill: University of North Carolina Press, 2010).

30. Indian affairs, not slavery, was the sticking point between union and disunion in 1830, though the two topics were clearly linked in the minds of Southern statesmen. Augustin S. Clayton, *A Vindication of the Recent and Prevailing Policy of the State of Georgia, both in reference to its internal affairs, and its relation with the General Government. In two series of essays, originally published in the 'Columbian Centinel' under the signature of 'Atticus.' To which is now prefixed a 'Prefatory Address,' by the Author* (Athens, Ga.: O. P. Shaw, 1827), 13, 17; John Rogers Vinton, "Journal of My Excursion to Georgia, & the Creek Nation—Also of My Tour with Genl Brown through the Southern & Western Borders, 29th Jany. 1827–30th July 1827," John Rogers Vinton Papers, 1814–1861, Duke University, Special Collections Library. See also Michael D. Green, *The Politics of Indian Removal: Creek Government and Society in Crisis* (Lincoln, Neb.: University of Nebraska Press, 1985), 147.

31. Walker, "Seeking the 'Remnant,'" 9–10, 13–14; T. Ward Frampton, "'Some Savage Tribe': Race, Legal Violence, and the Mormon War of 1838," *Journal of Mormon History* 40, no. 1 (Winter 2014): 183.

32. "Gathering of Israel," *Evening and Morning Star* (Independence, Mo.), vol. 2, no. 13, June 1833, 101, Mormon Publications: 19th and 20th Centuries, Harold B. Lee Library Digital Collections, Brigham Young University, accessed January 5, 2017, http://contentdm.lib.byu.edu/cdm/ref/collection/NCMP1820-1846/id/5919. On the sufferings of the Delawares and Kickapoos during successive removals, see generally John P. Bowes, *Land Too Good for Indians: Northern Indian Removal* (Norman: University of Oklahoma Press, 2016).

33. U.S. Congress, *Cherokee Indians. Memorial of a Delegation of the Cherokee Tribe of Indians, January 9, 1832*, 22nd Congress, 1st Sess., 1832, p. 1, 5; "Gathering of Israel," *Evening and Morning Star*, 101.

34. "The Elders in the Land of Zion to the Church of Christ Scattered Abroad," *Evening and Morning Star* (Independence, Mo.) vol. 1, no. 2, July 1832, p. 13, Mormon Publications: 19th and 20th Centuries, Harold B. Lee Library Digital Collections, Brigham Young University, accessed January 5, 2017, http://contentdm.lib.byu.edu/cdm/ref/collection/NCMP1820-1846/id/5919.

35. Robert Dockery Covington, *History of Robert Dockery Covington* (Provo, Utah: Brigham Young University Library, 1954), 2.

36. Robert Lang Campbell, "Robert Campbell Journal, 1843–48," 58, L. Tom Perry Special Collections, Brigham Young University (hereafter LTPSC); Hosea Stout, *On the Mormon Frontier: The Diary of Hosea Stout, 1844–1861*, vol. 1, ed. Juanita Brooks (Salt Lake City: University of Utah Press, 1982), 244. See also Stanley B. Kimball, *Heber C. Kimball: Mormon Patriarch and Pioneer* (Urbana: University of Illinois Press, 1986), 145.

37. Farmer, *On Zion's Mount*, 59–60.

38. Jesse Moss quoted in Staker, *"Hearken, O Ye People,"* 83. On "playing Lamanite," see Smith, "Playing Lamanite."

39. Robert Berkhofer Jr., *The White Man's Indian: Images of the American Indian from Columbus to the Present* (New York: Vintage Books, 1978), 25–27.

40. Jared Farmer, "Crossroads of the West," *Journal of Mormon History* 41, no. 1 (Winter 2015): 160.

41. Farmer, *On Zion's Mount*, 39, 59–61. Farmer notes that the Omaha claim to the land at Winter Quarters was disputed by the Otoes, an important point, considering that Brigham Young and the Mormons apparently made no attempt to negotiate with the latter group, suggesting either a willful or unintentional oversimplification of complicated territorial and social relationships between indigenous groups in the region.

42. Hyde, *Empires, Nations, and Families*, 358.

43. Sarah Barringer Gordon, *The Mormon Question: Polygamy and Constitutional Conflict in Nineteenth-Century America* (Chapel Hill: University of North Carolina Press, 2002), 56–57.

44. Reeve, *Religion of a Different Color*, 64.

45. Pratt, *Late Persecution of the Church*, 26.

46. Lilburn W. Boggs, Missouri Executive Order Number 44, October 27, 1838.

47. Gen. Winfield Scott, Orders, No. 25, Head Quarters, Eastern Division, Cherokee Agency, Tenn., May 17, 1838.

48. The official in question was Major General Edmund P. Gaines. Black Hawk, *Life of Black Hawk*, ed. Milo Milton Quaife (1916; repr., New York: Dover Publications, 1994), 50.

49. *Warsaw Signal*, Warsaw, Ill., June 12, 1844, and "Extra," June 14, 1844, both quoted in Kenneth Winn, *Exiles in a Land of Liberty: Mormons in America, 1830–1846* (Chapel Hill: University of North Carolina Press, 1989), 215.

50. Frampton, "'Some Savage Tribe,'" 186–87.

51. Elias Hutchings, "Autobiography, ca. 1842," 30, LTPSC.

52. Pratt, *Late Persecution of the Church*, xviii.

53. Eliza Whitmire quoted in Patrick Minges, ed., *Black Indian Slave Narratives* (Winston-Salem, N.C.: J. F. Blair, 2004), 34.

54. See, for example, Interview with J. W. Stephens, March 22, 1938, Indian-Pioneer Papers, 87:190–205.

55. Joseph Smith, Sidney Rigdon, and Elias Higbee, Petition, Washington, D.C., to United States Congress, Washington, D.C., ca. November 29, 1839, p. 30. Joseph Smith Papers, Church History Library, accessed January 20, 2017, http://www.josephsmithpapers.org.

56. James Mulholland, *An Address to Americans a Poem in Blank Verse . . . intended as a brief exposure of the cruelties and wrongs, which the Church has lately experienced in the state of Missouri* (Nauvoo, Ill.: E. Robinson, 1841), 3.

57. Josiah B. Conyers, *A Brief History of the Leading Causes of the Hancock Mob, in the Year 1846* (St. Louis: Printed for the Author by Cathcart and Prescott, 1846), 31.

58. Evan Jones, June 16, 1838, quoted in William G. McLoughlin, *Champions of the Cherokees: Evan and John B. Jones* (Princeton, N.J.: Princeton University Press, 2014), 174.

59. Conyers, *A Brief History*, 31.

60. "The Articles of Agreement and Cession," April 24, 1802, in *American State Papers, Public Lands*, 2 vols. (Washington, 1834), vol. 1, 125–26.

61. Major Ridge and John Ridge, Letter to Andrew Jackson, June 30, 1836.

62. Hutchings, "Autobiography," 19–20, LTPSC.

63. Conyers, *A Brief History*, 64.

64. Smith, 1840, quoted in Frampton, "'Some Savage Tribe,'" 175.

65. Lavina Fielding Anderson, ed., *Lucy's Book: A Critical Edition of Lucy Mack Smith's Family Memoir* (Salt Lake City: Signature Books, 2001), 691–92.

66. Joseph Holbrook, "Joseph Holbrook autobiography, 1806–1846," 41, LTPSC; *Cattaraugus Republican* (Ellicottville, Cattaraugus County, N.Y.), September 17, 1851, p. 3.

67. Levi Jackman, Journal, 1847, quoted in Farmer, *On Zion's Mount*, 60.

68. Farmer, *On Zion's Mount*, 58. Farmer describes an episode in which Saints traveling from Ohio to Missouri disinterred a skeleton from a burial mound, causing Joseph Smith Jr. to have a vision identifying the bones as those of Zelph, a "'white Lamanite' who had fallen in battle."

69. The phrase "description by deficiency" comes from Berkhofer, *The White Man's Indian*, 26.

70. This specific phrase comes from The Treaty of Fort Laramie with the Sioux, etc. (1851), *Indian Affairs: Laws and Treaties*, vol. 2, comp. and ed. by Charles J. Kappler (Washington: Government Printing Office, 1904), accessed July 11, 2017, http://digital.library.okstate.edu/kappler/Vol2/treaties/sio0594.htm.

71. Farmer, "Crossroads of the West," 160.

72. Mark Rifkin, *Settler Common Sense: Queerness and Everyday Colonialism in the American Renaissance* (Minneapolis: University of Minnesota Press, 2014).

73. Ann Eliza Young, *Wife No. 19, or The Story of A Life in Bondage, Being a Complete Expose of Mormonism, and Revealing the Sorrows, Sacrifices and Sufferings of Women in Polygamy, by Ann Eliza Young, Brigham Young's Apostate Wife* (Hartford, Conn.: Dustin, Gilman, 1875), 112–13.

74. Interestingly, Randi Lynn Tanglen suggests that Young desired the "eradication" of both Mormons and American Indians in order to enable the westward expansion of white Protestants. Tanglen, "The Indian Captivity Narrative: A Narrative of the Southwest," in *Southwestern Literature*, ed. William Brannon (Hackensack, N.J.: Salem Press, 2016), 69–70.

75. James A. Little, *From Kirtland to Salt Lake City* (Salt Lake City: James A. Little, 1890), 48–49.

76. Young, *Wife No. 19*, 116.

77. Farmer, "Crossroads of the West," 160.

78. Smith, et. al, Petition, 12.

79. Pratt, *Late Persecution of the Church*, xiii, xix.

80. The song was witnessed and recorded by John H. Jones, who accompanied a party of Creeks emigrating from Georgia to the West in 1835. Jones, "Autobiography of John H. Jones, 1814–1882," quoted in Christopher D. Haveman, *Rivers of Sand: Creek Indian Emigration, Relocation, & Ethnic Cleansing in the American South* (Lincoln, Neb.: University of Nebraska Press, 2016), 145–46.

81. Haveman, *Rivers of Sand*, 93. The petition in question was sent by eleven Creek headmen to Secretary of War John Eaton in the spring of 1831.

82. Haveman, *Rivers of Sand*, 93.

83. Peter Nabokov, *A Forest of Time: American Indian Ways of History* (New York: Cambridge University Press, 2002), 148.

84. James Taylor Carson, "Ethnogeography and the Native American Past," *Ethnohistory* 49, no. 4 (Fall 2002): 770.

85. For a useful overview, see Clara Sue Kidwell, Homer Noley, and George Tinker, *A Native American Theology* (Maryknoll, N.Y.: Orbis Books, 2001), 44–48.

86. Keith Basso, *Wisdom Sits in Places: Language and Landscape among the Western Apache* (Albuquerque: University of New Mexico Press, 1996), 7.

87. Vine Deloria Jr., *God is Red: A Native View of Religion* (Denver: Fulcrum Publishing, 2003), 66.

88. Nabokov, *A Forest of Time*, 130.

89. Glen Coulthard, "Place Against Empire: Understanding Indigenous Anti-Colonialism," *Affinities: A Journal of Radical Theory, Culture, and Action* 4, no. 2 (Fall 2010): 79.

90. Basso, *Wisdom Sits in Places*, 7.

91. Anonymous, *Cahawba Press and Alabama State Intelligencer* (Cahawba, Ala.), vol. 1, no. 27, March 19, 1825, p. 2.

92. Lewis Cass, "Indians of North America," *North American Review* 22, no. 50 (1826), 113.

93. Kerry A. Trask, *Black Hawk: The Battle for the Heart of America* (New York: Macmillan, 2006), 102.

94. Clayton, *A Vindication of the Recent and Prevailing Policy*, 19.

95. Andrew Jackson, Second Annual Message to Congress, December 6, 1830.

96. West, "Becoming Mormon," *The Essential West*, 188.

97. Tiya Miles, *Ties that Bind: The Story of an Afro-Cherokee Family in Slavery and Freedom* (Berkeley: University of California Press, 2015), 159.

98. There are many scholarly studies on historical trauma that are directed to psychologists, social workers, and health care providers. A short accessible introduction for readers unfamiliar with the concept in connection to American Indian populations is Tina Deschenie, "Historical Trauma," *Tribal College Journal* 17, no. 3 (Spring 2006): 8–11.

99. Farmer, *On Zion's Mount*, 16; see also R. H. Jackson, "The Mormon Experience: The Plains as Sinai, the Great Salt Lake as the Dead Sea, and the Great Basin as Desert-cum-Promised Land," *Journal of Historical Geography* 18, no. 1 (1992): 41–58. As Eric Eliason points out in chapter 8 of this volume, while Jackson County, Missouri remains in the minds of many Mormons *the true* Zion, modern interpretations increasingly tend to shy away from fixing it in such a bounded place, opting instead to emphasize Zion as an expansive realm or even a spiritual posture.

100. Patrick Wolfe, "Race and the Trace of History: For Henry Reynolds," in *Studies in Settler Colonialism: Politics, Identity and Culture*, ed. Fiona Bateman and Lionel Pilkington (Basingstoke, Hampshire, United Kingdom: Palgrave Macmillan, 2011), 283–84.

101. West, "Becoming Mormon," 190.

102. Sandy Grande, "Refusing the University," in *Toward What Justice?: Describing Diverse Dreams of Justice in Education*, ed. Eve Tuck and K. Wayne Yang (New York: Routledge, 2018), 53.

103. William Mulder, "Immigration and the 'Mormon Question': An International Episode," *Western Political Quarterly* 9, no. 2 (June 1956), 416–33.

104. Excerpt of a letter from Thomas L. McKenney to the Secretary of War, dated Nov. 29, 1827, *The Cherokee Phoenix*, New Echota, Cherokee Nation, February 21, 1828, p. 2.

105. Thomas L. McKenney, *History of the Indian Tribes of North America, with Biographical Sketches and Anecdotes of the Principal Chiefs, Embellished with One Hundred and Twenty Portraits, from the Indian Gallery in the Department of War, at Washington.* (Philadelphia: F. W. Greenough, 1838–44),

106. John Mack Faragher, "Commentary: Settler Colonial Studies and the North American Frontier," *Settler Colonial Studies* 4, no. 2 (2014): 185.

107. West, "Reconstructing Race," 119.

108. Hokulani K. Aikau, *A Chosen People, A Promised Land: Mormonism and Race in Hawai'i* (Minneapolis: University of Minnesota Press, 2012), xii, 42–45, 53.

109. Farmer, *On Zion's Mount*, 57.

110. Melanie Benson Taylor, *Reconstructing the Native South: American Indian Literature and the Lost Cause* (Athens, Ga.: University of Georgia Press, 2011), 4.

= 2 =

Constructing a National Marital and Sexual Culture

Reconsidering the "Twin Relics of Barbarism"

Christine Talbot

In 1856, the Republican Party platform connected slavery and polygamy as "twin relics of barbarism," which they promised to prohibit in the U.S. territories.[1] In 1890, a lawyer from San Francisco, John A. Wills, claimed to have coined the phrase "the twin relics of barbarism," referencing polygamy and slavery. He reported that while some Republican delegates at the 1856 convention hesitated to pair the two, "the rapturous enthusiasm with which the resolution was received . . . was the first convincing evidence that the committee had acted wisely in determining to preserve it [the language] in its original form."[2] From their very beginnings, Republicans argued that the federal government should exercise its sovereign powers over the territories to rid them of these two barbarous practices. In the West, the federal government could exercise in the territories power that it could not exercise in the states. The 1856 Republican Party platform acknowledged this and claimed that "it is both the right and the imperative duty of Congress" to prohibit the twin relics in the territories.[3] They did so in the context of developing national debates not only over the authority of the federal government but also over the proper nature of the American family.

To some extent, Republican links between slavery and polygamy were driven by rhetorical political opportunism.[4] Wills claimed that "in order to make war upon polygamy, and at the same time strengthen the case against slavery as much as possible, by associating the two together, I determined to couple them together in one and the same resolution."[5] The 1856 platform likely linked the two practices in part to broaden the base of the Republican Party beyond its antislavery origins. Moreover, Wills and the Republicans who enthusiastically embraced his phrase no doubt knew the value of political phraseology. Challenged by one senior senator to remove the phrase, another senator came to Wills's defense because, as a former newspaper editor, "he knew the value of political phrases, as instrumentalities in political warfare."[6]

However, the links Republicans made between slavery and polygamy were not simply rooted in the political opportunity of a catchy phrase. They became an appealing phrase and good fortune for Republicans because the connections made sense to the people creating and consuming the rhetoric. The rationale behind the connection between polygamy and slavery remained hazy in the Republican platform precisely because many people already understood it; clever political phraseology has little bite without preceding political perceptions. Examining themes in antipolygamy and antislavery writings shows that slavery and polygamy in the antebellum period were imagined to threaten emerging northern marital, filial, and sexual structures in similar ways. As wage labor moved northern men out of the home and into the workplace, new economic structures gave rise to new gender and family ideals among northern reformers to whom "large families and patriarchal control . . . made little economic or social sense."[7] This process was likely accelerated by the 1849 gold rush, in which patriarchs lost domination over sons who had economic opportunity to escape paternal home rule. In a context in which wage labor had begun to replace agricultural labor, patriarchal power over the family waned and sons had more flexible economic opportunities. New ideals of companionate marriage and democratic families emerged. Properly ordered democratic households came to be (theoretically) held together not by patriarchal relations of authority and dependence, but by feelings of love and affection between spouses and between parents and children. As new ideas of companionate marriage emerged, abolitionists especially looked to a family model, which historian Michael D. Pierson refers to as "free hearts and free homes" to replace patriarchy as the glue that held marriages and families together. Family affection, of course, depended on ideas of female consent to marriage, a consent that antislavery and antipolygamy writers juxtaposed to the coercion they found characteristic of slavery and polygamy.

Companionate families were imagined to free the hearts of those within the home from the patriarchal control so characteristic of southern plantations and,

I would add, of fictional portrayals of Mormon polygamy. "Advocates for their changing world, [abolitionists] pressed all Americans to accept their model as normative and warred against those who held onto gender ideas different from their own."[8] Antipolygamy writers joined this cause as well, as their novels combatted alternative families in the West. The new marriage and family ideals antipolygamy and antislavery reformers advocated were both a measure of the progress of northern civilization as set against the barbarisms of the South and the West and a prescription for the direction the entire nation should take. As Pierson argues, "dramatic social and rhetorical divisions on personal issues like gender roles and family structures helped to produce the image that two very different societies were in competition with each other," North and South.[9] I would add that similar conflicts over gender roles and family structures put Northeast and West in competition with each other as well.

This essay examines the conceptual territories traversed by antebellum writings that constituted slavery and polygamy as the "twin relics of barbarism." Looking at antislavery and antipolygamy rhetoric together demonstrates how northern reformers conceptualized a model of marriage, family, and sexuality they wanted to nationalize. They hoped that the project of nationalizing this new model would happen, at least in part, through ridding the nation of two central challenges to the democratic family—slavery and polygamy. Antislavery writings illustrate that the practice of slavery in the South, widely termed the "patriarchal institution," endangered companionate marriage and family, trapped women in sexual bondage, and failed to contain men's sexual excesses and patriarchal rule. Early antipolygamy writers saw polygamy as slavery's equal in this regard; polygamy, or "patriarchal marriage," trapped women in sexual bondage and powerlessness. It was a backward affront to the companionate households that northern reformers associated with the progress of civilization. For anti-Mormons, Latter-day Saints (by and large northern white converts in the 1850s) had returned to a backward, uncivilized "patriarchal" state reminiscent in many ways of southern slavery. That is, Utah's gender roles and family structures appeared to anti-Mormon reformers to be very much in line with the South.[10]

Both antipolygamy and antislavery writers claimed that polygamy and slavery were threats to marriage, family, and women's sexual virtue as central institutions of American life. Both slavery and polygamy enabled the depravity of men of power—slaveholders and polygamists—to break up marriages and families for their own licentious purposes, resulting in the trafficking of women for men's depraved objectives. Slavery endangered both black and white women's sexuality by making black women entirely at the disposal of depraved slave owners, and betraying white women's trust and fidelity in their husbands. Polygamy endangered white women's sexuality by making it subject to the demands of depraved husbands. Legal historian Sarah Barringer Gordon notes, "The division of society into a pampered and much-married male aristocracy at one end, and oppressed wives and poor men at the other, combined with the licentiousness and violence of plural husbands and the death of those wronged by an abusive social and sexual system, all pointed to a connection that antipolygamists drew early and often—polygamy was a form of slavery."[11]

Antipolygamy and antislavery writings demonstrate northern reformers' attempts to turn American sentiments against the institutions that in 1856 would be called the "twin relics of barbarism."[12] For antislavery and antipolygamy authors, neither slavery nor polygamy allowed free hearts or free homes. Ideas about sexuality, marriage, and the home, then, were deeply embedded in the rhetoric of the "twin relics of barbarism." It was in part because slavery and polygamy destroyed companionate marriages and families and endangered women's sexuality that northern reformers and Republican politicians alike linked the two systems.

In 1861, Henry Sumner Maine, a British legal scholar, situated the context for the transition to companionate, democratic families in a broader movement of "progressive" societies from status to contract. Status, he argued, represented older models of family in which individuals were enveloped in filial ties of dependence and obligation that determined their social position. The growth of individualism in progressive societies meant that, increasingly, individuals could determine their relationships and obligations on their own terms by free agreement—contract. Marriage, he argued, was increasingly such a contract.[13] On the other hand, slavery and polygamy, their opponents argued, was very much a vestigial holdover of status-based societies, and so was incompatible with modern democracies. Republican reformers, thus, opposed polygamy and slavery as domestic relations that violated the terms of contractual societies.

Antislavery writings in the antebellum period took many forms—fiction, short story, essay, pamphlet, and book—and the ways slavery threatened marriage, family, and women's sexuality were consistent themes from the 1830s until the Civil War. Antipolygamy, though not as popular a genre, took similar forms to antislavery—fiction, short story, essay, pamphlet, and book—and also demonstrated the dangers polygamy posed to marriage, family, and women's sexuality. In many ways, these sources built on the ground established by antislavery rhetoric, forging the links between the two practices that informed the language of the "twin relics." This essay draws widely from these sources, focusing especially on writings that demonstrate the threat slavery posed to companionate marriage, the democratic family, and women's sexuality. I am particularly concerned with narrative and storytelling, here, because both fictional and real-life accounts of slavery and polygamy served particular functions in calls for state action. Fictional accounts allowed writers to mobilize the power of imagination to cultivate ideas about what families, and by extension societies, could be like if they were organized along a companionate, democratic model. For these writers, properly organized families could change the world with what literary scholar Jane Tompkins has called "sentimental power." For these writers, the ideal home was a model for democratic social organization, guided by women's moral superiority.[14]

Both antislavery and antipolygamy writers were anxious to demonstrate that the events they described were at least based in fact. Antislavery writers gave readers a look at how writers imagined the subjective experience of slaves. Because the evils of slavery often took place in the privacy of the household, these writers struggled to show the truth of incidents of which there was little public record.[15] Many narratives in *The Liberty Bell*, an antislavery gift book of short stories and essays published annually from 1839 to 1858, began with some claim to truth—"a meeting with the hero or heroine, an account of events in the newspaper, or most often and simply just having been told."[16] Stories from other sources often began with similar claims. Even Harriet Beecher Stowe identified the roots of her novel, *Uncle Tom's Cabin*, in events she either witnessed or heard about. Her characters and their experiences, Stowe claimed, both in her novel and later in *The Key to Uncle Tom's Cabin*, had real parallels in the world.[17] To be sure, antislavery writings served the agendas of their authors, but their accounts of the experiences of slaves were more often based on accounts they heard from former slaves than antipolygamy writers' narratives were on Mormon accounts. As Manisha Sinha suggests, "If slave narratives are accepted as authentic black testimony about the workings of slavery, then the abuse of female slaves was an essential component of fugitive slave abolitionism rather than a figment of the supposed prurient and pornographic imagination of white abolitionists."[18] Slave and former slave women testified of the sexual assaults of their masters in personal testimonies and autobiographies. That is, antislavery authors' claims to the truth of their accounts were much more veritable than antipolygamy writers' claims.

Antipolygamy accounts, though, did give their readers glimpses of how writers fancied, often with prurient imaginations, the experience of women and men practicing polygamy, which were in many ways far removed from actual realities. This may account for antipolygamy writers' anxious justifications for their writings in which they expressed a profound need to demonstrate the truth of what they had written. These novelists, according to literary and religious scholar Terryl Givens, seemed to lack "a sense of themselves *as* a novelist or of their task as being novel writing."[19] Indeed, they may have imagined themselves telling the truth about a phenomenon most of them had likely not even witnessed. On another level, however, the apologetic tone of many of these writers' truth claims also suggests an ulterior motive: to provide justification for their audience to encounter the portrayals of sexuality, violence, and crime they were about to read. Maria Ward, among the most apologetic of antipolygamy writers, justified her writings with fervor: "Knowing, as I do know, the evils and horrors and abominations of the Mormon system, the degradation it imposes on females, and the consequent vices which extend through all the ramifications of the society, a sense of duty to the world has induced me to prepare the following narrative for the public eye."[20] By framing her book as an anonymous memoir, Ward, as both character and author, could frame her "observations" as fact, even though they had little basis in the realities of Mormon women's experiences of polygamy.[21] Last, Nelson Winch Green was perhaps most clear in apologizing to readers for the smut they were about to encounter. In his recounting of the story of Mrs. Ettie V. Smith, complete with a reprint of her affidavit of its truth, Green claimed that nothing had been written to arouse "morbid curiosity." In fact, he claimed to have omitted details "from a wish to avoid offence."[22] Clearly, these apologies and justifications served dual purposes—to protect authors from accusations of poor taste while attracting audiences interested but unwilling to claim that interest in the scandalous tales they were about to consume.

Many antislavery and antipolygamy writers were much more invested in what Sarah Gordon has called "emotional fact" than actual.[23] It was the truths of the heart that writers wished to convey—hearts enslaved, broken, and destroyed by polygamy and slavery. Harriet Beecher Stowe was particularly deliberate about telling the "emotional facts" about slavery, telling her readers that she has "given only a faint shadow, a dim picture, of the anguish and despair that are, at this very moment, riving thousands of hearts, shattering thousands of families, and driving a helpless and sensitive race to frenzy and despair. There are those living who know the mothers whom this accursed traffic has driven to the murder of their children; and themselves seeking in death a shelter from woes more dreaded than death."[24] These, for Stowe, were among the emotional facts of slavery, and in Stowe's final chapter, readers were called to *feel* correctly about slavery with sympathy for the downtrodden and outrage that such a system prevailed in the United States.[25]

Antipolygamy writer Metta Victoria Fuller was also especially clear about telling the emotional facts of polygamy, inviting her readers "to pause over this little record of *one* history, and then, multiplying it by tens of thousands, say if he can find it in his heart to fellowship with such a moral monster as Deseret now is."[26] The many experiences to which Fuller was witness in her novel were meant to evoke this sympathy and to call readers to action against polygamy.[27] Antipolygamy and antislavery writers alike wanted their readers first to feel correctly about polygamy, with sympathy for the victims of polygamy and slavery, and outrage that these systems continued to exist, and second to call for federal action to resolve the relics causing Republican unease.

The emotional facts antislavery and antipolygamy writings attempted to communicate to their readers were cut from the same cloth, circulating around the dangers both systems posed to changing marital, familial, and sexual values that were emerging in the Northeast. Slavery and polygamy endangered companionate marriage, imperiled the democratic family held together by bonds of affection rather than patriarchal control, and threatened women's sexual purity. Polygamy, antipolygamy writers claimed, was equivalent to slavery, and endangered marriage, family, and women's sexuality in ways similar to slavery. Both rhetorics called for state intervention to outlaw the twin systems that so violated companionate democratic family life.

The connections antislavery writers made to polygamy were less explicit and less frequent than those connecting polygamy to slavery, but the ways antislavery writers called up images of plantation polygamy were still important in establishing the links between the two practices. In one early rhetorical association between slavery and polygamy, George Bourne's 1837 treatise, *Slavery Illustrated in Its Effects Upon Woman and Domestic Society*, claimed that the slave states were a vast brothel in which "multiform incest, polygamy, adultery, and other uncleanness are constantly perpetrated."[28] Central to the threat slavery posed to marriage was that, like in polygamous marriages, the state had no role in validating slave family or sexual relationships. Slave marriages were illegal in the antebellum period, and this made both the institution of marriage itself and the people in such marriages, especially women, vulnerable. Extralegal marriages could be both established and broken up by slave masters with little concern for the filial affection of those involved. Although marriage among slaves was illegal, many slaves established extralegal forms of marriage and established families that provided much needed forms of support and affection. At times, slave owners allowed slaves to select their own partners, and at others, slaves were forced into partnerships they may not otherwise have chosen. Nonetheless, the conditions of slavery in antebellum America made slave marital and family life difficult and the threat of separation was ubiquitous. As antislavery writers pointed out, the dissolution of slave marriages was done almost entirely at the whim of slave owners, and the consequences for slaves were disastrous.

Multiple polygamous slave marriages showed up in antislavery writings as simply a fact of slave life. In many stories, black slave women were sometimes forced to participate in a kind of polygamy under a slave breeding system that declared slave marriages illegal, ignored slaves' extralegal attempts to establish filial ties, and forced slaves into marital and sexual relations they did not want. In one example, a short story by Caroline W. Healey Dall, the main character, a slave named Annie Gray, was married to one man who was a hired hand. Upon his disappearance, Annie's master simply told Annie to prepare again to be a wife with no regard to her previous marriage.[29] In another tale, also by Dall, after bearing eighteen children and seeing them taken from her and sold, one slave purchased the possession of her only remaining child by agreeing to marry the new Negro her master was to bring home that night. "She was to meet him for the first time at that altar that the institution of Slavery so utterly desecrates."[30] Thus, slave women like the ones in these stories were sometimes forced to participate in several extralegal marriages over the course of a lifetime, a kind of polygamy that debased the institution of marriage.

In antislavery writings, slavery presented a threefold danger to marriage. Some of those dangers were echoed in later antipolygamy writings. First, writers claimed that because slave marriages were illegal, whatever relationships slaves could establish were inherently fragile and vulnerable to the whims of masters. Second, writers also claimed that the moral and spiritual development that occurred within marriage and family sometimes did not occur among slaves who had either no or extremely limited marital and filial ties. Third, a genre of narratives known as "tragic mulatta" stories demonstrated that light-skinned black women, in particular, were vulnerable to seduction by and sometimes tricked into extralegal marriages to white men who then, by will or by circumstance, left the women in tragic conditions. These dangers resulted from the fact that slavery made slave marriages and the establishment of slave families illegal.

In 1837, George Bourne declared, as antipolygamy writers would later affirm, that "the domestic union preceded all other relations and laws," and was the foundation of human society.³¹ The objective of marriage, he believed, was "to preserve the native purity of woman in all its unsullied freshness and primitive vigor."³² However, he affirmed that "slavery, as it is established by law among us, cannot possibly co-exist with marriage, female chastity, and domestic relationship."³³ He pointed out that even when slaves managed to establish a semblance of marital and family life, it was easily torn apart by the whim and will of slave masters.³⁴

Twenty years later, an anonymous author, who called him- or herself "A Native of the South-West," echoed Bourne's early sentiments more thoroughly. This writer, whose purpose was to "trace, in a kind, candid, and truthful manner, the influence of slavery upon the diversified relations and interests of the Family," extolled the virtues of the proper companionate Christian marriage, while condemning its absence among slaves.³⁵ Society, this author argued, "has risen to the highest elevation, or sunk to the deepest debasement, as family obligations have been respected or violated."³⁶ In a statement about the nature of filial emotion, the author claimed, "The manifestation and reciprocation of sympathy, affection, and kind offices, should be tender, and constant, and secure from all interference."³⁷ This iteration of family life was responsible for "prosperous, refined, and happy people." However, under slavery, "No provision can be made for its [marriage's] formation, celebration, or continuance; ... The voluntariness and independence necessary to take the conjugal vow cannot belong to slaves."³⁸ Slave marriages would, this author argued, impair the control of slave masters over slaves, and thus could not be permitted. In a society without marriage, slaves lacked the refining influence of marriage and the resulting "wretched system of concubinage inevitably produces the most revolting licentiousness."³⁹ Thus slaves, lacking marriages and families, also lacked a "whole class of purifying, cheering, ennobling, and consoling influences and sentiments."⁴⁰ In the absence of these influences, slaves degenerated into base, blunted beings ruled by passions and licentiousness. This author concluded, "The family is the head, the heart, the fountain of society, and it has not a privilege that slavery does not nullify, a right that it does not violate, a single facility for improvement it does not counteract, nor a hope that it does not put out in darkness."⁴¹ The absence of legal marriage among slaves, then, had dire consequences not only for individual slaves' moral and spiritual development, but for the development of slave society.

Some light-skinned black women were subjected to false marriages in a genre of narratives known as the "tragic mulatta" stories. In many of these narratives, unsuspecting biracial women were seduced into marriage, often extralegal, by beguiling white men in ways similar to the ways polygamous husbands mesmerized their wives. In one early example, published in 1839, Lydia Maria Child told the story of a young physician who, unknowingly, married another man's light-skinned slave. Upon discovering she was a slave, the physician purchased his wife from her owner, who also confessed that she was his daughter.[42] As American studies scholar Karen Sánchez-Eppler demonstrates, the story perverts courtship into ownership. Once purchased by her husband, the slave's husband and owner are the same man. "It is the collapse of the assumed difference between family and slavery that makes this anecdote so disturbing; in this story the institutions of marriage and of slavery are not merely analogous, they are coextensive and indistinguishable."[43] Narratives like this one intended to show readers that for many a "tragic mulatta," family and slavery were undifferentiated from each other. The bonds of love and the exigencies of economic transaction and property ownership were entangled together.

In Child's later story, "The Quadroons," published in 1842, a quadroon (someone having one quarter black ancestry) woman, Rosalie, and a white man, Edward, fall in love. While the marriage was not a legal one, Edward tells Rosalie, "Let the church that my mother loved sanction our union, and my own soul will be satisfied without the protection of the state." For him, "It was a marriage sanctioned by Heaven though unrecognized on earth."[44] Edward and Rosalie live together in peace for ten years, and have a daughter they name Xarifa. After ten years, Edward develops political ambitions and Charlotte, the daughter of a powerful wealthy man, "awakened thoughts of the great worldly advantages connected with a union" with her.[45] Edward becomes betrothed to Charlotte. Just before his legal marriage to Charlotte, he professes his love to Rosalie and suggests "she would ever be his real wife, and they might see each other frequently." Rosalie, however, refuses, her spirit "too pure to form a selfish league with crime."[46] Brokenhearted, Edward nonetheless enters a loveless marriage with Charlotte, who, "fortunately . . . could not miss the impassioned tenderness she had never experienced." During a chance meeting of Charlotte and Rosalie and Xarifa, Charlotte figures out that she is looking at the Rosalie whose name Edward had been uttering in his fitful sleep, and "from gossiping tongues" Charlotte learns of Edward's previous relationship with Rosalie. "She wept, but not as poor Rosalie had done, for she never had loved, and been beloved, like [Rosalie]."[47] A year after Edward's marriage to Charlotte, Rosalie is found dead, likely murdered by Charlotte. Edward, reunited with his daughter Xarifa, attends the funeral and weeps profusely. He returns to live with Xarifa for some time but drinks his grief for Rosalie away. When Edward dies in a drunken accident, it is discovered that Rosalie had been the daughter of a slave of a wealthy master and his heirs discover their claim to ownership of Xarifa and sell her at auction to a master bent on desecrating her. Xarifa plans an escape, but is betrayed by another slave, is injured in the attempt, and eventually dies. She is buried, and "no one wept at the grave of her who had been so carefully cherished, and so tenderly beloved."[48]

This story profoundly illustrated the role of slavery in destroying companionate marriages and families. The idyllic setting and loving family in which Child placed Edward, Rosalie, and Xarifa for ten years was destroyed by Edward's ambitions and his willingness to sacrifice love for political gain. The nature of Edward's extralegal "marriage" to Rosalie facilitated Edward's betrayal by allowing him easy escape, illustrating the dangers of marriage without a legal contract. Moreover, Child's narrative juxtaposed Edward's loveless legal marriage to Charlotte to his loving relationship with Rosalie, clearly demonstrating Child's mandate that love serve as the defining feature of marriage. The noble Rosalie refused to accept the duplicity of Edward's loveless marriage to Charlotte and, as the tragic heroine of the story, died unsullied but betrayed by the feckless Edward. Upon his death, Edward's beloved daughter was resigned to a life of slavery and sexual desecration, once again demonstrating the dangers of extralegal marriages. Edward had no legal claim to Xarifa and thus, even in death, could not protect her from this terrible fate.

The lack of legal ties among slaves disrupted not only marriages, but families as well. Many slaveholders demonstrated complete disregard for black families and the affective ties that bound them together. As literary scholar Julie Husband points out, between 1820 and 1860, nearly one third of American slave families were separated; other slaveholding societies did not separate family members from each other on this scale.[49] Partly in response to the very real destruction of families under slavery and partly to generate sympathy for the antislavery cause, abolitionists of the 1830s launched what Husband calls a "family protection campaign," publicizing the destruction of slave families by the slave trade, the vulnerability of slave women to sexual exploitation, and the spectacle of white masters selling their own biracial children to other owners.[50]

In keeping with Husband's claims, Pierson demonstrates that the charges of 1830s abolitionists illustrated the worst offenses against the family. Abolitionists like George Bourne rightly claimed that slaveholders destroyed slave families, raped the women they enslaved, and viewed their own daughters, borne of their slaves, as commodities.[51] Bourne declared, "Slavery abolishes all the ties of consanguinity, for no relationship is admitted to exist between the white and the colored members of the same household." Slaveholding men had sexual relations with slave women and, in turn, the daughters that resulted from such unions. The sons of slaveholders also had relations with their half-sisters and their mothers.[52] Moreover, for Bourne, slave breeding destroyed both intergenerational and marital ties, replacing family structures with commercial relations.[53] The commercial nature of slavery meant that husbands, wives, mothers, and children were sold away from their families for profit.

The theme of families being broken up by slavery continued through antislavery rhetoric until the Civil War. In one 1854 short story, Anne P. Adams declared that in the slave market, "Husbands would be torn from their wives, mothers from their children, and *all* from everything they loved most dearly."[54] Julie Husband points out that the family protection campaign that started in the 1830s and continued through the 1850s "succeeded in connecting slavery, sexual exploitation, and the separation of families in the public mind." This, Husband claims, "prepared the public to receive" Harriet Beecher Stowe's *Uncle Tom's Cabin*.[55] According to literary scholar Philip Fisher, in antislavery novels like Stowe's, "The central psychological and social evil of slavery is the separation of families: the selling of children or wives or uncles or fathers to separate buyers and with such sales, the permanent severing of family ties."[56] For Stowe, this theme is briefly encapsulated by the statement of a white woman stranger on a steamboat carrying the character Tom further south, who states "The most dreadful part of slavery, to my mind, is its outrages of feelings and affections—the separating of families, for example."[57]

In her analysis of *Uncle Tom's Cabin*, literary scholar Gillian Brown argues, "The real horror that slavery holds for the 'mothers of America' to whom Stowe addressed her antislavery appeal is the suggestion that the family life nurtured by women is not immune from the economic life outside it."[58] For Stowe, Brown claims, the problem with slavery was that it introduced the world of the male, public marketplace into the arena of the female, private home. While slaveholders defended slavery in patriarchal filial terms, figuring slaves as their domestic dependents, the economic exigencies of slavery belied that claim and laid bare the crudely economic relations between owners and slaves.[59]

Beginning a meditation on the separation of families, Stowe demonstrated the relationship between the economic exigencies of slavery and the disruption of slave family ties. In the beginning of the novel, readers are introduced to

George and Eliza, two married slaves from plantations near each other. Eliza's otherwise relatively benevolent master, Mr. Shelby, sells Eliza's son, along with the protagonist, Uncle Tom, to a slave trader to pay off Shelby's debt, demonstrating the carelessness with which even the most benevolent of slave owners separated families. Shelby permits the ruthlessness of the marketplace to invade the sanctity of the home, demonstrating that "the slave economy always subjects the home and family to market contingencies."[60]

At the same time, Eliza's husband, George, who had been leased out to a factory, is forced to return to a cruel master. Their family broken, Eliza and George escape, but not together, and are reunited in a Quaker settlement where George feels the pleasures of home for the first time.[61] This feeling compels George and Eliza to continue to Canada, where they reestablish their family. George's sister and Eliza's mother Cassy, formerly a sexual slave on the depraved Legree plantation, find Eliza and George five years free in Canada, which Stowe likens to heaven for slave families: "These shores of refuge, like the eternal shore, often unite again, in glad communion, hearts that for long years have mourned each other as lost." All of this Stowe calls "truth stranger than fiction," and remarks, "How can it be otherwise, when a system prevails which whirls families and scatters their members, as the wind whirls and scatters the leaves of autumn?"[62] But Eliza and George are among the lucky in Stowe's novel, as additional scenes of ancillary characters feature children being sold out of the arms of mothers, never to be seen again. In Stowe's narrative, slavery, even under the best of conditions, disrupted almost any attempt slaves might have of establishing families, while escape enables George's and Eliza's heavenly family reunion, establishing their "free home" in Canada and later Liberia. Most slaves, however, were not so fortunate.

Besides the breaking up of slave families, another threat the twin relics shared was the threat to women's virtue constituted by the ways slavery and polygamy both exposed women to the evil of licentious men who could buy and sell female flesh for sexual purposes. Bound up with antislavery ideas about marriage and family were deep concerns about the dangers slavery posed to black women's sexuality. In 1833 Lydia Maria Child's book, *An Appeal in Favor of that Class of Americans Called Africans*, began to explore a subject that would soon become popular in antislavery discourse—the sexual exploitation of slave women and its "degrading effect . . . on the morals of both blacks and whites."[63] In this book, Child declared of the slave woman, "She is the property of her master, and her daughters are his property. They are allowed to have no conscientious scruples, no sense of shame, no regard for the feelings of husband, or parent; they must be entirely subservient to the will of their owner, on pain of being whipped as near unto death as will comport with his interest, or quite to death, if it suit his pleasure."[64] Slavery, Child argued, made women the property of lustful owners and left them powerless to protect their virtue. Although controversial in the early 1830s, the book gave antislavery writers ammunition that would prove valuable over the coming decades.[65]

As historian Carol Lasser demonstrates, depictions of sexual assault in antislavery discourse shifted over the antebellum period from what she calls "voyeuristic abolitionism" in the 1830s to a tamer and more respectable abolitionism by the late 1840s and early 1850s. In the 1830s, when women were more fully integrated throughout the antislavery movement, both men and women writers graphically described the sexual exploitation of female slaves as part of their antislavery appeals to women.[66] Antislavery writers justified their more explicit descriptions of the sexual threats slavery posed by accompanying them with calls to action against slavery. However, as antislavery activism shifted from moral suasion to electoral politics, women's place in the movement became less clear as concerns about gendered respectability in the political arena surfaced. By the late 1840s "both the language of voyeuristic abolitionism and the mobilization of women around the highly sexualized content of the rhetoric that had, in the 1830s, helped rally them to the cause, receded."[67] That is, "sexualized antislavery rhetoric moved from center to margin."[68] Antipolygamy rhetoric, on the other hand, maintained a voyeuristic flavor well into the late 1850s, demonstrating the sexual threats to women that polygamy legitimated.

In one example of voyeuristic abolitionism, George Bourne articulated similar concerns to Child's early writings about the sexual dangers slave women faced and he linked them to companionate marriage and family relations. "The sexual relation is of God's appointment," he declared, suggesting that the emotions and sensibilities that accompany the sexual relationship "are of the purest and most refining character."[69] For Bourne, "Female chastity is the cornerstone of society. *It is a woman's instinct to be undefiled.*"[70] He went on to show that female chastity leads to the wife's affection, the mother's love, the sister's tenderness, and is entirely eradicated by slavery.[71] The purpose of marriage, Bourne argued, was "to preserve the native purity of woman in all its unsullied freshness and primitive vigor."[72] Slavery, he claimed, "abrogates the law and institution of marriage" among slaves, such that women's purity could not be preserved. Slave women were "despoiled of all protection; exposed to every indignity; obliged to submit to the brutal demand of any lawless white man; coerced to degradation by heartrending tortures; doomed to sacrifice the tenderest affections; scourged to conceal their instinctive sensibilities; and . . . they are merely human tools to pander to the sensuality, and to gratify the unclean desires of their inhuman task-masters."[73]

Not only did slavery endanger the virtue of black women and families, but white ones as well. Everyone in the South, Bourne claimed, knew about sexual relations between masters and slaves; "The facts are as public as the houses in which the parties resided."[74] The mothers and sisters of southern white men "are acquainted with the flagrant sensuality of their sons and brothers. Wives and daughters are certified of the constant adulterous intercourse of their husbands and fathers."[75] These sexual sins "dissolve the bonds of society, eradicate the safeguards of domestic peace and enjoyment, and pollute the very fountains of human existence."[76] In addition to these evils, slavery also encouraged owners to sell the daughters conceived through intercourse with their slaves; "Men and even professing Christians will sell their own daughters for the express purposes of an impure life."[77] Thus, slave owning men not only raped and assaulted their slaves, but sold the daughters conceived through such contact into lives of sexual servitude.

The theme of women's sexual exploitation under slavery continued, though in tamer language, into the 1840s and 1850s. One story, written by Frances H. Green in 1845, illustrates the consequences of slave women's sexual victimization for slave marriages. Green claims she heard the story from a man who knew a former slave named Laco, who had married a slave named Clusy who could pass as white. Clusy's master attempted to assault her and her refusals earned her forty lashes immediately after her and Laco's baby was born. Laco and Clusy escaped forthwith, but Clusy died shortly thereafter.

Like many antislavery writers, Green punctuated her narratives with calls to action, particularly directed at women. Indeed, Laco himself implores Green to narrate his tale with pleas to "all ye virtuous—all you pious women of the land; and if your virtue, your piety, are not a mere sham—are not a damning lie—give speedy help to the thousands of women—all of them your sisters in the bonds of humanity—many of them your sisters in the bonds of Christianity—who are daily prostituted on the alter [sic] of slavery!"[78] Laco continued, "For if any woman can hear it without a wish—a determination to labor with all her might to abolish THE SLAVERY OF WOMAN, I impeach her virtue—She is *not* TRUE—she is NOT PURE."[79]

Carol Lasser points out that by the 1850s, in antislavery rhetoric, "sexual transgressions are sketched and suggested, but never graphically depicted or explicitly named." This is especially true in Stowe's novel, *Uncle Tom's Cabin*. As part of a broader attempt to expand the audience of antislavery rhetoric, "Stowe's moderate prose allowed the book to enter northern parlors" without offending middle-class sensibilities.[80] Stowe addressed the sexual threat slavery posed to slave women, but always circuitously, never directly, naming the offenses. The endangered virtue of slave women is most demonstrated when the beautiful Emmeline is sold to the malignant slave master, Simon Legree, for sexual service. When Emmeline arrives on the Legree plantation, she meets Cassy, who has been serving as Legree's sexual concubine for some time. Cassy's backstory reveals a lengthy history of sexual servitude to various masters. Moreover, in "the most extreme manifestation possible of the corruption of the maternal ethic that chattel slavery, by definition, necessitates," Cassy had murdered her infant to prevent his enslavement and sale.[81] Literary scholar Eve Allegra Raimon argues that Cassy was perhaps the most self-possessed and agentic character in the tradition of tragic mulatto characters, but her backstory nonetheless illustrated the sexual danger of slavery for beautiful "mulatta" women. For Stowe, Emmeline's and Cassy's positions were but a few examples of the widespread "shameless sale of beautiful mulatto and quadroon girls" for sexual slavery.[82]

In 1860, Lydia Maria Child expanded upon themes she had first explored in 1833. Quoting a woman named Margaret Douglass, Child declared that the female slave "knows that she is a *slave*, and, as such, powerless beneath the whims or fancies of her master. If he casts upon her a desiring eye, she knows that she *must* submit . . . [S]he *feels* her degradation, and so do others with whom she is connected. She has parents, brothers, sisters, a lover, perhaps, who all suffer through her and with her."[83] Child also pointed out that vulnerability of slave women to sexual assault by masters threatened not only the integrity of slave families, but the integrity and peace of slaveholders' families as well. The slave children of slave masters who assaulted and impregnated their slaves served to their white wives as constant reminders of their husbands' infidelities, threatening the affective ties that undergirded the democratic family. "White mothers and daughters of the South have suffered under this custom [the sexual assault of slaves] for years; they have seen their dearest affections trampled on, their hopes of domestic happiness destroyed. . . . They know the fact, and their hearts bleed under its knowledge, however they may have attempted to conceal their discoveries."[84]

Michael D. Pierson argues that antislavery rhetoric in the 1830s and 1840s was concerned primarily with the material conditions in which slaves lived. By the 1850s abolitionists attacked slavery because it reinforced patriarchal dependence on a white patriarch and made it impossible for slaves to achieve individual fulfillment, particularly for slave women who were subject to that patriarch's sexual control.[85] In this sense, over the 1850s, antislavery rhetoric became more like emerging antipolygamy rhetoric. Hence, in the 1850s, critiques of slavery and polygamy were also critiques of patriarchal family models that denied both slaves and women individual freedom. Indeed, many of the reform efforts of the 1850s, Pierson suggests, were critiques of patriarchs themselves. "Inherently exploitive social practices and regulations—the widespread availability of alcohol, the system of chattel slavery, or Mormon polygamy—lured men who might otherwise have been model husbands into vice and destruction of the home."[86] The new family ideals emerging in the Northeast required the manly restraint of men who respected the sanctity of the family, dissuading husbands from using arbitrary power over their wives and children.[87] Affection, not domination, drew these families together. The contractual family was imagined as a more civilized alternative to traditional patriarchal families because its bonds were consensual.

Writers claimed that polygamy in the West and slavery in the South perpetuated patriarchal models of family life and enabled male tyranny in the home. They agreed that male domination of households placed hearts and homes in bondage, in one way or another, under both systems. Empowered by the twin relics of barbarism to dominate their households, slaveholding and polygamous men became depraved by this power. Writers demonstrated the enslavement of women in the South and in the West to illustrate the implications of unfettered male authority over the household. Slaveholding and polygamous households dominated by men could not, by nature, be "free" because they trapped slaves and women in servitude, denying and betraying the freedom of their hearts. Both antipolygamy and antislavery argued that patriarchal dependence was always flawed because the inherent sexual nature of men led them to exploit women under their control.[88] For antislavery writers, the sexual assault of female slaves now became evidence of the lustful nature of men. For antipolygamy writers, the sexual exploitation of wives served as that evidence. Both sets of writers concluded that if all men were lustful, all women needed the freedoms and protections companionate marriage provided.[89]

One meditation of the effect of slavery on slaveholding men came in Stowe's *Uncle Tom's Cabin*. For Stowe, even the best of slaveholders cannot help but be depraved by the system itself. Augustine St. Clare, Tom's second owner, is one of the more humane slaveholders. St. Clare is a decent fellow and "no planter."[90] At one point early in the novel he declares that all slaveholders "know better" than to participate in slavery, but are compelled by the institution itself to participate.[91] In another scene, strangers on a boat headed to the Legree plantation discuss how not all masters are as depraved and violent as Simon Legree, but mention that even humane slaveholders are responsible for the brutality of slavery because they participate in and support the system. One young man declares, "It is you considerate, humane men, that are responsible for all the brutality and outrage wrought by these wretches; because, if it were not for your sanction and influence, the whole system could not keep foot-hold for an hour."[92] That is, St. Clare's complicity enables Legree's cruelty and depravity. Slavery turned good men bad by making them over into controlling patriarchs.

One of the privileges of slavery's patriarchs was their sexual access to slaves. The rampant sexual activity between masters and slaves on many plantations encouraged antislavery writers to characterize plantations as Oriental harems. American studies scholar Amy Kaplan, in her groundbreaking essay "Manifest Domesticity," argues that the genre of domestic fiction performed its cultural work by linking household domesticity to the national domestic, in opposition to that which was foreign. Household and national "domestics," she argues, mirrored each other in nineteenth-century discourse, suggesting that the national domestic sphere, the borders of the nation, were marked, especially in domestic fiction, by the appropriate practice of domesticity in the home. A proper home was fundamental to the performance of national identity and belonging. Kaplan further claims that "domesticity not only monitors the borders between the civilized and the savage but also regulates traces of the savage within itself."[93] That is, the improper practice of domesticity marked those within the borders of the nation as savage, backward, and barbaric. Perhaps nowhere is this truer than in the use of Orientalist metaphors in antipolygamy and antislavery writings. Mormon historians Leonard J. Arrington and Jon Haupt point out in their early analysis of antipolygamy literature that the image of the harem was familiar to many if not most literate Americans.[94] In fact, the imagery of the Oriental harem was so familiar to American readers that antislavery and antipolygamy writers used it to mark both practices as foreign and barbaric, thus making slaveholders and Mormons cruel foreigners.

Antislavery writers deployed the image of the Oriental seraglio in their descriptions of southern plantations. As Pierson points out, "the abolitionist sexual critique of slavery that positioned masters as sultans of harems and enslaved women as rape victims" was widespread in the 1830s.[95] George Bourne quoted a Virginia woman, who declared, "We are called wives, and as such we are recognized in law; but we are little more than superintendents of a colored seraglio."[96] A few years later, Bourne declared that "a northern citizen, when he visits the slave-holder's domain, is at once struck with the harem-like aspect of the large mansion in which he is sojourning."[97] He continued, "Neither Asiatic polygamy, nor even the Popish celibacy is equally nefarious and execrable in its reference to the law of chastity, and the transgressions of the seventh commandment as the accursed system of slavery in the United States."[98] Thomas Wentworth Higginson reportedly also declared that, compared to the South, "a Turkish harem is a cradle of virgin purity."[99] Plantations, antislavery writers asserted, were more like Turkish seraglios than American homes, marking plantations as foreign and backward.

The Orientalism of the South was not only reflected in the harem-like quality of southern plantations, but also in the seclusion of white women. Lydia Maria Child frequently discussed the Orientalist repercussions of slavery for slaveholding women. In one 1842 essay, she declared, "A seclusion, almost Mahommedan, is demanded of [woman] by the exactions of southern fashion."[100] She further claimed that "there is apparent, upon a close observation of southern life, a species of lurking and secret jealousy of women—an oriental desire of confining her to a state of restriction and surveillance—an overweening anxiety in man to engross all her social as well as domestic relations to himself alone."[101] In her 1843 short story, "Slavery's Pleasant Homes," Child described one white slaveholding woman as "nurtured in seclusion, almost as deep as that of the oriental harem."[102] Thus the Oriental nature of slavery not only trapped black women in the harems of their masters, but white women in the households of their husbands. Southern white women were adornments to their husbands' households, and southern men presided over their wives with as much dominion as their slave harems.[103] Slavery, for antislavery writers, not only made the southern household an Oriental harem or seraglio, but made slaveholding women its secluded prisoners. This, Child asserted, occurred in a context in which many nineteenth-century thinkers measured civilization by the treatment of women, "by whose position and estimate the degree of civilized culture is usually measured."[104]

Even Harriet Beecher Stowe's *Uncle Tom's Cabin* contained traces of Orientalism. Her description of the St. Clare mansion conflates the Orient, the Moors, and Spain all together. According to literary critic Jennifer L. Jenkens, this conflation "constructs a body of images that, for her, describe the non-white, non-American, non-Calvanist world." Stowe's South is "more European than American but even more Oriental than European."[105] Thus, the St. Clare mansion becomes representative of the South more broadly as a "seductively, dangerously feminized and decadent place" that can "only produce corrupt and horrific versions of the family."[106]

The broad concerns about marriage, family, and sexuality that animated antislavery campaigns in the antebellum era also roused antipolygamy writers after the Mormons publicly announced the practice of plural marriage in 1852, for polygamy, too, produced corrupt and horrific versions of the family. Antipolygamy writers often used slavery as a kind of trope to demonstrate the marital, familial, and sexual evils of polygamy. At times, the equation of polygamy with slavery was simply asserted. This is clearest in Metta Victoria Fuller's preface to her novel: "Repulsive as slavery appears to us, we can but deem polygamy as a thing more loathsome and poisonous to social and political purity."[107] Lumping polygamy with slavery and untidily with temperance, Fuller continued to claim that "as citizens of this country, we owe it as a duty, not only to the Constitution but to humanity, that we sternly oppose slavery in all its forms—intemperance and its hideous deformities, and polygamy with its train of evils which no man can truly conceive, but which surely will end in animalizing man, in corrupting the very founts of virtue and purity and, finally, in barbarism."[108] Here, slavery worked as a broad metaphor for both intemperance (which reformers believed enslaved men to alcohol and their wives to their husbands' drinking) and polygamy, which antipolygamy reformers believed enslaved women.

Other authors claimed that polygamy enslaved women by requiring them to labor as slaves labored, and by subjecting women to corporal punishment like that which slaves endured. Alfreda Eva Bell asserted that under polygamy, "The women are treated as but little better than slaves; they are in fact white slaves; are required to do all the most servile drudgery; are painfully impressed with their nothingness and utter inferiority, in divers [sic] ways and at all seasons; and are frequently . . . subjected to personal violence and various modes of corporeal punishment."[109] By way of example, one character, Lizzie Price's husband, "flew into a violent rage at the sight of her grief, when he proposed bringing another wife into the house, and actually beat her—*beat her with his fists*—so violently as to bring on a hemorrhage, which, being repeated, ended her days."[110]

Maria Ward also claimed that polygamous women are "treated little better than slaves, were required to do all the drudgery, were frequently subjected to corporeal punishment, and painfully impressed with a sense of their inferiority in a thousand ways."[111] By Ward's account, no family in Utah hires servants; a few have slaves, but most who are in need of additional labor simply take another wife.[112] One buyer even comments that the two young women he is purchasing as wives are better and cheaper than hired hands.[113] In another instance, a plural wife, Mrs. Clarke, declares that she is "compelled, by stripes and punishment, to perform the most menial drudgery."[114] Yet another character in Ward's book sells his daughter into polygamy. The daughter resists, telling her father, who is only interested in profiting from her sale, "I dare disobey any man, who seeks to make me a slave, and whose tyranny would embitter my whole life."[115] Lastly, one figure who appeared in Ward's novel was the polygamous wife, tied nude to a tree, beaten, and abandoned. This figure echoed the familiar figure of the black bondswoman.[116] This reference to slavery, as Nancy Bentley points out, would have been clear enough to most nineteenth-century readers as to need no explanation; Mormonism punished its disobedient women like masters punished slaves.[117]

Also in Ward's novel, women disenchanted with polygamy are disciplined by what Ward calls "lynch law," a phrase that invoked punishments of runaway and disobedient slaves.[118] Ward claims that if a woman should denigrate either polygamy or the men who practiced it, she would meet with some "hideous punishment."[119] Few women recover from the effects of these punishments, "and many are rendered nervous, and half insane, from apprehension of the like."[120] Maria Ward pointed out that under polygamy no law prohibited the punishment of women.[121] This was also true of slavery, as few laws in the South prohibited or even limited, the punishment of slaves. Moreover, some women in Ward's novel escape and are pursued by the Mormons in a manner reminiscent of runaway slaves. Thus, in these novels, women were slaves under polygamy first because they were compelled by tyrannical husbands to labor as slaves, second because they were punished corporally as were slaves, and third because runaway wives were pursued in much the same manner as runaway slaves.

One problem with such a direct equation between polygamy and slavery was that, unlike slaves, at least some Mormon women appeared to consent to the slavery of polygamy.[122] Antipolygamy writers thus had to manufacture coercion that, on the surface, could look like consent. They did this in two primary ways: mystical influence and deception. As Increase and Maria van Deusen argued, polygamy could only be "accomplished by the artifice and deception successfully practiced upon the yielding susceptibilities and pliant nature of the female sex."[123] For example, in Ward's novel the protagonist Mrs. Ward, upon meeting Mr.

Ward, "soon became aware of some unaccountable power exercised over me by my fellow traveler.... I felt bewildered and intoxicated, and partially at least lost the sense of consciousness, and the power of motion."[124] Later in the novel, Joseph Smith seduces a woman named Ellen with a mystical influence that deprived her of free will.[125] Indeed, antipolygamy novels abounded with women over whom some sort of mystical influence or magnetism is exercised to convert them to the practice of Mormon polygamy. In this way, writers attempted to show that Mormonism denied women of their free will.

In antipolygamy novels, Mormon men also simply tricked unsuspecting women into plural marriage, often by declaring their love and then simply marrying again without their wives' knowledge or consent. In Metta Victoria Fuller's book, her protagonist Margaret Fletcher, is deceived by her husband and tricked into polygamy. Convinced her husband would never take another wife, Margaret accompanies Richard to join the Mormons in Salt Lake City. However, Richard marries another woman in secret and Margaret is ushered into polygamy by the duplicity of her husband. In Bell's novel, the husband of Bell's main character, Boadicea, also promises his wife he will never enter polygamy, and then simply appears one day with a new wife. Thus, men's duplicity and betrayal of women's affections ushered many women into plural marriage without their consent.

Some antipolygamists were quick to point out that legal marriage had little significance among the Mormons, whose marriage ceremonies were primarily religious and only sometimes and secondarily also civil. They argued that the Prophet approved and controlled the performance of plural marriages.[126] Orvilla Belisle was most vocal on this point, declaring of marriage that "they [the Mormons] abrogated all moral and civil law, set at defiance customs that we learned to view as sacred as law, and the common codes of decency."[127] The fact that men could marry second wives extralegally failed to protect first wives from betrayal and allowed men to seduce or coerce unsuspecting young women into plural marriage. One such young woman, Maud Hatfield, after being deceived into plural marriage, declared that "no sane Englishwoman can so far forget the dictates of virtue, of what is due to themselves and the claims of others, as to defend such monstrous outrages of decency, virtue, and both moral and civil law."[128] The civil law of marriage, in Utah, failed to protect Maud and other women like her from the sexual outrages of polygamy. Under polygamy, as under slavery, women lacked the protection and sanction of the state in marriage.

The extralegal nature of polygamy, antipolygamists claimed, not only failed to protect women from marital and sexual abuses but also informed how Mormons thought about the nature of marriage itself. As Austin Ward (purportedly the husband of Maria Ward) declared, "The Mormons seem to regard marriage not as a means for promoting social happiness, but solely as a method for the most convenient propagation of the race."[129] Austin Ward claimed that polygamous marriage was based not on romance or sentiment, but on expediency and sexual desire.[130] That Mormons performed plural marriage without civic endorsement resulted in perverted sensibilities about the very nature and purpose of marital contracts. Polygamy was about sex, not happiness or love. Hence, it enabled the sexual abuse of women and undermined the companionate, democratic family.

Like antislavery writings, antipolygamy novels clearly endorsed emerging northern ideas about romantic, companionate marriage, foregrounding love and consent as the only legitimate basis for marriage. In Ward's novel, one central character, a young woman named Emily, is in love with a noble young man, Harmer. However, the prophet Brigham Young desires Emily for his own wife and attempts to coerce her to marry him. Young tells Emily that in Utah, only he can perform marriages, and he will never allow her marriage to Harmer. Emily responds that polygamy is concubinage. She declares, "Without love, without sympathy, without congeniality of mind, or appropriateness of age sensibility on one side and compulsion on the other, what else could it be?" Young, however, is quick to minimize the role of love in marriage, declaring, "These sympathies and congenialities of which you speak, are nothing, and only exist in the distempered fancy of silly young women."[131] Emily continues throughout the novel to resist Young's advances, and at one point speaks clandestinely to one of his wives, who tells Emily, "I ought to have been aware that polygamy would destroy all that was holy, and beautiful, and tender, in married life. I ought to have foreseen how all the sweet and familiar confidence of that most endearing relation, when rightly considered, all the reciprocal sympathies, and tendernesses, and cares, which constitute, more than anything else, the true happiness of the conjugal state must be necessarily wanting, where the affections were divided."[132]

Fuller's novel contains another endorsement of companionate marriage. Fuller's main protagonist, Margaret, moves to Utah after the Mormons convince her husband, Richard Wilde, he can acquire easy money there. Near the beginning of Richard's and Margaret's story comes a critique of Richard's love for Margaret: "He adored her with a kind of passion and unrest which did not promise as well for duration as for strength; but of this the pure and single-hearted woman never dreamed."[133] Eventually in Utah, Richard takes Margaret's lifelong friend, Sarah, as his second wife. Upon learning this news, Margaret declares that "now that wedlock was no longer made sacred by one faith, one love, one purpose, it was not wedlock."[134] Ultimately, Margaret dies of a broken heart. Upon Margaret's death, Sarah realizes the damage she has done, and swears, "Always, always, my voice shall rise in defense of one love, constant through life, and faithful in death—one home—one father and mother for the children—one joy on earth—one hope in heaven. Always my spirit shall burn in defense of the purity of womanhood, against these specious pleaders who would make it a thing of chance and change."[135] This, it seems, was the ultimate message of the novel. Sarah is redeemed through her endorsement of the companionate marriage made possible only by monogamy.

Companionate marriage was, for both antislavery and antipolygamy writers, accompanied by the democratic family. Both writings critiqued a patriarchal family model that was quickly being replaced in the Northeast by the companionate family. In the words of Nancy Bentley, "Like slavery, the institution of polygamy was said to violate the Christian family, or what historians today call the contractual family, whose members are to be bound by affection rather than subordination to the patriarchal head and governed by ideals of consent rather than obedience and corporeal force. Slavery and polygamy were thus conjoined as nearly identical crimes against the family."[136]

Torn from their happy New England families, the main characters of antipolygamy novels all enter polygamy in one way or another, which, "besides proving the ruin of all domestic peace, had been the destroyer of all household affection. It was the natural result of that abominable system."[137] In Utah, many men were obsessed with getting more wives. These were mostly middle-aged men "already blessed with several wives and a multitude of children; if an institution could be called a blessing which made a home much more resemble a hospital or asylum, than a quiet scene of domestic peace."[138] For Alfreda Eva Bell, "Among the Mormons the peculiar sanctity of home is unknown. There is not that privacy, that secluded retreat, that makes every house, where things are as they should be, a sort of Penetralia, or Inner Temple, a *Sanctum Sanctorium*."[139]

Polygamy not only ruined the peace and privacy of the home, it confused marital and parental ties as well. Novelists accused polygamists of marrying each other's wives profusely. Belisle theorized, "Thus, a husband became privately the husband of as many of his neighbors' wives as he chose, provided they acquiesced in the private arrangement; and in *all things* except publicity, they were identical with ordinary marriages!"[140] In this sort of situation, as Mrs. B. G. Ferris confirmed, "These miserable creatures have houses where they stay, and a discordant and disunited association of women and children, but no *families*—there are none of the comforts and delights of home with the polygamist."[141] Although different in structure than the profligate sexuality under slavery, the end result of polygamy was the same—the confusion and profusion of consanguineous ties among Mormons that disrupted not only the structure of the family but its affective bonds as well.

Antipolygamists also made tacit connections to slavery in their novels by accusing polygamists of buying and selling women and girls for sex. In Ward's novel, this is done under the guise of marriage, either deceiving or coercing women into a form of sexual slavery without their knowledge or consent. Especially after the Saints' arrival in Utah denies women any legal recourse or chance of escape from polygamy, the young women of the settlement are bought and sold.[142] Indeed, as Mrs. Ward's central Mormon female acquaintance, Mrs. Bradish, admits to Mrs. Ward, husbands essentially exchange a wife for payment to the church. "And so the church is to derive profit from the enslavement of its females? Abominable!"[143] Polygamy, then, was cast as a form of slavery in which women were bought and sold for sex by their husbands, their cruel masters.

Antipolygamy novels illustrate that, like slavery, polygamy endangered women's sexuality from the get go. Novelists claimed that polygamy enslaved otherwise virtuous, unsuspecting women in licentiousness and left them to bear their shame. Orvilla Belisle claims that when in Illinois, the Mormons kept polygamy secret so that the non-Mormon residents "little knew that these women had been lured from home, friends, and virtue, and bearing in their arms the price of their shame to remind them how low they had fallen, cared for nothing now; that they were lost to all a true woman prizes, but the gratification of the moment, whether it plunged her deeper in wo, or drowned her senses in appalling lethargy."[144] Polygamy thus alienated women from their true, pure sexuality.

In Ward's novel, Mrs. Ward says, "This polygamy is only another name for the most abhorrent licentiousness, and no pure-minded woman would ever consent to have any part or lot in such a system."[145] As if to demonstrate her point, one of prophet Brigham Young's many wives declares that polygamy "makes the domestic altar a shrine of legal prostitution."[146] In the same novel, one new arrival to Utah, whose fate readers can see coming, remarks that the polygamous household she observes is "no better than a house of ill-fame, and she felt degraded by having entered its doors."[147] Within a few weeks, this character's husband takes another wife. Lastly, in a final, climactic confrontation with her husband, Mrs. Ward declares, "This place is a perfect Sodom, of that you must beware. How unhappy and miserable are the women, how degraded the children. And your two daughters here, in this abominable sink of iniquity, to be perhaps the tenth or twentieth wife of some sensual animal, who only lives for licentious gratification."[148] Polygamy, then, was sexual slavery by another name, and Mormon fathers sold their daughters into sexual servitude.

In the 1850s, antipolygamy writers also examined the problem of patriarchal dependence and shared with antislavery writers a critique of white patriarchs themselves, this time of Mormon patriarchs in the West.[149] Antipolygamy writers claimed that in the absence of the social and filial controls of northeastern society and the families they had left behind, Mormon men lost all restraint. In one instance, Fuller's leading man, Richard's "natural tendencies had been restrained by education and example, but now that these were torn away, his actions would not always bear the clear light of an accusing conscience; and presently, conscience no longer intruded herself."[150] As the Mormons moved to Utah, the brutality and depravity of Mormon men came more to the foreground of Ward's novel as well: "Indeed, I observed that the further we removed from the civilized settlements, the more tyrannical the husbands became, and I finally began to wonder what would be the end of it."[151] As Mormon men moved away from the social controls of northeastern society, antipolygamists argued, they returned to their natural tyrannical and depraved patriarchal natures.

Antipolygamy writers claimed that Mormonism only worked to inflame and exaggerate men's natural passion for power. One character in Ward's novel, Mrs. Murray, claims that Mormonism "addresses itself to the venal desires of men, encourages their superstitions, and gratifies their passions. Hence is the secret of its strength."[152] Mormon men, like Brigham Young, according to one of his wives, were "utterly devoid of all the finer and gentler feelings. He is incapable of sentiment and degrades marriage to a mere means of propagating the human species."[153] Toward the end of the novel, Mrs. Ward herself comes to the troubling conclusion "that a Mormon, if he acted out the principles of his church, must be hypocritical, sensual, devoid of all conscience, and devilish."[154]

Belisle says of her main male character, Arthur Guildford, "The poison that had been working in his heart had blunted the finer sensibilities of his nature, and he was no longer capable of entering into the *penetralia* of a sensitively high-toned, pure heart, without jarring its chords. The unhallowed tenets he had espoused had marred the purity of his soul and tainted the atmosphere around him, while it lulled him with its mystic vapours, made him oblivious to the downward path in which he was fast hastening."[155] Mormon polygamy facilitated the depravity of men who ruled their households as patriarchal tyrants, destroying any semblance of a free home. Moreover, they betrayed their wives' affections by taking on additional wives, leading lives of licentious gratification.

The spectacle of polygamous men's sexuality run rampant among women powerless to resist lent itself to the same kinds of Orientalist metaphors antislavery writers used.[156] While references to the harems of Mormon leaders and the "customs of Constantinople" abound in many antebellum antipolygamy writings, no antipolygamy author was more successful at deploying the trope of the harem against polygamy than Orvilla Belisle.[157] She repeatedly refers to the most favored wife of a polygamous family as a "sultana," invoking Orientalist visions of sultans and their harems.[158] Mormondom was even worse than the Turkish Orient, though, for Mormons "set at nought the laws alike of God and man, had made Nauvoo a modern Sodom, which had no parallel even in Turkey, where women are bought and sold, not forcibly seized and imprisoned in a harem, and where a bashaw's passions are under more restraint than during the reign of Mormonism at Nauvoo, in civilized, Republican America."[159] In Turkey, Belisle imagined with little evidence or rationale, at least women were paid for and not stolen, and men's passions were under greater restraint than among the Mormons. Also, implied in Belisle's conclusions was that Mormonism is a greater threat because it exists "in civilized, Republican America." Mormonism's geographic location within the boundaries of the United States made it more threatening to Americans than the distant Orient, for it threatened to pollute America with its improper domestic relationships.

Metta Victoria Fuller also noted the backward and barbaric nature of the practice of polygamy. Echoing the Republican platform's language of the "twin relics of barbarism," Fuller argued, "Half-civilized states have ceased [the practice of polygamy] as dangerous to happiness, and as outraging every instinct of the better nature within the breast; and as ages rolled away they left the institution behind as one of the relics of barbarism which marked the half-developed state of man as a social being."[160] Here, Fuller implied that Americans, through a more proper practice of monogamy, had moved beyond the backward barbarism of polygamy, while Mormonism threatened to return the nation to a half-developed state. She also implied that the other relic of barbarism, slavery, continued to illustrate the backward nature of the South.

The connections reformers made between slavery and polygamy ran deep and, in part, compelled the linking of the two practices as the "twin relics of barbarism" in the 1856 Republican Party platform. While Republicans claimed the rhetoric of the "twin relics" linking slavery and polygamy, Democrats could not alienate their southern base with those connections. While Democrats agreed that polygamy was a moral abomination, they were hesitant to support federal intervention in Utah because to do so would endanger the doctrine of popular sovereignty upon which slavery proponents depended. Moreover, both polygamy and slavery were classified as "domestic institutions" under the purview of state governments, not federal, so to turn one over to federal supervision, even in the territories, endangered state sovereignty over the other.[161] Nonetheless, a Democratic administration conducted the first federal intervention in Utah in 1857. In April 1857 a southern Democratic strategist intimated that Democratic President James Buchanan might "supersede the Negro-Mania with the almost universal excitements of an Anti-Mormon crusade." Perhaps hoping to divorce slavery from polygamy, displacing one with the other, Buchanan sent troops to Utah to suppress the "Mormon rebellion."[162] Later called "Buchanan's blunder," the Utah War was, for the most part, a failure, although Brigham Young did surrender the governorship of Utah to a federal appointee, Alfred Cumming.[163]

Linkages between slavery and polygamy outlasted the 1856 Republican platform, and even the demise of slavery and the end of the Civil War. In the spring of 1860 Representative Justin Morrill of Vermont introduced a bill that would criminalize polygamy in the U.S. territories. By this time, the rhetorical links writers had established between polygamy and slavery meant that politicians and reformers alike associated slavery and polygamy together as challenges to marriage, family, and women's sexuality. In the words of Nancy F. Cott, "When Mormon polygamy was discussed, slavery was never far from politicians' minds, and the reverse was also true."[164] As Cott points out, as Congress debated the Morrill bill, Senator Charles Sumner stressed the ways slavery and polygamy posed similar threats to both marriage and women's sexual purity. He declared, "There are many disgusting elements in Slavery which are not present in Polygamy. By license of polygamy, one man may have many wives, all bound to him by marriage-tie, and in other respects protected by law. By license of Slavery, a whole race is delivered over to prostitution and concubinage, without the protection of any law."[165]

Ironically, after both the Morrill Act and the federal victory over slavery, antipolygamy writers mobilized slavery in the service of opposing polygamy more vociferously. Even after the manumission of African American slaves, antipolygamy writers argued, women in Utah remained slaves to their husbands.[166] Harriet Beecher Stowe wrote the preface to Fanny Stenhouse's 1874 antipolygamy treatise, *"Tell It All": The Story of a Life's Experience in Mormonism*. There Stowe declared that "our day has seen the glorious breaking of fetters. The slave-pens of the south have become a nightmare of the past." Polygamy, however, remained, and Stowe asked, "Shall we not then hope that the hour is come to loose the bonds of a cruel slavery [polygamy] whose chains have cut into the very hearts of thousands of our sisters—a slavery which debases and degrades womanhood, motherhood, and the family?"[167] Images of polygamy as against companionate marriage, the democratic family, and the sexual purity of woman continued to animate antipolygamy writings well after the demise of slavery as antipolygamy reformers attempted to spread their vision of marriage, family, and sexuality across the nation. It was not until the Mormons gave up plural marriage in 1890 that these campaigns faded, and not until the early twentieth century that they disappeared entirely.

In examining "Greater Reconstruction" in the West, particularly in relationship to the Mormons, the narrative easily becomes more about social control than liberation. In the South, Reconstruction was, among other things, fundamentally about the liberation of black Americans from slavery, the facilitation of the establishment of black families, and the guaranteeing of black citizenship rights. As Julie Novkov points out, Freedmen's Bureau officials in the South, tasked with helping freed people transition from slavery to freedom, were fundamentally invested in "regularizing marital relationships for black couples."[168] Black couples, however, were also invested in regularizing their marital relationship and flocked to the altar.[169] For both federal officials and black Americans themselves, normative marital contracts were imagined to protect black women from sexual violence.[170] Among the Mormons, however, Greater Reconstruction was about controlling Mormon behavior, breaking up polygamous families, and disciplining Mormons through the revocation of citizenship rights.[171] Mormons responded to attempts to reconstruct their marital relationships with recalcitrance until finally, in 1890 under threat of the dissolution of the church, prophet Wilford Woodruff capitulated to federal demands to abandon the practice (though polygamy continued unofficially into the twentieth century). In the end, both reconstructions, in Novkov's terms, built the capacity of the federal government for "managing and controlling the configuration of families and the proper performance of familial roles."[172] Moreover, these campaigns "reconfigured the national state's posture toward the regulation of private individuals' lives, and established a national-state interest in families and their construction as civic institutions."[173] The performance of democratic family norms became more central to notions of national belonging. In this sense, the efforts of antislavery and antipolygamy writers to make normative their vision of companionate, democratic families across the nation succeeded.

Notes

1. Kirk H. Porter, comp., *National Party Platforms* (New York: MacMillan, 1924), 48.
2. John A. Wills, "The Twin Relics of Barbarism," *Historical Society of Southern California, Los Angeles* 1, no. 5 (1890): 42.
3. Porter, *National Party Platforms*, 48.
4. I am grateful to John Mack Faragher for the phrase "rhetorical political opportunism."
5. Wills, "Twin Relics," 41.
6. Wills, "Twin Relics," 42.
7. Michael D. Pierson, *Free Hearts and Free Homes: Gender and American Antislavery Politics* (Chapel Hill: University of North Carolina Press, 2003), 6–7, quoted material on 7.
8. Pierson, *Free Hearts and Free Homes*, 20.
9. Pierson, *Free Hearts and Free Homes*, 23.
10. Pierson, *Free Hearts and Free Homes*, 23.
11. Sarah Barringer Gordon, "'Our National Hearthstone': Anti-Polygamy Fiction and the Sentimental Campaign against Moral Diversity in Antebellum America," *Yale Journal of Law and the Humanities* 8, no. 2 (Summer 1996): 327. See also Sarah Barringer Gordon, *The Mormon Question: Polygamy and Constitutional Conflict in Nineteenth-Century America* (Chapel Hill: University of North Carolina Press, 2002), 51–116.
12. In her study of antipolygamy novels, Sarah Barringer Gordon demonstrates the connection between sentiment and law, suggesting that mid-nineteenth-century sentimental campaigns against polygamy were also calls to legal action. See Gordon, "'Our National Hearthstone,'" 309–10.
13. Henry Sumner Maine, *Ancient Law: Its Connection with the Early History of Society and Its Relation to Modern Ideas* (London: John Murray, 1861), 168–70.
14. Jane Tompkins, "Sentimental Power: *Uncle Tom's Cabin* and the Politics of Literary History," in *Sensational Designs: The Cultural Work of American Fiction, 1790–1960*, ed. Jane Tompkins (New York: Oxford University Press, 1986), 122–46.
15. Michael D. Pierson, "'Slavery Cannot Be Covered Up with Broadcloth or a Bandanna': The Evolution of White Abolitionist Attacks on the 'Patriarchal Institution,'" *Journal of the Early Republic* 25, no. 3 (Fall 2005): 394.
16. Karen Sánchez-Eppler, "Bodily Bonds: The Intersecting Rhetorics of Feminism and Abolition," *Representations* 24 (Autumn 1988): 35.
17. Harriet Beecher Stowe, *The Key to Uncle Tom's Cabin* (1853; repr., New York: Arno Press, 1969).
18. Manisha Sinha, *The Slave's Cause: A History of Abolitionism* (New Haven, Conn.: Yale University Press, 2016), 457.
19. Terryl Givens, *Viper on the Hearth: Mormons, Myths, and the Construction of Heresy* (New York: Oxford University Press, 1997), 114–15, his emphasis.

20. Maria Ward [pseud.], *Female Life among the Mormons: A Narrative of Many Years' Personal Experience* (New York: J. C. Derby, 1855), iii-iv.

21. See Gordon, "'Our National Hearthstone,'" 306.

22. Nelson Winch Green, *Fifteen Years among the Mormons: Being the Narrative of Mrs. Mary Ettie V. Smith, Late of Great Salt Lake City; a Sister of One of the Mormon High Priests, She Having Been Personally Acquainted With Most of the Mormon Leaders, and Long in the Confidence of the "Prophet," Brigham Young* (New York: H. Dayton, 1860), x.

23. Gordon, "'Our National Hearthstone,'" 305-6.

24. Harriet Beecher Stowe, Henry Louis Gates, and Hollis Robbins, *The Annotated Uncle Tom's Cabin* (New York: W. W. Norton, 2007), 466-67.

25. Stowe, *Uncle Tom's Cabin*, 467-68.

26. Metta Victoria Fuller, *Mormon Wives: A Narrative of Facts Stranger than Fiction* (New York: Derby and Jackson, 1856), iii.

27. Gordon, "'Our National Hearthstone.'"

28. George Bourne, *Slavery Illustrated in Its Effects Upon Woman and Domestic Society* (Boston: Isaac Knapp, 1837; repr., Freeport, NY: Books for Libraries Press, 1972), 27.

29. Caroline W. Healey Dall, "Annie Gray: A Tale," in *The Liberty Bell* (Boston: Massachusetts Anti-Slavery Society, 1848), 292.

30. Dall, "Annie Gray," 27.

31. Bourne, *Slavery Illustrated*, 33.

32. Bourne, *Slavery Illustrated*, 39.

33. Bourne, *Slavery Illustrated*, 29.

34. Bourne, *Slavery Illustrated*, 26-27.

35. A Native of the South-West, *The Family and Slavery* (Cincinnati: American Reform Tract and Book Society, 1857), 5.

36. A Native of the South-West, *The Family and Slavery*, 1.

37. A Native of the South-West, *The Family and Slavery*, 5.

38. A Native of the South-West, *The Family and Slavery*, 6.

39. A Native of the South-West, *The Family and Slavery*, 7.

40. A Native of the South-West, *The Family and Slavery*, 10.

41. A Native of the South-West, *The Family and Slavery*, 23.

42. Lydia Maria Child, *Antislavery Catechism*, 2nd ed. (Newburyport: Charles Whipple, 1839), 16-17.

43. Sánchez-Eppler, "Bodily Bonds," 28.

44. Lydia Maria Child, "The Quadroons," in *The Liberty Bell* (Boston: Massachusetts Anti-Slavery Fair, 1842), 118.

45. Child, "The Quadroons," 122.

46. Child, "The Quadroons," 125.

47. Child, "The Quadroons," 129.

48. Child, "The Quadroons," 141.

49. Julie Husband, *Antislavery Discourse and Nineteenth-Century American Literature: Incendiary Pictures* (New York: Palgrave MacMillan, 2010), 4.

50. Husband, *Antislavery Discourse*, 1.

51. Pierson, "'Slavery Cannot Be Covered Up,'" 397.
52. Bourne, *Slavery Illustrated*, 64.
53. Pierson, "'Slavery Cannot Be Covered Up,'" 394–95.
54. Anne P. Adams, "Christine," in *Autographs for Freedom*, ed. Julia Griffiths (Auburn: Alden Beardsley, 1854), 139.
55. Husband, *Antislavery Discourse*, 1.
56. Philip Fisher, "Making a Thing into a Man: The Sentimental Novel and Slavery," in *Hard Facts: Setting and Form in the American Novel* (New York: Oxford University Press, 1985), 101.
57. Stowe, *Uncle Tom's Cabin*, 132.
58. Gillian Brown, "Getting in the Kitchen with Dinah: Domestic Politics in *Uncle Tom's Cabin*," *American Quarterly* 36, no. 4 (Autumn 1984): 505.
59. Amy Schrager Lang, "Feel Right and Pray," in *Prophetic Woman: Anne Hutchinson and the Problem of Dissent in the Literature of New England*, 193–214 (Berkeley: University of California Press, 1987), 198.
60. Brown, "Getting in the Kitchen," 509.
61. Stowe, *Uncle Tom's Cabin*, 143–51.
62. Stowe, *Uncle Tom's Cabin*, 453.
63. Lydia Maria Child, *An Appeal in Favor of That Class of Americans Called Africans* (Boston: Allen and Ticknor, 1833), 19.
64. Child, *An Appeal*, 23. See also Carolyn L. Karcher, "Rape, Murder, and Revenge in 'Slavery's Pleasant Homes': Lydia Maria Child's Antislavery Fiction and the Limits of Genre," *Women's Studies International Forum* 9, no. 2 (1986): 325.
65. Controversy swirled around the publication of Child's early book, and Child had a hard time finding publishers for her subsequent work. In response to Child's claims, people also canceled subscriptions to Child's magazine, *Juvenile Miscellany*. See Karcher, "Rape, Murder, and Revenge," 324–25.
66. Carol Lasser, "Voyeuristic Abolitionism: Sex, Gender, and the Transformation of Antislavery Rhetoric," *Journal of the Early Republic* 28, no. 1 (Spring 2008): 91.
67. Lasser, 'Voyeuristic Abolitionism," 92.
68. Lasser, "Voyeuristic Abolitionism," 104.
69. Bourne, *Slavery Illustrated*, 13–14.
70. Bourne, *Slavery Illustrated*, 34, his emphasis.
71. Bourne, *Slavery Illustrated*, 34.
72. Bourne, *Slavery Illustrated*, 38–39.
73. Bourne, *Slavery Illustrated*, 26.
74. Bourne, *Slavery Illustrated*, 48.
75. Bourne, *Slavery Illustrated*, 22–23.
76. Bourne, *Slavery Illustrated*, 15.
77. Bourne, *Slavery Illustrated*, 64.
78. Frances H. Green, "The Slave Wife," in *Liberty Chimes* (Providence: Ladies' Anti-Slavery Society, 1845), 100.
79. Green, "The Slave Wife," 107, her emphasis.

80. Lasser, "Voyeuristic Abolitionism," 109.

81. Eve Allegra Raimon, *The "Tragic Mulatta" Revisited: Race and Nationalism in Nineteenth-Century Antislavery Fiction* (New Brunswick: Rutgers University Press, 2004), 109–10.

82. Stowe, *Uncle Tom's Cabin*, 464.

83. Lydia Maria Child, *The Patriarchal Institution, as Described by Members of Its Own Family* (New York: American Anti-Slavery Society, 1860), 29.

84. Child, *The Patriarchal Institution*, 29.

85. Pierson, "'Slavery Cannot Be Covered Up,'" 399.

86. Gordon, "'Our National Hearthstone,'" 315.

87. Gordon, "'Our National Hearthstone,'" 343–44.

88. Pierson, "'Slavery Cannot Be Covered Up,'" 402.

89. Pierson, "'Slavery Cannot Be Covered Up,'" 407.

90. Stowe, *Uncle Tom's Cabin*, 241.

91. Stowe, *Uncle Tom's Cabin*, 230–43, quoted material on 239.

92. Stowe, *Uncle Tom's Cabin*, 358.

93. Amy Kaplan, "Manifest Domesticity," *American Literature* 70, no. 3 (September 1998): 582.

94. Leonard Arrington and Jon Haupt, "Intolerable Zion: The Image of Mormonism in Nineteenth-Century American Literature," *Western Humanities Review* 22 (Summer 1968): 247.

95. Pierson, "'Slavery Cannot Be Covered Up,'" 387–88, quoted material on 388.

96. George Bourne, *Picture of Slavery in the United States of America* (Middletown, Conn.: Edwin Hunt, 1834), 92.

97. Bourne, *Picture of Slavery*, 74.

98. Bourne, *Picture of Slavery*, 44.

99. Quoted in Ronald G. Walters, *The Antislavery Appeal: American Abolitionism after 1830* (Baltimore: Johns Hopkins University Press, 1976), 74.

100. Lydia Maria Child, "Peculiar Traits of Southern Life—Condition of Woman—Her Strange Seclusion—True and False Civilization—Southern Chivalry," *Portsmouth Journal*, reprinted in *Anti-Slavery Standard*, December 8, 1842, p. 18.

101. Child, "Peculiar Traits of Southern Life," 18.

102. Lydia Maria Child, "Slavery's Pleasant Homes," in *The Liberty Bell* (Boston: Massachusetts Anti-Slavery Society, 1843), 148.

103. Child, "Peculiar Traits of Southern Life," 18.

104. Child, "Peculiar Traits of Southern Life," 18.

105. Jennifer L. Jenkins, "Failed Mothers and Fallen Houses: The Crisis of Domesticity in Uncle Tom's Cabin," *ESQ* 38 (2nd Quarter, 1992): 169.

106. Jenkins, "Failed Mothers," 170.

107. Fuller, *Mormon Wives*, vi.

108. Fuller, *Mormon Wives*, viii.

109. Alfreda Eva Bell, *Boadicea: The Mormon Wife, Life-Scenes in Utah* (Baltimore: Arthur R. Orton, 1855), 54.

110. Bell, *Boadicea*, 55.
111. Ward, *Female Life*, 103.
112. Ward, *Female Life*, 321.
113. See Ward, *Female Life*, 356–64.
114. Ward, *Female Life*, 105.
115. Ward, *Female Life*, 358.
116. Ward, *Female Life*, 429.
117. Nancy Bentley, "Marriage as Treason: Polygamy, Nation, and the Novel," in *The Futures of American Studies*, ed. Donald E. Pease and Robyn Wiegman (Durham: Duke University Press, 2002), 345–46. See also Amy Dru Stanley, *From Bondage to Contract: Wage Labor, Marriage, and the Market in the Age of Slave Emancipation* (New York: Cambridge University Press, 1998), 27.
118. Ward, *Female Life*, 428.
119. Ward, *Female Life*, 428.
120. Ward, *Female Life*, 429.
121. Austin Ward, *The Husband in Utah; or, Sights and Scenes among the Mormons; with Remarks on Their Moral and Social Economy* (New York: Derby and Jackson, 1857), 96.
122. Bentley, "Marriage as Treason," 347.
123. Increase van Deusen and Maria van Deusen, *Spiritual Delusions; Being Key to the Mysteries of Mormonism, Exposing the Particulars of that Astounding Heresy, the Spiritual-Wife System, as Practiced by Brigham Young, of Utah* (New York: Moulton and Tuttle, 1854), 40.
124. Ward, *Female Life*, 12.
125. Ward, *Female Life*, 65.
126. J. W. Gunnison, *The Mormons, or Latter-Day Saints, in the Valley of The Great Salt Lake: A History of Their Rise and Progress, Peculiar Doctrines, Present Condition, and Prospects, Derived from Personal Observation during a Residence among Them* (Philadelphia: J. B. Lippincott, 1856), 70–71.
127. Orvilla S. Belisle, *The Prophets: Or, Mormonism Unveiled* (Philadelphia: Wm. White Smith, 1855; repr., Primary Source Edition, n.p.: Ulan Press, 2012), 148.
128. Belisle, *The Prophets*, 203.
129. Ward, *The Husband in Utah*, 205.
130. Ward, *The Husband in Utah*, 61–62.
131. Ward, *Female Life*, 292.
132. Ward, *Female Life*, 312–13.
133. Fuller, *Mormon Wives*, 85.
134. Fuller, *Mormon Wives*, 242–43, quoted material on 243.
135. Fuller, *Mormon Wives*, 316.
136. Bentley, "Marriage as Treason," 346–47. For an analysis of the contractual family, see Michael Grossberg, *Governing the Hearth: Law and the Family in Nineteenth-Century America* (Chapel Hill: University of North Carolina Press, 1985).
137. Ward, *Female Life*, 410.
138. Ward, *Female Life*, 385.

139. Bell, *Boadicea*, 24.

140. Belisle, *The Prophets*, 256, her emphasis.

141. Mrs. B. G. Ferris, *The Mormons at Home: With Some Incidents of Travel from Missouri to California, 1852–1853, in a Series of Letters* (New York: Dix and Edwards, 1856), 129.

142. Ward, *Female Life*, 295.

143. Ward, *Female Life*, 307.

144. Belisle, *The Prophets*, 233.

145. Ward, *Female Life*, 306–7.

146. Ward, *Female Life*, 314.

147. Ward, *Female Life*, 390.

148. Ward, *Female Life*, 434.

149. Pierson, "'Slavery Cannot Be Covered Up,'" 399–402.

150. Fuller, *Mormon Wives*, 198.

151. Ward, *Female Life*, 168.

152. Ward, *Female Life*, 94–95.

153. Ward, *Female Life*, 312.

154. Ward, *Female Life*, 425.

155. Belisle, *The Prophets*, 177.

156. For a more extensive discussion of the use of Orientalism in antipolygamy literature, see Christine Talbot, *A Foreign Kingdom: Mormons and Polygamy in American Political Culture, 1852–1890* (Urbana: University of Illinois Press, 2013), 130–36

157. The phrase "customs of Constantinople" comes from William John Conybeare, *Mormonism: Reprinted from the "Edinburgh Review," No. 202, For April 1854, Printed by Subscription* (Cuttack, Ind.: Orissa Mission Press, W. Brooks, 1855), 361.

158. See Belisle, *The Prophets*, 252, 263, 289–90, 338–40, 372.

159. Belisle, *The Prophets*, 351–52.

160. Fuller, *Mormon Wives*, vi.

161. For a thorough discussion of issues of popular sovereignty in Utah, see Brent M. Rogers, *Unpopular Sovereignty: Mormons and the Federal Management of Early Utah Territory* (Lincoln: University of Nebraska Press, 2017).

162. Robert Tyler to James Buchanan, April 27, 1857, quoted in William P. Mackinnon, ed., *Kingdom in the West: The Mormons and the American Frontier*, vol. 2, *At Sword's Point, Part 1: A Documentary History of the Utah War to 1858* (Norman: University of Oklahoma Press, 2008), 124 (spelling and punctuation modernized).

163. For a discussion of the Utah War in the context of debates over popular sovereignty, see Rogers, 135–269.

164. Nancy F. Cott, *Public Vows: A History of Marriage and the Nation* (Cambridge: Harvard University Press, 2002), 73.

165. Senator Charles Sumner of Massachusetts, *Congressional Globe*, 36th Cong., 1st Sess. (June 4, 1860), 2592. See Cott, 74.

166. Talbot, *A Foreign Kingdom*, 116–19.

167. Harriet Beecher Stowe, preface to Fanny Stenhouse, *"Tell It All": The Story of a Life's Experience in Mormonism. An Autobiography . . . Including a Full Account of the Mountain Meadows Massacre, and the Life, Confession, and Execution of Bishop John D. Lee* (Hartford, Conn.: A. D. Worthington, 1874), vi.

168. Julie Novkov, "Making Citizens of Freedmen and Polygamists," in *Statebuilding from the Margins: Between Reconstruction and the New Deal*, ed. Carol Nackenoff and Julie Novkov (Philadelphia: University of Pennsylvania Press, 2014), 36–38, quoted material on 37.

169. See Laura F. Edwards, "'The Marriage Relation Is at the Foundation of All Our Rights': The Politics of Slave Marriages in North Carolina after Emancipation," *Law and History Review* 14 (Spring 1996): 81–124; Katherine Franke, "Becoming a Citizen: Reconstruction-Era Regulation of African-American Marriages," *Yale Journal of Law and the Humanities* 11 (Summer 1999): 251–309; Nancy Bercaw, *Gendered Freedoms: Race, Rights, and the Politics of Household in the Delta, 1861–1875* (Gainesville: University Press of Florida, 2003); and Elizabeth Regosin, *Freedom's Promise: Ex-Slave Families and Citizenship in the Age of Emancipation* (Charlottesville: University Press of Virginia, 2002).

170. Novkov, "Making Citizens," 40–41.

171. See Talbot, *A Foreign Kingdom*, 147–60.

172. Novkov, "Making Citizens," 61.

173. Novkov, "Making Citizens," 34.

= 3 =

Disciplinary Democracy

Mormon Violence and the Construction of the Modern American State

Patrick Q. Mason

It is tempting to speak of the reconstruction of Mormonism in the antebellum period. In 1857 President James Buchanan, acting on widely believed reports that the Latter-day Saints were in open revolt against the government of the United States, dispatched some 2,500 troops to quell the supposed rebellion. Following the mostly peaceful resolution of the Utah War, federal troops remained stationed near Salt Lake City, and a new political regime was installed with little or no say from the local population. Popular sovereignty and self-rule gave way to a government of political appointees dispatched from and ultimately answerable to Washington, with the occupying military force stationed at Camp Floyd and then Camp Douglas keeping a watchful eye. These antebellum parallels to the postbellum period of Reconstruction in the South are readily apparent, and instructive.

Yet it is not only anachronistic but also analytically slippery to refer to the reconstruction of Mormonism occurring as early as the 1850s. Legal historian Sarah Barringer Gordon is more accurate when she dubs the antipolygamy crusade of the 1880s as a "second 'Reconstruction' in the West."[1] Indeed, numerous developments in postbellum Utah offer parallels to the experience of the Reconstruction South, including the transfer of the territorial militia's command from Latter-day Saint leaders Brigham Young and Daniel H. Wells to the avowed anti-Mormon Patrick Edward Connor, property seizures by federal receivers in the late 1880s, the disfranchisement of Latter-day Saint voters in Utah and Idaho, and the 1889 ruling by Judge Thomas Anderson that Mormons could not become naturalized American citizens.[2] A good case can therefore be made for a second reconstruction proceeding in Utah particularly after the Hayes administration ended Reconstruction in the South in 1877.

If, however, reconstruction is taken to mean rebuilding in the wake of severe damage and destruction, then in fact the reconstruction of Mormonism did not occur until after 1890, when the Church of Jesus Christ of Latter-day Saints officially abandoned polygamy and theocratic politics. Thus ended the four-decade conflict between the federal government and the Latter-day Saints, characterized by fear-inducing raids and incarceration, attenuated political and religious rights, property seizures, and anxieties that provoked violence on all sides. It was only after the federal government had brought the weight of its newly discovered power to bear on a recalcitrant Mormon population and polity that the *re*-construction of Mormonism truly commenced. Mormonism was not fully formed when its founding prophet Joseph Smith was assassinated in 1844. The religion would not reach a steady state, both in terms of doctrinal stability and an equilibrium with the surrounding society, until the twentieth century. Therefore, prior to 1890 it is more accurate to consider the historical processes attendant to the *construction* of American Mormonism, forged in a period of sustained cultural opposition and governmental coercion.

The construction of Mormonism from 1830 to 1890 was intimately linked to the construction of the American state, which was predicated on securing a monopoly on the use of public violence within the borders of its claimed territory.[3] Throughout the nineteenth century Americans grappled with the question of whether violence in the public sphere could be legitimately deployed by any corporate body other than the duly authorized agents of the state. The reality and specter of Mormon violence in the first several decades of the religion's existence provided both an actual and perceived threat to the nascent American statebuilding project. Mormons were not alone in posing this question. The newly expansive, confident, and disciplinary proto-modern state apparatus also turned its attention to limiting and eventually squelching violence by other groups deemed to be illegitimate practitioners of violence, including various vigilante groups, African Americans, abolitionists, Confederates, and American Indians. Reconstruction in the South from 1865 to 1877 marked the federal state's most substantial effort at coercively establishing its authority in the face of an existential threat, but stopped tragically short of eliminating all alternative forms of public violence. Indeed, federal and state officials tolerated the extralegal violence of southern white vigilantes well into the twentieth century, long after authorities in other regions of the country had stopped tacitly or explicitly relying on vigilantism to provide a form of social or political order where the arm of regular law enforcement did not yet fully reach.[4]

Mormonism's history of violence—both real and perceived, perpetrated and received—precipitated a series of increasingly coercive responses from federal and state governmental authorities throughout the nineteenth century. The state's use of forceful, even violent, tactics against Latter-day Saints was done in the name of the (non-LDS) people and received widespread if never unanimous public support. State violence against Latter-day Saints could therefore claim to be democratic in nature. I use the term "disciplinary democracy" to describe this process whereby the putatively democratic state employs its coercive power to subject an internal group with alternative claims to sovereignty or political organization with the aim of subsequently incorporating the subjected group into the body politic. This process is in many ways related to but nevertheless distinct from other coercive expressions of state power, particularly against racialized groups that the state deems to be fundamentally unassimilable. The disciplinary democracy applied toward Latter-day Saints in the late nineteenth-century United States, or toward Catholics during the German *Kulturkampf* of the 1870s, thus had a different logic than the settler colonialism wielded against indigenous peoples in the United States, Australia, South Africa, Canada, and elsewhere.[5]

The processes by which the American state disciplined and (re)constructed Mormonism in the second half of the nineteenth century are brought into further relief by referencing sociologist Max Weber's theory of the state's monopoly on violence and theologian William Cavanaugh's theory of the "myth of religious violence." Latter-day Saints were by no means the only group subject to disciplinary democracy, but the disciplining and (re)construction of Mormonism serves as a useful lens to better comprehend the construction of the modern American nation-state.

The State's Monopoly on Violence

Among the principal architects of modern notions of state power was the seventeenth-century English philosopher Thomas Hobbes, whose 1651 masterpiece *Leviathan* is one of the foundational texts in Western political philosophy. Hobbes argued that in their natural state humans are guided by unenlightened self-interest that would, if left unchecked, have highly destructive consequences. In envisioning what society would be like "without a common power to keep them all in awe," he concluded that it would sooner or later devolve into "a time of war, where every man is an enemy to every man." The utter lack of security would thwart sustained efforts toward industry, culture, and every other vestige of civilization: "no arts, no letters and no society. Worst of all there is continual fear and danger of violent death, and the life of man is solitary, poor, nasty, brutish and short."[6]

In Hobbes's estimation, the only way to stave off the endemic violence of humanity is to "erect such a common power" that will be given full authority to establish conditions to preserve "the common peace and safety." The desire for self-preservation drives people to accept the constraints of a sovereign commonwealth ruled by law, in which they renounce their personal right to violence against others so that they in turn may also be protected. Each person submits their will to the sovereign—in Hobbes's formulation, the ideal was an absolute monarch—and in so doing "the multitude is united in one person that is called a commonwealth. . . . This is the generation of that great Leviathan, or rather, to speak more reverently, of that mortal god, to which we owe our peace and defense under the immortal God." Possessing "the authority given him by every particular man in the commonwealth," the sovereign uses "his strength and any means he thinks is expedient for the multitude's peace and common defense," far more effectively than competing clans or disaggregated individuals could.[7]

More than three and a half centuries later, in the winter of 1918–19 German sociologist Max Weber delivered a talk to a student club at Munich University that was later translated into English as *Politics as a Vocation*. He began his lecture by asking the deceptively simple question, "What is a 'state'?" Arguing that the state cannot be defined in terms of its ends but rather its particular means, specifically "the use of physical force," Weber noted the "especially intimate" relationship of violence and the modern state:

> A state is a human community that (successfully) claims the *monopoly of the legitimate use of physical force* within a given territory. . . . Specifically, at the present time, the right to use physical force is ascribed to other institutions or to individuals only to the extent to which the state permits it. The state is considered the sole source of the "right" to use violence. . . . The state is a relation of men dominating men, a relation supported by means of legitimate (i.e., considered to be legitimate) violence. If the state is to exist, the dominated must obey the authority claimed by the powers that be.[8]

Weber's observations, expanding on both the Hobbesian notion of a social contract and Trotsky's dictum that "Every state is founded on force," came after World War I and at the conclusion of the long nineteenth century, which was up to that point the most successful period of statebuilding in world history. That the culmination of the modern Euro-American statebuilding project was the most devastating war in human history (until the next one) only underscored the "intimate" relationship between the modern state and violence.

Though it established a government by virtue of securing independence from Great Britain and then ratifying a new Constitution, the United States did not emerge fully formed. It took many decades before the American state consolidated its monopoly on violence within its claimed territories. The Revolution actually created something of a quandary for the emergent American state. As historian Richard Maxwell Brown pointed out, "Aside from the fact that violence was a *sine qua non* for gaining independence, the Revolution was the supreme lesson to Americans that in practical terms violence pays. For many later generations the Revolution legitimized violence when used for what was deemed a good cause."[9] The principles of majority rule and popular sovereignty secured by the nation's founding revolutionaries were frequently invoked by subsequent rioters and vigilantes. A pair of Missourians observing the expulsion of Latter-day Saints from Clay County acknowledged the tension between the rule of law and the democratic spirit that sometimes led to mob action: "We defend these principles at all hazards, although we are trampling on our law and Constitution. But we can't help it in no way while we possessed the spirit of 76."[10] Americans thus inherited a dual legacy from the Revolution: on the one hand, it was the means by which an independent nation-state emerged; on the other hand, it furnished citizens with a powerful rationale for public violence legitimized by the will of the people.

The Jacksonian period witnessed an alarming rise in social violence, manifested largely by urban riots in the Northeast and a spreading vigilante impulse along the frontier.[11] A number of conditions and changes in society such as industrialization and urbanization, immigration, the absence of local professional paramilitary police forces, westward expansion and frontier settlement, and intensified debates over slavery and the growing abolitionist movement all combined to make it a particularly volatile period.[12] What made Jacksonian-era rioting distinctive was "not its sources, however, but the frequency of its occurrence, its effectiveness, and the relative inability of public authorities to control or suppress it."[13] For instance, in 1835 alone there were nearly 150 riots in America, 109 of them between July and October.[14] In a seminal 1972 article, historian David Grimsted established that the political and cultural ideologies of the age, celebrating the sovereignty of the individual and the ascendancy of the common man, encouraged riotous responses to threatening situations and made subduing them difficult. "The Jacksonian experience," Grimsted concluded, "suggests that riot is not antithetical to, or abnormal in, a democracy but a result of the very basic tendencies and tensions within it. Because of these the riot situation poses in stark form many of the deepest dilemmas a democracy faces."[15]

The "mobocracy" that Joseph Smith and his followers so often complained of was not an isolated phenomenon unique to the Western Reserve of Ohio, the upper counties of western Missouri, and western Illinois. In fact, people throughout the country were lamenting the mob epidemic that seemed to infect the entire nation in the antebellum period. A Columbia, South Carolina, newspaper opined, "Our whole community seems to be under an unnatural excitement. Mobs, strikes, riots, abolition movements, insurrections, Lynch clubs seem to be the engrossing topics of the day." The Richmond *Whig* decried "the present supremacy of the Mobocracy," and the Philadelphia *National Gazette* grumbled, "The horrible fact is staring us in the face, that, whenever the fury or the cupidity of the mob is excited, they can gratify their lawless appetites almost with impunity."[16] Governor James F. Thomas of Maryland appealed to the same principles of democracy and popular sovereignty invoked by the mob, claiming that "in a country like ours where the people are acknowledged to be supreme . . . there can be no apology, there is no extenuation or excuse for such commotions, and their occurrence stains the character of the government and wounds deeply the cause of equal government."[17]

In January 1838 Abraham Lincoln delivered an address titled "The Perpetuation of Our Political Institutions." A little over a year after the expulsion of Mormons from Clay County, Missouri, and less than three months after the murder of abolitionist editor Elijah Lovejoy in Alton, Illinois, Lincoln recognized the prevailing mob spirit of the day and warned of the threat it posed to the integrity of the American state:

> I hope I am over wary; but if I am not, there is, even now, something of ill-omen amongst us. I mean the increasing disregard for law which pervades the country; the growing disposition to substitute the wild and furious passions, in lieu of the sober judgement of Courts; and the worse than savage mobs, for the executive ministers of justice. . . . Whenever

the vicious portion of population shall be permitted to gather in bands of hundreds and thousands, and burn churches, ravage and rob provision stores, throw printing presses into rivers, shoot editors and hang and burn obnoxious persons at pleasure, and with impunity; depend on it, this Government cannot last.[18]

Lincoln was far too obscure a figure in 1838 for these words to have had much of a direct impact, but his outlook was prescient. By the late 1850s one of the few things that most Americans could agree on was that the very fabric of the state—the union—seemed threatened by lawlessness, disorder, and violence. The fugitive slave controversy, the brutal attack on Charles Sumner on the Senate floor, "bleeding Kansas," the Utah War, and John Brown's raid on Harpers Ferry all combined to paint a portrait of a conflict-wracked nation in serious crisis. One of President Millard Fillmore's friends complained of threats to the nation arising in seemingly every quarter. "We talk of the anarchy and confusion prevailing in Mexico," he wrote, "but we overlook the infamy and treason in Utah, and the disgraceful conduct of the Representatives in Congress. The John Brown raid on Harpers Ferry, and the lynching and tarring and feathering now taking place in the South, for a mere expression of opinion, is disgraceful to our annals."[19]

One of the major challenges faced by the antebellum federal government in asserting anything like a monopoly on violence—and thus constituting a proper Weberian state—was that it simply lacked administrative capacity. Progressive Era theorist Frank Goodnow defined this capacity as "the expression of the will of the state and the execution of that will." Political scientist Kimberley S. Johnson expanded upon Goodnow's definition by observing, "Administrative capacity is what government does; it bridges the gap between enactment and enforcement." The challenge for policy makers is not simply to devise policies but also to implement them. The limited administrative capacity of nineteenth-century American government created continual frustration for reform-minded state builders. "America's small, bounded, and fragmented governmental sphere," Johnson notes, "was an impediment to the creation of a 'strong' state.... The goal of many of these state builders was Hamiltonian in its scope—a truly national government with significant powers and resources to address what reformers saw as the moral and political ills of the day."[20]

The decentralized antebellum American state did muster the administrative capacity to handle slave revolts and the rare outbreak of abolitionist violence such as the raid on Harpers Ferry precisely because the states themselves had developed such capacity in regard to the regulation and maintenance of slavery. As the nation rapidly pushed westward, however, the administrative capacity of the state simply could not keep up. Congress had a constitutional mandate "to dispose of and make all needful Rules and Regulations" in U.S. territories, but the limited American state was ill-equipped to actually govern the massive tracts of land acquired in the Louisiana Purchase and Treaty of Guadalupe Hidalgo.[21] As historian Anne Hyde observed, "Imposing order [in the West] became an unending nightmare to the armies of federal officials charged with the task." California in particular "became proof of the need for a national project to create, integrate, and dominate the West," but many of the early experiments in statebuilding "failed entirely." Even when the nascent state identified clear threats to its white citizens—namely, American Indians who attacked mining settlements or raided cattle—it "had little legislation or cash to do much." Limited in its own capacity, the state relied on local militias who were often brutal, even genocidal, in their treatment of Native peoples.[22] In some locales, most famously San Francisco in the 1850s, public order devolved to the point that self-appointed vigilance committees replaced democratically elected governments.[23]

The federal government's attempt to impose order in territorial Utah and thereby discipline the Mormons was the clearest, most concerted, and most successful attempt at statebuilding in the West prior to the Civil War. Though arguably unnecessary, unquestionably ham-fisted, and very nearly a humanitarian disaster, President Buchanan's Utah Expedition did accomplish its goal of installing a federally appointed governor not of the Latter-day Saints' choosing and thereby rebuffing the Saints' apparent challenge to the federal government's sovereignty. Yet even this achievement of the antebellum American state must be qualified. The fact is that the territorial government in Utah worked only insofar as the Saints cooperated, and only because they had already built the foundations of a functioning state before the army installed Governor Alfred Cumming. That the Utah War was followed by another three decades of concerted Latter-day Saint resistance to federal authority only further demonstrates that whatever administrative capacity the state established in Utah in the late 1850s was, if not quite ephemeral, certainly fragile and conditional.[24]

The precariousness of state power in the West in 1860 underscores how rapidly and dramatically the situation changed over the next thirty years. The U.S. Census Bureau's 1890 declaration that the frontier was closed can be interpreted as a signal of the state's successful campaign to establish its monopoly on violence in all western states and territories. The advent and application of communications and transportation technologies such as the telegraph and railroad were instrumental. They complemented and enabled the state's newfound harnessing of executive, legislative, judicial, and military power to impose its will in the Reconstruction South and "second Reconstruction" West. The three major alternative polities in the nineteenth-century West—American Indian nations, Mormon theocracy, and white vigilantism—had all been predicated at least in part on their ability to deploy violent force either parallel to or in resistance to federally approved structures. As of the end of 1890, Indian resistance had been crushed, the Mormons had been cowed into submission, and vigilantes had been stripped of political (if not always social) legitimacy. By the last decade of the nineteenth century, the American state's monopoly on violence, and therefore its very existence, was secure if not quite complete.

The Myth of Mormon Violence

Violence perpetrated both against and by the Latter-day Saints significantly shaped the first three decades of Mormonism's existence. The new religion originated in 1830 as a nonviolent millenarian Christian sect. Even after he became disenchanted and left the movement, early convert and church historian John Corrill offered written testimony of the Saints' pacifism, asserting that until 1833 "the Mormons had not so much as lifted a finger, even in their own defence, so tenecious [sic] were they for the precepts of the gospel—'turn the other cheek.'"[25] The violent expulsion of the Saints from Jackson County, Missouri, in the summer of 1833 led the Mormons to take up arms in self-defense.[26] This initiated a logic and cycle of violence that would over the next twenty-five years manifest in recurrent conflict with neighboring settlers in Missouri from 1833 to 1838 and in Illinois from 1844 to 1846. It would lead to violent clashes with American Indians especially in the first decade of settlement in Utah, extralegal violence against dissenters and "Gentiles" in 1850s Utah, the Mountain Meadows Massacre in 1857, and the Utah War in 1857–58. To risk overgeneralization, the Latter-day Saints were mostly on the receiving end of violence in Missouri and Illinois but primarily on the giving end once they arrived in Utah and quickly established themselves as the regional power.

Mormon violence did not go unnoticed, and it left a legacy that has dogged the religion and its adherents long past the point at which Latter-day Saints stopped using violence to promote or defend the kingdom of God.[27] One strand of nineteenth-century anti-Mormon discourse assigned "both sociopolitical coherence and malevolent intent" to the religion. As historian Spencer Fluhman observes, "Political anti-Mormonism crystallized in the conviction that Mormonism constituted an ideology inherently at odds with republicanism and was thus unassimilable within American society." Channeling anxieties about the "fanatical" conflation of religion and politics with roots in their own history, American Protestants "violently opposed Mormon visions for fear of Mormonism's tyrannical and violent potential."[28]

Opponents had plenty of evidence with which to build the case against apparent Mormon fanaticism. After vigilantes drove Mormons out of Jackson County, Missouri, in 1833, Joseph Smith (unsuccessfully) led an armed band that called itself "Zion's Camp" or the "armies of Israel" to redeem their lost properties. When the conflict in Missouri escalated in 1838, Latter-day Saints formed their own militia in harmony with state law and local custom. However, a smaller but influential subset of Saints also created their own secret vigilante band called the "Danites," which Latter-day Saint Albert Rockwood said earned that designation "because the Prophet Daniel had said they shall take the kingdom and possess it for-ever." The Danites' more aggressive tactics against both internal dissenters and external foes earned them—and their religion—a reputation for the dangers of zealous excess. In the midst of the battles between the Saints and Missourians in late October 1838, Rockwood enthusiastically appealed to his father to "come to Zion and fight for the religion of Jesus. . . . The Prophet has unsheathed his sword and in the name of Jesus declares that it shall not be sheathed again untill [sic] he can go unto any County or state in safety and in peace."[29]

The imagery of a martial Mormonism was further enhanced when in their sanctuary city of Nauvoo, Illinois, the Latter-day Saints formed an army called the Nauvoo Legion with Joseph Smith as its commanding officer. The Legion turned out to have more bark than bite, its displays of force limited to the parade ground. But after Joseph Smith was assassinated and Brigham Young assumed leadership over the Latter-day Saints, he revived the tradition of Mormon vigilantism. In Nauvoo and then 1850s Utah, Young authorized individuals and groups (sometimes called Danites) to intimidate dissenters and perceived enemies, which in some cases turned lethal and may have even included targeted assassinations.[30] The most horrific episode of Mormon violence came in September 1857, when Latter-day Saint settlers along with some Paiute allies brutally slaughtered an emigrant company of 120 men, women, and children at Mountain Meadows in southern Utah. The Mountain Meadows Massacre seemed to prove what many of Mormonism's critics suspected, namely that theocratic violence resided at the heart of the religion.[31]

Those same critics could also point to Latter-day Saint ritual and doctrine to locate religiously inspired violence. Joseph Smith's murder gave rise to revenge fantasies within the religion; for many decades the Saints swore sacred ceremonial oaths to "avenge the blood of the prophets upon this nation."[32] In the 1850s Brigham Young and other leaders also publicly preached a doctrine of "blood atonement," in which a person's own blood would have to be shed in order to gain forgiveness for certain severe sins. Historians debate to what extent both the blood oath and blood atonement translated into physical violence. Yet even if such statements remained purely ceremonial, hyperbolic, or metaphoric, decades of belligerent discourse produced a religion rich with symbolic violence.

The combined weight of discursive and actual Latter-day Saint violence provided ample fodder for the growing chorus of anti-Mormon critics that included everyone from ministers to politicians to novelists. In 1887 Arthur Conan Doyle introduced Sherlock Holmes to the world in the murder mystery *A Study in Scarlet*. The novel's backstory took the reader across the ocean from Victorian England to the "Country of the Saints" in Utah. In Doyle's rendering, the residents of the territory lived in perpetual fear under the theocratic iron grip of a cold, stern Brigham Young, who readily dispatched his secret police—the dreaded Danites—to enforce his reign of terror. "The man who held out against the church vanished away," wrote Doyle, and "a rash word or a hasty act was followed by annihilation." Everyone spent their days and especially nights "in fear and trembling," daring not to speak a word out of line for fear that their neighbor, or even a member of their own family, might be one of Young's enforcers.[33]

As *A Study in Scarlet* exemplified, precise facts did not get in the way of the construction of a myth of Mormonism as an oppressive, expansive, and violent system. Late nineteenth- and early twentieth-century authors wrote of Mormonism as a "religious despotism" intent on "conquest."[34] One writer stated confidently, "It has been the settled policy of the Mormons to control Utah and the adjacent Territories, and from there to conquer the United States, and, subsequently, the whole world."[35] Rather than a fringe view, this fear of an expansionist and conquest-driven Mormonism reached the very highest levels of American society, with President Rutherford B. Hayes stating in his 1880 annual message to Congress, "The political power of the Mormon sect is increasing. It is extending steadily into other Territories. Wherever it goes it establishes polygamy and sectarian power."[36] Hayes and his successors Chester Arthur, Grover Cleveland, and Benjamin Harrison each put their weight behind legislative and judicial efforts to suppress, in Arthur's words, "this barbarous system."[37]

Much of the national discourse about Mormonism centered of course on polygamy. Early opponents of the practice sometimes struggled to articulate why the Saints' peculiar marriage institution should rise to the level of national attention, let alone congressional and executive power. Polygamy's apparent offense toward moral sensibilities alone seemed insufficient to mobilize effective public opposition, just as arguments based on a broadly shared Christian morality had proven inadequate for abolitionists seeking to end slavery. Antipolygamy activists landed on a more successful strategy when they framed polygamy as the violent subjugation of helpless women by oppressive patriarchs and priests. Literary scholar Terryl Givens has demonstrated how violence and cruelty, especially toward women, became regular features in nineteenth- and early twentieth-century novelistic portrayals of Mormonism, complete with lurid accounts of beatings, whippings, forced imprisonment, torture, and strangulation, punctuated by the occasional targeted killing.[38] This sentiment found its way into oral arguments before the Supreme Court in the 1878 *Reynolds v. United States* case, when Attorney General Charles Devens drew a series of parallels between Latter-day Saint polygamy and a range of other atrocities committed in the "name of religion," including the burning of Hindu widows on their husbands' funeral pyres, the abandonment of newborn infants by "East Islanders," and "gruesome murders" committed by Indian Thugs.[39]

In seeking precedents and parallels to help conceptualize the Mormon menace, in which the dangers of false or excessive religion congealed in both polygamy and theocratic violence, it became commonplace for writers to fashion Joseph Smith as a latter-day Muhammad, intent on fanatically spreading his false religion at the point of the sword. An 1877 article in an African American Methodist periodical comparing Mormonism and Islam claimed that "both resort to the sword for the subjugation of the individual judgment to the voice of the Church."[40] A 1906 book subtitled *Mormonism the Mohammedanism of the West* echoed the same theme: "Mormons are the Mohammedans of America. . . . Both proselyte by violence, as they have opportunity to use their power. . . . Both systems aim at universal domination."[41]

Tales of Mormon violence also circulated at the grassroots level. When proselytizing in the American South, Latter-day Saint missionaries were confronted with accusations that "you have compelled infants to kill their own mothers because they attempted to escape from your territory." Other missionaries heard that "the 'Mormons' sacrificed a child every year, for each family in their Church, and that women who become useless through old age, for slaves and other purposes were eaten or boxed up and thrown into some river."[42]

The myth of Mormon violence clearly peddled in significant novelistic excess. Anti-Mormon accounts typically consisted of wild flights of fancy and strained analogies far more than carefully researched histories or ethnographies. Nevertheless, the myth was useful, which explains its potency, pervasiveness, and perpetuity.[43]

One of the principal ends to which the myth of Mormon violence was deployed was in the construction of the modern American state. To understand how, it is helpful to consider the theory developed by theologian William Cavanaugh in his book *The Myth of Religious Violence*. Without denying the obvious fact that religious institutions and individuals have often been perpetrators of violence, Cavanaugh asserts that "one of the foundational legitimating myths of the liberal nation-state" is that religion, as "an irrational and dangerous impulse," is inherently prone to violence. The Enlightenment distinction between the religious and secular is thus justified by positing the latter as ethically superior to and as an essential guard against the former. There is a clear payoff for the secular state in such a construction, according to Cavanaugh, as "revulsion toward killing and dying in the name of one's religion is one of the principal means by which we become convinced that killing and dying in the name of the nation-state is laudable and proper." The myth of religious violence serves to marginalize religious discourse and actors in the public sphere by associating them with irrationality and violence, and furthermore reinforces the nation-state's monopoly on violence by framing it, in part, as a shield against religious fanaticism. Hobbes's "mortal god" thus demands the ultimate loyalty otherwise reserved for the divine. As Cavanaugh contends, "The fact that Christianity is construed as a religion, whereas nationalism is not, helps to ensure that the Christian's public and lethal loyalty belongs to the nation-state."[44]

As a specific application of the myth of religious violence in nineteenth-century America, the myth of Mormon violence contributed to the construction of the United States as a liberal nation-state in which religion would enjoy private freedom but no determinative public role.[45] One way that we can see how the myth of religious violence operated in the Latter-day Saint case is to consider the specific instances in which the state deemed Mormon violence to be either legitimate or illegitimate. For example, after Missourians first attacked Mormon settlements in 1833, Governor Daniel Dunklin encouraged the Mormons to organize themselves into armed companies to defend their homes and property—a directive that both legitimated the Mormons' complaints and underscored the state's inability to regulate violence within its borders through its own properly constituted law enforcement or military forces. Despite repeatedly affirming the Mormons' "clear, and indisputable right" to organize in self-defense for the reclamation of their homes after having been expelled, Dunklin finally balked when faced with the prospect of a band of armed religious zealots led by a prophet marching across his state. A militia comprised of wronged Mormon settlers could help keep the peace, but a Mormon militia calling itself "the armies of Israel" represented a fundamental threat to the state and would have to be turned back.[46]

A similar dynamic played out in 1850s Utah. When Latter-day Saints directed their violence against dissenters, non-Mormons, and the U.S. Army—in other words, when the actions could be construed as being motivated by religious sentiment or ordered by religious authorities in the interest of a particular religious body—then the violence was considered illegitimate, dangerous, and even treasonous. However, when the Saints used violence against American Indians as part of the Euro-American conquest of the American continent—in other words, when it served the interests of the expanding state—then the violence was characterized both at the time and by later (white) generations as normal and even heroic. More often, the violence was simply ignored and forgotten, as if it never occurred in the first place.[47] These examples of Mormon violence in Missouri and Utah are classic illustrations of the way the myth of religious violence operates, in Cavanaugh's formulation: "Violence that is labeled religious is always peculiarly virulent and reprehensible. But violence that is labeled secular hardly counts as violence at all, since it is inherently peace making."[48]

Understanding how the myth of religious violence has been operationalized is not intended to minimize the reality or harmfulness of violence perpetrated by religious actors. It is important, however, to recognize that the modern liberal state has a strong interest in promoting a narrative in which religious violence is obvious, inherently dangerous, especially brutal, and conducive to increased disorder. The state's own violence, on the other hand, is often rendered invisible or victimless. Even when state violence is seen, it is characterized as justified, normal, and ultimately contributive toward peace and social order. The state secures a monopoly on violence by claiming—and convincing its citizens—that its violence is either unremarkable or laudatory. The myth of Mormon violence contributed to the construction of the modern American state by demonstrating that Mormons' violence was hardly worthy of the name when conducted on behalf of or in line with the goals of the state but constituted a fundamental threat to the republic when pursued for apparently religious ends.

Monopoly Achieved

In the quarter century following Appomattox, the United States expanded its administrative capacity, and therefore its very credentials as a modern state, by pursuing two overlapping projects of coercive political and social reconstruction—from 1865 to 1877 in the South, and from the 1870s until 1890 in the West.[49] As political scientist Julie Novkov has argued, "The capacity and scope of interest built in the early days of Reconstruction did not evaporate as the national government lost its will to enforce black rights to manly citizenship. It shifted to the making of other citizens," and in so doing "brought about significant growth in the federal government's scope of regulatory authority, and depended upon major expansions of state capacity for their implementation."[50] The government's campaign to subdue the Indians rested primarily on military conquest followed by an administrative and bureaucratic reordering of Native life, politics, and society. That same raw edge of state power was never fully activated against the Mormons, but the persistent presence of federal troops and then federal marshals in Utah Territory beginning in the late 1850s made clear that the state's disciplinary power was not merely persuasive and benevolent. In both cases, the establishment of state power required the abandonment of violence as a public option for anyone but the state's agents. Utah thus became a site where the postbellum reconstructive state flexed its newfound muscles and realized that it could, with concerted effort, impose its will and achieve genuine sovereignty in a region that had previously successfully resisted American statebuilding.

One of the signal accomplishments of this "second Reconstruction" was that it helped secure the loyalty and participation of Southerners who had been on the receiving end of the first Reconstruction. As I have argued elsewhere, anti-Mormonism became a uniting factor in a fractured American republic following the Civil War, giving common cause to Southerners and Northerners, states and the federal government, and Democrats and Republicans. Having railed against the federal exercise of power in their own local affairs in the 1860s and 1870s, by the 1880s Southern Democrats joined with Northern Republicans in passing punitive anti-Mormon legislation in Congress and cheering on federal marshals and activist judges to quash the Mormon menace. "Opponents of the first Reconstruction," I argue, "white southerners now became agents and supporters of a second."[51]

Latter-day Saints themselves participated in formalizing the state's monopoly on violence. As early as 1835, Joseph Smith's followers adopted and then canonized a declaration of belief regarding governments and laws. In distinctly Lockean and Madisonian terms, the declaration affirmed that one of the primary responsibilities of proper government is to maintain freedom of conscience and worship. At the same time, the declaration insisted that "religious opinions do not justify sedition nor conspiracy," and that the disciplinary authority of religious bodies extended only to internal ecclesiastical matters. Church courts and leaders did not possess "authority to try men on the right of property or life, to take from them this world's goods, or to put them in jeopardy of either life or limb, or to inflict any physical punishment upon them."[52] Early Mormons did not always conform to their stated principles. As outlined above, Latter-day Saints did use violence toward religious ends at various points from 1838 to 1858, contradicting their own stated position and thus constituting one of early Mormonism's fundamental challenges to the state.

A crucial component of the state's imposition of authority on Utah was therefore to establish its monopoly on violence. That monopoly was secured when in December 1889 the First Presidency and Twelve Apostles of the Church of Jesus Christ of Latter-day Saints, led by prophet-president Wilford Woodruff, issued an official declaration disavowing the church's right to violence or temporal political authority. They declared that "this Church views the shedding of human blood with the utmost abhorrence," and denounced any notion that "our Church favors or believes in the killing of persons who leave the Church or apostatize from its doctrines." The church hierarchs disclaimed any notion of religiously inspired sedition, acknowledging that expressions to the contrary had been made more than three decades earlier in the context of the Utah War but now were of no effect. The statement concluded that "this Church does not claim to be an independent, temporal kingdom of God, or to be an *imperium in imperio* aiming to overthrow the United States or any other civil government." Returning to the sentiments of the 1835 church, the declaration insisted, "Church government and civil government are distinct and separate in our theory and practice, and we regard it as part of our destiny to aid in the maintenance and perpetuity of the institutions of our country."[53]

Historians have rightly emphasized the importance of Wilford Woodruff's "Manifesto," issued nine months after this declaration, in which the church president announced the cessation of plural marriage. While polygamy had been at the center of the conflict between Latter-day Saints and the federal government for four decades, it was the December 1889 declaration, even more than the Manifesto, that represented the church's ultimate acknowledgment of state sovereignty and the state's monopoly on violence. In considering the significance of the 1889 "Manifesto of the Apostles," historian Thomas Alexander concluded that "although the manifesto on plural marriage of September 1890 has received more attention, it was not as important as the Manifesto of the Apostles in laying the basis for the restructuring of Mormonism and its relationship with American society."[54] Plural marriage was the publicly presenting symptom of a longer and deeper conflict of sovereignties and authorities. In resolving the contest decidedly in favor of the state, Wilford Woodruff's dual declarations in 1889 and 1890 completed Mormonism's construction as a religion suited for full participation in the modern state—in other words, a religion that is constructed as "essentially interior, and essentially distinct from public, secular rationality."[55]

The work of the state's disciplinary democracy in Utah came to full fruition when in 1898, less than a decade after Woodruff's two manifestos, Latter-day Saints enthusiastically supported the Spanish-American War. The *Improvement Era* confidently declared, "It is gratifying to know that in the issues involved our country is wholly right," and the First Presidency issued a statement affirming the full loyalty of Latter-day Saints to the national cause. Utah, which had finally gained statehood only two years previous, quickly fulfilled its quota of volunteers, and some of the troops departed Salt Lake City after having received special blessings of protection in the temple.[56] William Cavanaugh suggests that the test for what a person considers to be of absolute value is "that for which one is willing to kill."[57] If so, then by 1898 the state had asserted its control over the Mormon moral imagination, as in word and deed Latter-day Saints expressed their willingness to kill for the state but not for their religion. As Mormon boys marched forth from Zion to fight for the new American empire, the state's disciplinary (re)construction of Mormonism was complete.

Notes

1. Sarah Barringer Gordon, *The Mormon Question: Polygamy and Constitutional Conflict in Nineteenth-Century America* (Chapel Hill: University of North Carolina Press, 2002), 144.

2. For the legal history of this period, see Edwin Brown Firmage and Richard Collin Mangrum, *Zion in the Courts: A Legal History of the Church of Jesus Christ of Latter-day Saints, 1830–1900* (Urbana: University of Illinois Press, 1988); and Thomas G. Alexander, *Things in Heaven and Earth: The Life and Times of Wilford Woodruff* (Salt Lake City: Signature Books, 1993), chap. 11.

3. In this essay I am concerned specifically with "public violence," as the state's interest in regulating private or domestic violence constitutes a separate (if related) narrative and set of issues. Throughout this essay, then, the "violence" I refer to should be understood as referring to violence in the public sphere.

4. The classic study of American vigilantism is Richard Maxwell Brown, *Strain of Violence: Historical Studies of American Violence and Vigilantism* (New York: Oxford University Press, 1975).

5. On the *Kulturkampf*, see David Blackbourn, *Marpingen: Apparitions of the Virgin Mary in a Nineteenth-Century German Village* (1993; repr., New York: Vintage Books, 1995). On settler colonialism, see Donald Denoon, "Understanding Settler Societies," *Historical Studies* 18 (1979): 511–27; Lorenzo Verancini, *Settler Colonialism: A Theoretical Overview* (New York: Palgrave Macmillan, 2010). I arrived at the term "disciplinary democracy" independently, but it has also been used in contemporary cultural studies, such as in the review essay by Charles McPhedran, "Cultural Studies in the Age of Disciplinary Democracy," *Cultural Studies Review* 14, no. 1 (March 2008): 225–31.

6. Thomas Hobbes, *Leviathan*, ed. Marshall Missner (New York: Pearson, 2008), 83. This edition is "a quasi-translation of Hobbes' language into a somewhat more contemporary form" (viii).

7. Hobbes, *Leviathan*, 116.

8. Max Weber, *Politics as a Vocation*, trans. H. H. Gerth and C. Wright Mills (Philadelphia: Fortress Press, 1965), 1–2.

9. Richard Maxwell Brown, ed., *American Violence* (Englewood Cliffs, N.J.: Prentice-Hall, 1970), 2.

10. Anderson Wilson and Emelia Wilson to Samuel Turrentine, Clay County, MO, July 4, 1836, quoted in Richard Lloyd Anderson, "Atchison's Letters and the Causes of Mormon Expulsion from Missouri," *BYU Studies* 26 (Summer 1986): 12.

11. See David Grimsted, "Rioting in Its Jacksonian Setting," *American Historical Review* 77, no. 2 (April 1972): 361–97; Brown, *Strain of Violence*; Michael Feldberg, *The Turbulent Era: Riot and Disorder in Jacksonian America* (New York: Oxford University Press, 1980); David Grimsted, *American Mobbing, 1828–1861: Toward Civil War* (New York: Oxford University Press, 1998).

12. See Sean Wilentz, *The Rise of American Democracy: Jefferson to Lincoln* (New York: W. W. Norton, 2005); Daniel Walker Howe, *What Hath God Wrought: The Transformation of America, 1815–1848* (New York: Oxford University Press, 2007).

13. Feldberg, *The Turbulent Era*, 6–7.

14. Grimsted, *American Mobbing*, 4.

15. Grimsted, "Rioting in Its Jacksonian Setting," 397.

16. All quotes from Grimsted, *American Mobbing*, 3.

17. Quoted in Grimsted, "Rioting in Its Jacksonian Setting," 366.

18. Abraham Lincoln, "The Perpetuation of Our Political Institutions," reprinted in *Journal of the Abraham Lincoln Association* 6, no. 1 (1984): 7, 9.

19. Letter from H. Cowpen to Millard Fillmore, quoted in Peter Knupfer, "A Crisis in Conservatism: Northern Unionism and the Harpers Ferry Raid," in *His Soul Goes Marching On: Responses to John Brown and the Harpers Ferry Raid*, ed. Paul Finkelman (Charlottesville: University Press of Virginia, 1995), 126.

20. Kimberley S. Johnson, *Governing the American State: Congress and the New Federalism, 1877–1929* (Princeton, N.J.: Princeton University Press, 2007), 2, 8.

21. U.S. Constitution, Article 4, Section 3, Clause 2.

22. See Anne F. Hyde, *Empires, Nations, and Families: A New History of the North American West, 1800–1860* (New York: Harper Collins, 2011), 462–65; Brendan C. Lindsay, *Murder State: California's Native American Genocide, 1846–1873* (Lincoln: University of Nebraska Press, 2012); and Benjamin Madley, *An American Genocide: The United States and the California Indian Catastrophe, 1846–1873* (New Haven, Conn.: Yale University Press, 2016).

23. On San Francisco, see Mary P. Ryan, *Civic Wars: Democracy and Public Life in the American City during the Nineteenth Century* (Berkeley: University of California Press, 1997), 139–45; Robert M. Senkewicz, S.J., *Vigilantes in Gold Rush San Francisco* (Stanford, Calif.: Stanford University Press, 1985).

24. See William P. MacKinnon, ed., *At Sword's Point, Part 1: A Documentary History of the Utah War to 1858* (Norman, Okla.: Arthur H. Clark, 2008); Matthew J. Grow, *"Liberty to the Downtrodden": Thomas L. Kane, Romantic Reformer* (New Haven, Conn.: Yale University Press, 2009), chaps. 9–10; David L. Bigler and Will Bagley, *The Mormon Rebellion: America's First Civil War, 1857–1858* (Norman: University of Oklahoma Press, 2011); and Brent M. Rogers, *Unpopular Sovereignty: Mormons and the Federal Management of Early Utah Territory* (Lincoln: University of Nebraska Press, 2017).

25. John Corrill, *A Brief History of the Church of Christ of Latter Day Saints (Commonly Called Mormons). . . .* (St. Louis: the author, 1839), 19, spelling as in original.

26. See Patrick Q. Mason, "'The Wars and the Perplexities of the Nations': Reflections on Early Mormonism, Violence, and the State," *Journal of Mormon History* 38, no. 3 (Summer 2012): 72–89.

27. A prominent modern example is Jon Krakauer, *Under the Banner of Heaven: A Story of Violent Faith* (New York: Anchor Books, 2004).

28. J. Spencer Fluhman, *"A Peculiar People": Anti-Mormonism and the Making of Religion in Nineteenth-Century America* (Chapel Hill: University of North Carolina Press, 2012), 82, 86, 88.

29. Dean C. Jessee and David J. Whittaker, eds., "The Last Months of Mormonism in Missouri: The Albert Perry Rockwood Journal," *Brigham Young University Studies* 28 (Winter 1988): 23, 25.

30. See John G. Turner, *Brigham Young: Pioneer Prophet* (Cambridge, Mass.: Belknap Press of Harvard University Press, 2012), 121–22, 184–88, 258–63; Polly Aird, "'You Nasty Apostates, Clear Out': Reasons for Disaffection in the Late 1850s," *Journal of Mormon History* 30, no. 2 (Fall 2004): 129–207; Ardis E. Parshall, "'Pursue, Retake & Punish': The 1857 Santa Clara Ambush," *Utah Historical Quarterly* 73, no. 1 (Winter 2005): 64–86; William P. MacKinnon, "'Lonely Bones': Leadership and Utah War Violence," *Journal of Mormon History* 33, no. 1 (Spring 2007): 121–78. For a first-person account of dubious reliability, see William Adams Hickman with John H. Beadle, *Brigham's Destroying Angel: Being the Life, Confession, and Startling Disclosures of the Notorious Bill Hickman, the Danite Chief of Utah* (Salt Lake City: Shepard Publishing, 1904).

31. See Juanita Brooks, *The Mountain Meadows Massacre* (Stanford, Calif.: Stanford University Press, 1950); Will Bagley, *Blood of the Prophets: Brigham Young and the Massacre*

at Mountain Meadows (Norman: University of Oklahoma Press, 2002); Sally Denton, *American Massacre: The Tragedy at Mountain Meadows* (New York: Vintage Books, 2004); and Ronald W. Walker, Richard E. Turley Jr., and Glen M. Leonard, *Massacre at Mountain Meadows: An American Tragedy* (New York: Oxford University Press, 2008).

32. Quoted in David John Buerger, "The Development of the Mormon Temple Endowment Ceremony," *Dialogue: A Journal of Mormon Thought* 20, no. 4 (Winter 1987): 52.

33. Arthur Conan Doyle, *A Study in Scarlet* (1887; repr., Garden City, N.Y.: Doubleday, 1974), 102–3.

34. Rev. G. L. Thompson, "The Mormon Problem," *Christian Advocate* (New York), Jan. 28, 1886; Rev. M. L. Oswalt, *Pen Pictures of Mormonism* (Philadelphia: American Baptist Publication Society, 1899), 11–12.

35. Willing, *On American Soil*, 5.

36. Rutherford B. Hayes, "Fourth Annual Message [1880]," in *A Compilation of the Messages and Papers of the Presidents, 1789–1897*, comp. James D. Richardson (Washington, D.C.: Published by Authority of Congress, 1899), 7:605–6.

37. Chester A. Arthur, "First Annual Message [1881]," in Richardson, *Compilation of the Messages and Papers of the Presidents*, 8:58. For a fuller treatment of federal anti-Mormon efforts in the 1880s, see Patrick Q. Mason, *The Mormon Menace: Violence and Anti-Mormonism in the Postbellum South* (New York: Oxford University Press, 2011), 59–62; and Gordon, *The Mormon Question*. On Mormon "barbarism," see Fluhman, *"A Peculiar People,"* chap. 4.

38. Terryl L. Givens, *The Viper on the Hearth: Mormons, Myths, and the Construction of Heresy*, updated ed. (New York: Oxford University Press, 2013), 157–60.

39. Quoted in Gordon, *The Mormon Question*, 126.

40. Untitled, *Southwestern Christian Advocate* (New Orleans), May 10, 1877.

41. Jennie Fowler Willing, *On American Soil, or Mormonism the Mohammedanism of the West* (Louisville: Pickett Publishing, 1906), 3–4. See also J. Spencer Fluhman, "An 'American Mahomet': Joseph Smith, Muhammad, and the Problem of Prophets in Antebellum America," *Journal of Mormon History* 34, no. 3 (Summer 2008): 23–45.

42. Southern States Mission Manuscript History, Church History Library, The Church of Jesus Christ of Latter-day Saints, Salt Lake City, Utah, April 18, 1889, and Aug. 7, 1889.

43. See Givens, *The Viper on the Hearth*; Gordon, *The Mormon Question*; Fluhman, *"A Peculiar People"*; Christine Talbot, *A Foreign Kingdom: Mormons and Polygamy in American Political Culture, 1852–1890* (Urbana: University of Illinois Press, 2013).

44. William T. Cavanaugh, *The Myth of Religious Violence: Secular Ideology and the Roots of Modern Conflict* (New York: Oxford University Press, 2009), 4–5, 9–10.

45. The formulation of a putatively secular liberal United States was complicated by the ways in which Protestant Christians built a "moral establishment" throughout the nineteenth century that wielded the power of the state against those (including Mormons) whose notions of the appropriate forms of public religion differed from the emergent evangelical consensus. See David Sehat, *The Myth of American Religious Freedom* (New York: Oxford University Press, 2011).

46. See Fluhman, *"A Peculiar People,"* 88.

47. See Jared Farmer, *On Zion's Mount: Mormons, Indians, and the American Landscape* (Cambridge, Mass.: Harvard University Press, 2008).

48. Cavanaugh, *The Myth of Religious Violence*, 13.

49. Historian Elliott West has persuasively argued for a "Greater Reconstruction" beginning as early as 1845 and first applied in the West before moving east (and south). See Elliott West, *The Last Indian War: The Nez Perce Story* (New York: Oxford University Press, 2009). While recognizing the usefulness of West's thesis, I employ the more traditional periodization here because of my lack of confidence that "reconstruction" is the proper name for federal action against Mormonism in the period of its early formation, as stated earlier in this article.

50. Julie Novkov, "Making Citizens of Freedmen and Polygamists," in *Statebuilding from the Margins: Between Reconstruction and the New Deal*, edited by Carol Nackenoff and Julie Novkov (Philadelphia: University of Pennsylvania Press, 2014), 63, 60–61.

51. Mason, *The Mormon Menace*, 100–101; see all of chap. 5 for a development of this argument.

52. *The Doctrine and Covenants of the Church of Jesus Christ of Latter-day Saints* (Salt Lake City: The Church of Jesus Christ of Latter-day Saints, 1981), 134:7, 10.

53. Wilford Woodruff, George Q. Cannon, and Joseph F. Smith, "Official Declaration," December 12, 1889, in *Messages of the First Presidency of the Church of Jesus Christ of Latter-day Saints, 1833–1964*, ed. James R. Clark (Salt Lake City: Bookcraft, 1966), 3:184–87.

54. Alexander, *Things in Heaven and Earth*, 259.

55. Cavanaugh, *The Myth of Religious Violence*, 9.

56. Ronald W. Walker, "Sheaves, Bucklers, and the State: Mormon Leaders Respond to the Dilemmas of War," in *The New Mormon History: Revisionist Essays on the Past*, ed. D. Michael Quinn (Salt Lake City: Signature Books, 1992), 278; see also D. Michael Quinn, "The Mormon Church and the Spanish-American War: An End to Selective Pacifism," *Pacific Historical Review* 43, no. 3 (August 1974): 342–66.

57. Cavanaugh, *The Myth of Religious Violence*, 56.

PART II
The Context of Reconstruction

Interlude 2

Racial Dimensions

Cathleen Cahill and Crystal N. Feimster

In 1935 W. E. B. Du Bois published *Black Reconstruction in America, 1860–1880* and challenged the historical narrative developed by William A. Dunning of Columbia University and his students. The Dunning School of historiography painted Southern Reconstruction as an abject failure; the honorable South, prostrate by the destruction of war, was overrun by corrupt federal officials, inept black politicians, and lazy and vicious newly freed black people. It was a history of Reconstruction that found full flower in D. W. Griffith's 1915 film, *Birth of a Nation*, an adaption of Thomas Dixon Jr.'s 1905 novel, *The Clansman: An Historical Romance of the Ku Klux Klan*.

Du Bois offered a history of Reconstruction that centered the lives and experiences of newly freed black people and argued that they brought the United States closest to its best ideals of justice and equality. In *Black Reconstruction*, Du Bois highlighted how the government was used as a tool for social good, pointing especially to the establishment of public school systems in the South. His most innovative historical departure (and the most controversial) was to frame slavery and the transition to freedom as "a general strike."[1] Eric Foner's 1988 publication, *Reconstruction: America's Unfinished Revolution*, drew heavily on Du Bois's ideas and quickly became the standard Reconstruction text. While the authors of these essays acknowledge Foner's history of Reconstruction, they leave us to wonder what Du Bois might think of their efforts to expand the bounds of Reconstruction during the postwar period into the western territory without centering newly freed black people.

While Du Bois did not write much about Indians or Asians and failed to mention Mormons in *Black Reconstruction*, he wrote briefly about relations between blacks and Indians. He showed how white legislators used state laws to disenfranchise and deny citizenship to Indians, Chinese, and African Americans alike.[2] Moreover, Du Bois called on scholars to examine how Reconstruction played out in the West. In his chapter titled "The Duel for Labor Control on Border and Frontier," he noted that "the border between slavery and free labor," including (and especially relevant for our purposes) Missouri and the Indian Territory, "was vitally affected by the abolition of slavery. Its history during and after the Civil War is not usually included in Reconstruction."[3]

Without question Du Bois would insist that a study of how Reconstruction played out in the West requires paying attention to African Americans. For example, it was the efforts of newly freed people and their allies that led to the passage of the Reconstruction Amendments that drastically changed the calculus of citizenship in the United States. In his essay, "'To Merge Them into More Wholesome Social Elements': The Greater Reconstruction and Its Place in Utah," Brett Dowdle recounts that before the Fourteenth Amendment established birthright citizenship (excepting Indians not taxed), the federal government controlled membership in the nation's citizenry through a variety of means including treaty stipulations, use of the territorial system and prolonged territorial status, reservation boundaries, and court decisions, especially the Dred Scott decision of 1857. In the Dred Scott decision, the Supreme Court ruled that only white persons could become citizens (though it left open the possibility that Indians could naturalize like other foreign citizens if they were "civilized").

Like Du Bois, Dowdle also reveals the significance of expanding the timeline of Reconstruction beyond 1877. Making a claim for "a Greater Reconstruction," Dowdle demonstrates how a much broader temporal and geographic model fits with how most people understood and experienced life in the decade following the Civil War. He shows that throughout the 1870s as policy makers in the newly strengthened federal government again turned to the West, they themselves often deployed the analogy of "reconstructing" the populations that did not fit into a perceived American identity. Such reconstructing often meant reforming their cultures to conform to presumed racialized and gendered national norms— especially the nuclear family ideal, wage labor, and Protestant Christianity.

Framing *Black Reconstruction* from 1860 to 1880, Du Bois leaves little doubt that the Civil War marked the beginning of Reconstruction. In "The Case for Containing Reconstruction," Rachel St. John argues that what happened in the American West before the Civil War was not Reconstruction, but rather efforts at construction; attempts to expand the nation through the incorporation of new territory and the conquest of the people who lived there. In "The Application of Federal Power in Utah Territory," Brent Rogers clearly argues that the lessons learned during the prewar incorporation period were important to policy makers and served as warnings for soon-to-be Confederates. Rogers also reveals that after the Civil War the federal government redeployed the strategies, tactics, and tools it had gained in the conflict and Southern Reconstruction toward populations in the West. Highlighting the links between West and South, Rogers provides new insights about the interregional dynamics of Reconstruction. As Elliott West writes in the introduction: "If we start with that—if, that is, the Reconstruction era is made continental—then all sorts of questions, or rather sets of questions, quickly arise. How does the western side of the story generally jibe with the usual—the Southern—side?" Indeed, both Dowdle and Rogers offer a few possibilities.

Rogers's and Dowdle's essays demonstrate that as the nation struggled to come to terms with the changes wrought by the Civil War and Reconstruction, white Americans, especially Northerners, did a great deal of reasoning through analogy. In this sense there was a dialogue or a dialectic across space and time moving from West to South and back to the West again. Drawing on Natalia Molina, Dowdle's analysis of tropes reveals how white Americans used stereotypes to "think with" as they addressed the "problematic" populations in the nation. (Christine Talbot's piece also reveals how literary narratives likewise borrowed from each other.) Dowdle argues convincingly that religious prejudice and racism were tropes that worked hand in hand. White Americans reasoned by analogy across populations: if Catholics following a church leader in Rome were undemocratic, then Mormon loyalty to their prophet was also a problem. If slavery as a labor system was bad, Chinese coolie labor, which was deemed akin to slavery, was also bad—bad enough to bar Chinese laborers from the country in 1882. Americans used such reasoning to find solutions as well. In the powerful example of General Sherman that opens Dowdle's essay, we see a Civil War general whose Field Order Number 15 famously gave rise to the dream of "forty acres and a mule" for former slaves in the South and emphasized a similar vision of free labor ideology and family configuration for Mormons and Indians in the West. But the vehemence behind Sherman's letter seems more akin to his determination to force the Confederacy into conformity.

Rogers also demonstrates the movement of ideas between the West and the South as the federal government sought to control different populations in each region. Highlighting the expansion of federal power and its impact on relations between Mormons and American Indians in the territory, he provides new insight into how the racial politics of Reconstruction played out in the territorial West. Beginning with antebellum ideas about popular sovereignty and political debates about slavery, the removal of Native peoples, and polygamy, Rogers reframes the 1857 Utah War as setting the stage for the expansion of federal action in western territories during the Civil War and Reconstruction. During the Civil War as the federal government grew stronger (especially with Republican control of Congress) it passed the 1862 Morrill Anti-Bigamy Act, denied Utah's request for statehood, reinforced its military presence at Fort Douglas, and created the Uintah Indian Reservation. Gaining power during the Civil War and picking up speed during Reconstruction, the federal government ultimately succeeded in wielding its authority in Utah. When compared to how Reconstruction played out in the South, Rogers provides new insight into how the racial politics of Reconstruction played out in the territorial West and raises a host of questions about the nation's reluctant commitment to equal citizenship.

In both essays the federal government takes center stage, as policy makers, negotiators, generals, and political leaders work to define Reconstruction. Du Bois, however, would remind us that a top-down political history that ignores those on the ground, especially black and working-class peoples, leaves us with more questions than answers. Yet, by focusing on the expansion of federal power in Utah Territory and bringing our attention to how Mormons and Indians informed postwar America, Rogers and Dowdle provide new angles of vision for understanding Reconstruction and the American West. Moreover, their essays remind us of the importance of not losing sight of the racialized and gendered politics of Reconstruction that emerged from the Civil War and the destruction of slavery.

Notes

1. W. E. B. Du Bois, *Black Reconstruction in America, 1860–1880* (1935, repr., New York: Atheneum, 1998), 55–83 and 128.

2. Du Bois, *Black Reconstruction*, 561. On Indians, see 6, 96, 282, 288–89, 303, 308, 374, and 629. On the Chinese, see 282, 288, 374, 569, and 629.

3. Du Bois, *Black Reconstruction*, 526 and 561. He would also quite likely be excited to see recent scholarship exploring the relationship between Native nations in Indian Territory and their former slaves. See, for example, Tiya Miles, *Ties that Bind: The Story of an Afro-Cherokee Family in Slavery and Freedom* (Berkeley: University of California Press, 2005); and Barbara Krauthamer, *Black Slaves, Indian Masters: Slavery, Emancipation, and Citizenship in the Native American South* (Chapel Hill: University of North Carolina Press, 2013). See also Tiya Miles, "The Long Arm of the South?" *Western Historical Quarterly* 43, no. 3 (August 2012): 274–82.

= 4 =

The Application of Federal Power in Utah Territory

Brent M. Rogers

The reconstruction era of American history was messy and complex, comprised of a web of processes and decisions that rarely had distinct victories.[1] Depending on one's point of view, however, one could mark the increase and consolidation of federal power, especially in the West, as a triumph. United States federal power had surfaced in episodes ranging from the Monroe Doctrine to the Treaty of Guadalupe Hidalgo and was extended in the 1850s management of western territories.[2] Still, the general government had not ascended to dominance. During the Civil War and reconstruction periods that changed. A multitude of interwoven processes involving ideological and political debates and on-the-ground exercises of power had westerners experiencing a difficult shift in the negotiation of authority that was ultimately marked by a watershed in favor of federal supremacy.

The inceptive increase in federal activity mirrored the developing processes of Washington's territorial administration. By necessity, the central government was continually strengthening its presence, authority, and infrastructure as it attempted to manage new peoples and lands in the West. The government's management of the territorial West led to larger questions and discussions about the use of federal power over a locality, particularly after the advent of the Republican Party and its 1856 platform, which called on Congress to use its sovereign powers over the territories to prohibit slavery and polygamy in those places. At precisely that moment, American people, pundits, and legislators strenuously debated the issues of federalism in the form of states' rights and popular sovereignty. The Civil War and subsequent decades of reconstruction efforts settled the matter, especially in the territorial West, as federal authority emerged dominant. The application of federal power in Utah Territory provides a useful lens through which to view these processes and the slow development of national will being imposed upon a local population. Seen another way, this history unveils the transition and evolution of the federal government from gingerly testing its authority to firmly demonstrating its sovereignty in the West, even as the application of its power flowed and then ebbed in the South.

Though uneven, contested, and lengthy, from the 1850s through the 1880s the government proved over and again that it would make the territory of Utah into a proper self-governing American state. The history of the federal government's relationship with Utah Territory and particularly the way it handled infrastructural development, statehood requests, Indian affairs, and polygamy legislation highlight this larger era of growth in federal power. This long undertaking in Utah can be understood as both a construction and a reconstruction. In the larger sense of territorial supervision, the central government sought to make the Great Basin a loyal American republican place. At the same time, it had to reconstruct the Mormon people in Utah, a religious community that had already constructed a government and society that other Americans deemed illegitimate.

The Territorial System and the Politics of Antebellum Federal Authority

In the American system of federalism, territories were not sovereign in themselves, but were under the jurisdiction of the federal government. In the process to prepare territories for statehood, the U.S. president appointed federal officers including governors, prosecutors, judges, Indian agents, surveyors, and others to supervise a territory's population, elections, and passage of territorial laws. These officers were constitutionally mandated to ensure that a properly functioning republican form of government operated within the bounds of each territory.[3] In addition, the president oversaw military operations and gave orders for any U.S. troops stationed in the territories.[4] Extending even further, the president and Congress had discretionary power to deprive a territory of representative government and to change local government when necessary. The potential to employ such arbitrary power was threatening, and, constitutionally speaking, proved the supremacy of the federal government over areas of national expansion.

Once a territory's inhabitants demonstrated they could responsibly and loyally implement a republican government, federal authority would give way to state sovereignty.[5] That route, however, was determined by authorities in Washington.

When the United States acquired the far West from Mexico at the end of the U.S.-Mexico War in 1848, the extent of the territorial lands under direct federal management eclipsed for the first time the mass of land in the individual states combined. In 1857 Secretary of War John B. Floyd described the vast territorial region: "From our western frontier of settlements to those of northern Oregon the distance is about 1,800 miles; from the same frontier to the settlements of California, *via* Salt Lake, is 1,800 miles; from the frontier of Arkansas, at Fort Smith, by Albuquerque or Santa Fé, to Fort Tejon, is about 1,700 miles; and from San Antonio, by El Paso, to San Diego, near the borders of the white settlements, is 1,400 miles; constituting an aggregate line of 6,700 miles which ought to be occupied."[6]

The organization of six territories in the 1840s and 1850s enlarged the federal superstructure over western lands and peoples. In governing and developing the West, the national state grew in power and influence in the form of administrative bureaucracies for the army, Indian affairs, and land management. Outside of bureaucratic growth in Washington, federal officers moved to western territories to govern, to introduce American political and cultural customs, to build roads and forts, to perform land and railroad surveys, and to engage in scientific explorations. Federal funding began to flow west, serving as the bedrock of territorial economies. The swelling of bureaucratic needs and movement of officers and money initiated a deepening and developing federal presence in the West. As historian Richard White has noted, "The West provided an arena for the expansion of federal powers that was initially available nowhere else in the country. By exercising power, the government increased its power."[7] Indeed, in the territorial West this experiment with power had the potential to develop, but the realities of time, space, and human resources left the government with a minimal presence to manage the region's diverse peoples, including Mormons and Mexican Catholics.

In the Great Basin, and in the absence of federal authority, Mormons, who had fled the United States to go to Mexico just two years earlier, openly practiced their unique religion and its attendant familial structure of plural marriage. The belief and practice of plural marriage, Americans came to believe, undergirded a perceived theocracy and system of Indian affairs that encouraged a Mormon-Indian alliance against the United States.[8] Seeing these institutions and relationships as threats, the federal government slowly began to expand its reach into Utah. This was part of a broader process initiated in Washington to establish its authority in the West. Congress organized new territorial administrations and appointed a higher number of permanent federal officials to oversee those geopolitical entities and divest them of the trappings of former systems. These officials from the eastern United States did not represent the will of the local population but imposed federal mandates. For example, in New Mexico, as historian Howard Lamar explained, the first task of federal officials was to "retire certain traditional political habits of the New Mexican populace" and replace them with American praxis.[9] The Utah territorial inhabitants decried such a system that removed local self-rule: "We claim that in a republican form of government, such as our fathers established, and such as ours still professes to be, the officers are and should be the servants of the people, and not their masters, dictators, or tyrants."[10] Though Brigham Young argued that theocracy was a truly republican form of governance, Mormon political and familial systems were deemed un-American and nonrepublican according to the Protestant Christian values that buttressed the United States democratic republic.[11] That being the case, the territorial system was inconsistent with the republican idea of natural rights and local self-rule, but it was considered necessary to establish proper American systems in place of the incumbents (Mormon or Mexican). Territorial management, however, did not square with the growing popularity of the Democrats' prevailing doctrine of popular sovereignty.

Popular sovereignty emerged because of the U.S.-Mexico War. In 1846, before the war had been decided, Pennsylvania Democrat David Wilmot proposed an amendment to legislation that would have prohibited the extension of slavery into any lands acquired from the Mexican conflict. The Wilmot Proviso, as it came to be known, led to some vigorous debate in Congress; some Southerners declared that if the government ever blocked slavery from new territories the Southern states would leave the Union.[12]

Though the Senate rejected the amendment on a couple of occasions and the proviso ultimately did not become law, the die was cast. It became very clear: the general government could indeed prohibit slavery expansion in the West and otherwise restrict territorial popular will. That was a genie that could not be bottled up despite the best efforts of Lewis Cass and Stephen Douglas, who proposed popular sovereignty as the solution. Let the people of the territory decide whether they would allow slavery in their jurisdiction, these two Democrats argued, and take the federal government out of the question. In other words, when it came to slavery, treat the territories like the states.[13] It sounded like a good idea to a great number of people, especially Democrats and those residing in the Southern states. But the language allowing people of the territories to decide for themselves their own "domestic institutions" eventually extended the conversation beyond slavery. The emergence of the Republican Party and the presidential campaign of 1856 refocused the discourse around territorial autonomy and the applicability of federal power in western territories. It was within this context that the negotiation of greater federal authority was tested out in practice.

The 1856 Republican Party platform brilliantly positioned slavery with polygamy, both of which existed in Mormon Utah Territory, calling them the "twin relics of barbarism."[14] The platform called for the federal government to use its rightful authority as territorial manager to prohibit both in all United States territories. Republicans favored free labor and did not want to see slavery expand beyond the states in which it already resided. The party put the nation on notice that these two domestic institutions were unacceptable in the West and that they intended to use federal power to prevent their growth. Adding the abhorred practice of plural marriage to slavery presented an almost irrefutable logic: if Congress could enact laws to eliminate plural marriage, the same federal power to regulate one domestic institution could be used against the other. Popular sovereignty was meant to keep power out of the national government's hands, but the Republican Party reminded Americans of the legitimacy of sovereign federal authority over the territories and began to expose flaws in the idea of popular sovereignty.[15]

When Republican representative Justin Smith Morrill of Vermont crusaded against polygamy in early 1857 he noted that if left unchecked, the Mormon system of plural marriage would become a threat to and would significantly weaken American society. Wanting to protect the nation and diminish the threat of Mormon power, he accordingly called on Congress to act "whereby our common country may be rescued from the great reproach of a barbaric age." Morrill insisted that the people of Utah Territory were hostile to republicanism, no longer recognized federal law, and were not properly subordinate to federal authority. A member of the House Committee on the Territories, Morrill advocated for the congressional rejection of Utah laws, the reduction of the territory's boundaries or complete annexation of the territorial lands to neighboring geopolitical entities, or the establishment of a colonial style government with non-Mormons in all federal offices. Furthermore, he requested that a strong military force be sent to Utah to support and sustain the civil officers—a clear argument for asserting federal power in and over the territory.[16] The Vermont congressman's plan, however, highlighted a dilemma facing the U.S. government: assertive action to crush Utah's domestic institutions would violate the Democratic Party's doctrine of popular sovereignty and exacerbate Southern fears about the power of the government to block the expansion of slavery.

Though Democrats lauded congressional noninterference for slavery in the territories and would have been happy to use federal authority to protect that peculiar institution, they incongruously exercised power in Utah, thereby demonstrating the correctness of the Morrill predicament. Shortly following the 1856 presidential election and the inauguration of James Buchanan, the new Democratic president appointed new federal officials, including a governor to replace Mormon incumbent Brigham Young, and ordered some 2,500 federal troops to Utah Territory to suppress an alleged Mormon rebellion and to establish the "sovereignty of the Constitution and laws over the Territory of Utah."[17] The president later delivered a message on Utah affairs in which he focused on the "despotic power" of Mormon leader Brigham Young, calling Young's gubernatorial administration theocratic and un-American. The president piled on, emphasizing that Young had tampered "with the Indian tribes and exciting their hostile feelings against the United States."[18] Buchanan's statement here alluded to letters and reports received in Washington that demonstrated the Mormon violation of federal Indian legislation. These documents indicated that Mormons were conspiring to ally with Indians and potentially even black slaves against the interests of the federal government; white Americans had long feared that interracial alliances, particularly among Natives and blacks, would wreak havoc in the West and the South.[19] This message resembled the thoughts of William W. Drummond, a federal judge who had recently returned to Washington from Utah. Drummond had strongly argued that Mormons were a threat to national sovereignty and to all non-Mormons in the territory. He wanted to see the army sent to Utah to assert command over the territory and its peoples.[20]

Such expedience in advancing power in Utah only grew after the Utah legislature submitted a consequential memorial to Congress. In that January 1857 document, the legislature demanded the application of popular sovereignty in the territory with greater autonomy and local control particularly in the selection of territorial officers; it also claimed that Utahns would no longer tolerate hostile federal appointees. This memorial demonstrated Mormon belief that local sovereignty outweighed federal dictation and verged on the assertion of

Mormon political independence.[21] Strong statements from Utah's citizens only inflamed Washington's concern about Mormon power.

According to President Buchanan's rationale, the Mormons, led by Young, had set national sovereignty at defiance by failing to establish a republican form of government and by breaking federal laws, all of which warranted action and a decisive exercise of power. Indeed, the Utah War and the introduction of new federal officials and a permanent army into Utah Territory was a legitimate intervention meant to alter the practices and behaviors of the territorial population and make it more acceptable to American society.

Another influential Democrat, Illinois Senator Stephen A. Douglas—a major proponent of federal noninterference in the territories—had, in June 1857, delivered a speech that also advocated the use of greater federal authority over Utah Territory. After referencing polygamy and the power of Congress to prohibit the practice, Douglas demanded no halfway measures. He called for the repeal of Utah's organic act and the removal of all Mormons from local government and civil authority from the territory.[22] While President Buchanan had shied away from any language concerning plural marriage, perhaps hoping that his political opponents would not so easily tie his action to the Republican twin relics rhetoric, Douglas, the popular sovereignty advocate, was much less delicate in his exposition to blot Utah out of existence. The little giant's proposal was a nuclear option. Repealing the territory's organic act would have put the land under martial law until a new territory or territories were organized, at which point the stamp of national authority would be even more firmly imprinted on the Great Basin. The possibility of reconstructing Utah through the annexation of its lands to newly created territories had been discussed, but the utter destruction of the present territorial government had not. That Douglas and surely others in Congress entertained such an idea was another stark reminder of the supremacy of the central government over the territories.

Obliterating the territory's government and geopolitical boundaries would certainly have had dangerous consequences for the republican nation, especially given the heated national debate over slavery extension into territorial lands of the West. Somehow Douglas, Buchanan, and the Democrats did not have the foresight to see the problems of their reactionary rhetoric and action in Utah. More astute Republicans, like Abraham Lincoln, did. In the weeks after Douglas's speech, Lincoln offered a rebuttal that highlighted the magnitude of such federal action in Utah. "To be sure," the future president stated, "it would be a considerable backing down by Judge Douglas from his much vaunted doctrine of self government for the territories; but this is only additional proof of what was very plain from the beginning, that that doctrine was a mere deceitful pretence for the benefit of Slavery. . . . There is nothing in the United States Constitution or law against polygamy? And why is it not a part of the Judge's 'sacred right of self government' for that people to have it, or rather to *keep* it, if they choose?"[23] The logical extension of Douglas's proposal for Utah, according to Lincoln and other detractors, placed the future of slavery in western territories in peril, especially if an antislavery Republican won the next presidential election.[24]

A *Harper's Weekly* article of July 4, 1857, made the point clearly: "This scheme of repealing Territorial Acts is open to grave objections. Suppose a new Territory carved, in any future year of grace, out of New Mexico, and organized on the basis of the Kansas and Nebraska acts; suppose that Territory peopled with slaveholders, and prepared for admission to the Union with a Slave Constitution; and suppose a Congress strongly imbued with hostility to the extension of slavery; how convenient a precedent this scheme of Senator Douglas's would be for the passage of an Act repealing the Territorial Act of the new Territory, and leaving the offending slaveholders in the attitude of 'alien enemies!'"[25] This would not be the last time that the idea of dismantling Utah's governing structure was contemplated by federal authorities, though by the time the idea was more fully put into action, the consideration for protecting slaveholder interests in the West had largely disappeared.

The outcome of the Utah War was not what most people expected. The army did not conquer the Mormon people with great force. Congress did not dismantle the territory. Instead, Buchanan offered a full presidential pardon for Utah's inhabitants excusing their rebellious activities.[26] The sending of the army did, however, change the dynamics of the government's presence in the Great Basin. Two federal army outposts—Fort Bridger and Camp Floyd—were established on the main roads of overland travel. Soldiers surveyed and built new routes through Utah to other western territories and to California. U.S. officials, backed by the presence of a large military force, moved to ensure the observance of national laws and the proper surveillance of the territory's white and Native populations. Washington also created a new federal army district, known as the Department of Utah, while land surveyors and agents enhanced the government's grip on the region. The new forts, officers, explorations, and agencies also added to federal spending in Utah and the West.

As a result of the Utah War, the general government was able to begin to overlay a scaffolding that would add to the advancement of national interests over local ones and facilitate more efficiency in communication, travel, and land management in the region.²⁷ Americans generally regarded the Utah action positively; some even wished the federal fist had struck harder at the Mormon heart, because the nation, North and South, pro- and antislavery, believed that Mormonism was too strange and repugnant a religion to remain in a region so important to the American future. Mormons needed to be monitored more closely and be remade in the American way—republican and monogamous. Undoubtedly, the Utah War was a display of power, though not as commanding a display as many Americans thought or perhaps had hoped for. It created an enduring atmosphere and continuum of federal presence and surveillance over a group of people deemed too unpredictable and potentially disloyal to American interests in the increasingly important American West on the eve of the Civil War. If the Utah War represented an early, impetuous federal effort to properly govern Utah, subsequent activities symbolized a stronger reconstructing of Utah and its peoples. These included the passage of the 1862 Morrill Anti-Bigamy Act, the stationing of a permanent military presence at Fort Douglas, the separation of Native peoples to reservations, and especially the ratification of intensifying federal legislation on marriage.

The Civil War in Utah: The Morrill Act and Fort Douglas

The gradual growth of federal presence in the West got a boost from the Utah War. That expedition also informed relevant debates over the national government's power to halt slavery in the West and ongoing debates over polygamy. The twin relics rhetoric continued into the 1860s. James Rusling, an officer in the army's quartermaster department, wrote that "peculiar institutions, whether slavery or polygamy, breed the same results, whether in South Carolina or Utah" and further opined that plural marriage was an outrage against civilization and truly was "slavery's hideous and exquisite 'twin relic of barbarism.'"²⁸ Because the government had already shown a willingness to send an army to Utah Territory in what most assumed was an attack on the Mormon religious practice of polygamy, even if it was not explicitly marketed as such, Americans largely understood that if a Republican was elected president he could and would apply that same force to halt slavery expansion in the West.²⁹

Southerners had rejected the power of the government when it came to limiting slavery expansion from at least the time of the Wilmot Proviso and assumed that if the Republican candidate (Abraham Lincoln) won the election of 1860, he would eliminate slavery and usher in greater federal control throughout the nation. Southerners claimed that tyranny would soon replace republicanism.[30] The Utah example demonstrated the government's willingness to enforce national over local interests upon a people without their consent. To a nation of peoples steeped in a tradition of self-government, use of federal authority signaled a threat to local self-government and a broader shift toward Washington's influence over politics, economics, and culture everywhere in the United States.

Lincoln's election led to the secession of seven states and the empowerment of Republicans in Congress. The absence of the Southern states cleared the path for members of the new party to reshape the national government according to its principles, including more coercive federal action to restructure the West. Congress soon approved the admission of Kansas as a free state and organized the territories of Colorado and Nevada, diminishing the boundaries of Utah Territory. These territories and their new governments ensured greater independence for non-Mormons in the region and tripled the number of federally appointed authorities in the West through a system of patronage that advanced national interests, albeit typically in-line with party politics.[31] The Republican Congress also used its discretion to deny statehood for Utah.

In what was perhaps the best time to do so, Utah Mormons petitioned Congress for admittance to the Union in early 1862, when the balance on slavery was no longer an issue and when Mormons could best prove their loyalty to a nation embroiled in the Civil War. They also remained anxious to trade territorial, subservient status for self-governing statehood. Believing the government had inadequately met "the wants of a rapidly increasing population," and conveying a strong desire for local self-government over national sovereignty, the people of Utah pled for the federal shackles to be removed from the territory, stating they wanted "to enjoy those inherent, inalienable, and constitutional rights guaranteed to every American citizen."[32] Congress denied Utah's statehood request.[33] Mormon beliefs and practices were viewed as un-American, and therefore Mormons were unfit to exercise sovereignty in their sphere. Instead, within months, the national legislative body approved laws further demonstrating the central government's surging strength over western territories.

In 1862, Republican leaders shepherded several bills through Congress that had been stalled by the conflict over the expansion of slavery, including the Homestead Act, Morrill Anti-Bigamy Act, Pacific Railroad Act, and a law outlawing slavery in the territories. Each legislative action strengthened the government's design to better develop the transcontinental country.[34] In June 1862, Congress enacted and President Lincoln authorized a statute outlawing slavery and involuntary servitude in U.S. territories, making good on the first half of the Republican promise of 1856 to prohibit the "Twin Relics of Barbarism" in western territories.[35] On July 1, 1862, President Lincoln approved the Pacific Railroad Act, which further promoted western migration as well as quicker transportation and communication from coast to coast. That act promoted the construction of the transcontinental railroad to aid the government in its postal, military, and economic purposes in the West. Seven days later, on July 8, 1862, Lincoln signed the Morrill Anti-Bigamy Act, introduced by Vermont Republican Justin Morrill, which outlawed plural marriage in the territories. It was the first federal law regulating marriage in the United States. The Morrill Act was thus the fulfillment of the Republican agenda to criminalize the twin relics. Taken with the other legislation passed, the Morrill Act further extended congressional reach and signaled the staying power of national institutions and authority in the West. These laws provided the foundation to fulfill expansionist dreams of a transcontinental nation filled with free, loyal American settlers. And with them, the question of the federal government's authority over the western territories was settled.

With this new legislation, Morrill and the Republicans put into motion the reconstruction of what they saw as a debased society in Utah.[36] However, enforcement of the Morrill Act and the implementation of the other major 1862 laws did not come quickly or easily. The disruption of the Civil War stalled progress on the national project to forge an American West particularly as many U.S. officials and military men returned east to participate in the war. However, officials in Washington believed that maintaining national sovereignty in Utah required a military presence.[37] So, in October 1862, War Department officials ordered Patrick Connor and a new military contingent from California to Utah. Once in the territory, Connor established Camp Douglas, later renamed Fort Douglas, a 2,500-acre fortification on the east bench overlooking Salt Lake City.[38] The creation of that U.S. military base and the reinforcement to Fort Bridger, an outpost still in federal hands from the Utah War, resumed the policy of the general government begun in 1857 to supervise Mormons and Great Basin Natives, to ensure the observance of law and order, and to protect and continue to develop trails and communications.[39] Most importantly, the troops stationed in Utah could defend the new telegraph line that passed through Salt Lake City against the threat of any Mormon rebellion. As of October 1861, the transcontinental telegraph efficiently linked the East and West together; it stood as a powerful tool for the general government's management of its western lands and people, especially in wartime.

Fort Douglas represented a renewed occupying force in Utah during the Civil War and after. Patrick Connor wanted to enlarge the military presence to forcefully prosecute violators of the recently passed antipolygamy law. The Irish firebrand despised the religious practice of polygamy. He argued to his superiors that his troops could get rid of this barbaric practice in Utah and free the nation of the stigma of polygamists.[40]

Abraham Lincoln and other high-ranking military officials chose to act more diplomatically. The president likened the Mormons in Utah to timber on a farm. He stated, "Occasionally we would come to a log which had fallen down. It was too hard to split, too wet to burn, and too heavy to move, so we plowed around it." By relaying this analogy to a Utah Mormon diplomat, Lincoln wanted Brigham Young to understand "that if he will let me alone I will let him alone."[41] Fearing that the ongoing Civil War would encourage Mormon rebellion against the United States and inflame the war on another front, the president sought the status quo. This rationale had been used by opponents of the Morrill Act in 1862. California Senator James A. McDougall argued against the antipolygamy bill, rehearsing the rationale that the nation was already embroiled in civil war and therefore had "trouble enough on our hands without invoking further trouble" with Utah Mormons.[42] Connor was ordered to avoid confrontations with the Mormons "for any cause whatever." Lieutenant Richard C. Drum, the assistant adjutant general for national military districts in the West, warned that a "war with the Mormons would be the opportunity which our domestic enemies would not fail to improve, and it is not too much to say that at this time such a war would prove fatal to the Union cause."[43] Due to the war atmosphere and the unwillingness to devote more resources to Utah, the marriage law was left largely dormant during the Civil War, though the law—along with the other 1862 legislation and the federal resources and infrastructure already in place in the West—provided the foundation on which to build federal muscle and enforcement in the decades that followed.

When the question was raised as to whether the fort should be discontinued following the war, military leaders in Utah and Washington and legislators in Congress largely agreed that the fort and a powerful presence must be retained in Utah. After all, Utah Territory remained a valuable portion of land to the country. It was a crucial "half-way house to the Pacific" and represented "the granary from which the surrounding territories are to receive their supplies."[44] "It is my opinion," Fort Douglas post chaplain Norman McLeod wrote, "that were the troops withdrawn grave interests would be imperiled, a reign of terror inaugurated, and the spirit of vengeance, fostered by the teachings of the hierarchy, break forth into acts that would precipitate a conflict in which much treasure would be expended, and many precious lives sacrificed. All who are suspected of sympathy for Gentileism would be persecuted. It would be disastrous to every interest but that of the *one man power*; retard mining, endanger travel, give license and a field of operations to the revengeful bands that for years have been restrained through fear of General Connor."[45] McLeod and others wrote to Washington asserting the need for the enforcement of laws against polygamy and to protect growing American interests in the West.[46] Washington decision-makers opted to maintain, and eventually strengthen, Fort Douglas and the Department of Utah as vital infrastructure for the future enforcement of polygamy laws and for monitoring the region's Native population.

Federal Influence in Utah's Indian Affairs

Actions toward American Indians were a crucial component in the expansion of federal command and went hand-in-glove with military operations in the West. The government had already been concerned about a potential Mormon-Indian alliance in the Great Basin as part of the Utah War, but during the Civil War and beyond, the government more actively moved to separate the two peoples to control their relations and land.[47] With the threat of a Mormon-Indian alliance renewed, fearing these two groups' unauthorized use of power against the state, and with too few officers to patrol and police the vast Utah Territory, Indian agents called for change. They supported the removal of the Indians to a more remote location for their protection, for easier supervision and control, and to eventually eradicate the perceived Mormon influence over the indigenous population.[48] It was part of the larger process the government initiated to subjugate, dispossess, and confine Native peoples in the West, a process that expanded U.S. sovereignty in the form of reservations and a larger bureaucracy even as it hamstrung local and Native sovereignties.[49]

In the early 1860s the commissioner of Indian affairs, William P. Dole, promoted the concentration of Indians on a few reservations, the application of severalty to Native homelands and reservations, and the assimilation of Indians into mainstream white society. For Utah, Dole recommended the creation of a reservation far away from Mormon settlements and to concentrate in a manageable area the Indian residents who had since "scattered themselves in various portions of the Territory."[50] Commissioner Dole argued that separating Mormons and Natives would protect both and would promote greater white (non-Mormon) settlement in Utah. Dole informed Caleb B. Smith, the secretary of the interior, that Utah's Indian agents had held interviews "with some of the chiefs of important tribes," who had apparently stated to the agents their desire "to come under treaty relations, and to cede their lands to the United States, thereby securing to themselves quiet homes, and the means of comfortable subsistence."[51] From the information he had received, Smith also saw the benefit of the reservation and sent a proposal to President Lincoln. On Smith's recommendation, Lincoln began the process of markedly altering the physical and social landscape of Utah by issuing an executive order on October 3, 1861, to create the Uintah Indian Reservation deep in the mountains southeast of Salt Lake City.[52]

The year following Lincoln's executive order, Utah's Indian agents described the "greatest advantage" of the new reservation: "its remoteness from white settlements, being separated from them by the Uintah mountains on the north, the Wausatch range on the west, and bounded by the deserts of Colorado river on the south and east."[53] The location of the reservation separated Native peoples from the primary overland travel routes and new telegraphic communications, which also served the interests of the general government. Moving Indians away from Mormon influence and white settlement was a vital shift in sovereignty. Doing so ultimately provided closer supervision of Native peoples.

By the end of 1862 the commissioner of Indian affairs stated that the movement to completely separate the main population of Utah's Native peoples onto the Uintah reservation had gained momentum, though the Indians remained in a "state of restlessness" because of Mormon interference.[54] It took time for federal officials, with assistance from Brigham Young and other Mormons, to negotiate the move of many Native peoples to the Uintah Reservation in 1865; a dispossession that curtailed the remaining vestiges of Ute sovereignty.[55] Many leaders such as Peteetneet favored a treaty, as they apparently understood that the survival of their people depended on their choosing to give up their homelands and remove to the reservation. More coercion was necessary for other Ute leaders, including Sanpitch and Sowiette, but they ultimately signed the Spanish Fork Treaty, relinquishing claim to their homelands and agreeing to move to the Uintah reservation.[56]

At this same time, a Ute leader known as Black Hawk led a resistance movement against the Mormons. Playing on the ongoing tensions and political struggle between Mormons and government officers, Black Hawk initiated raids on Mormon settlements to procure livestock and other necessities. The perceptive Ute did not believe that the Mormons could effectively organize forces against his raiders because of their fear that the federal army would retaliate, nor did he believe that the Mormons would ask either the army or territorial officers for their assistance. Exploiting this political situation, Black Hawk determined that the army would not retaliate against the Utes for attacking Mormons. He was right.[57] The Mormon-Indian conflict lasted, intermittently, until the early 1870s.

During those years Mormon power in actual military might was exposed, and the limitation of their influence with the Utes was seen. This was particularly evident after Utah governor J. Wilson Shaffer, an appointee sent by president Ulysses S. Grant to diminish the vestiges of Mormon power in the territory, outlawed the Mormon militia in 1871. With no armed force to protect the territory's white people, the Mormons became reliant on federal troops to shield them against Native attacks.[58] By 1872 it was federal power that triumphed when the U.S. Army stationed in Utah, which had purposely let the Black Hawk conflict ensue, abruptly put an end to the Utes' resistance and forced their relocation to Uintah.[59] Authority in the form of the army and an Indian affairs bureaucracy ensured the confinement of a significant number of Utah's Native peoples to reservation lands. Mormons were increasingly marginalized in their relations with Great Basin Natives by the army's presence, and the supreme role of the federal government over Utah's Indian affairs was largely achieved by the end of the 1870s.[60]

The military campaign in Utah did not match the ferocity and brutality of General James H. Carleton's against Apaches and Navajos in New Mexico and other Indian wars in the West, but the goal was ultimately the same: move Natives to reservation lands away from white settlement and teach them to be Christian farmers.[61] Still, federal power was never total as some Utes, Paiutes, Goshutes, and bands of Northwestern Shoshones in Utah did not immediately relocate to reservations. Some Shoshones continued to live on privately owned land while Paiute and Goshute reservations were not established for several more decades. Thus, the government's objective in this facet was delayed, layered, and enforced in uneven waves for Utah's diverse Native population.[62]

Parallels of Federal Power in the Reconstruction South and West

In the post–Civil War reconstruction period, the government expanded its authority over populations that had challenged it in both the West and the South. In this period the South was treated like a territory, a geopolitical extension of national sovereignty that required federal directives and the exercise of power. The Republican-led Congress passed Reconstruction Acts, which provided for greater federal military power to guarantee that slavery was in fact extinguished and to help in the administration of African American rights. The United States government had the unenviable task of ensuring that readmitted Southern states, like the western territories, operated loyal and republican governments. Just as that government had the responsibility to prepare new territories like Utah, it initiated a process to reintroduce, reshape, and repair Southern state governments, thereby confirming national sovereignty.[63] Federal power came in a variety of forms and interventions. A strong military presence was needed for black suffrage and to safeguard all freed persons in their rights and property.[64] Other interventions offered new forms of accessibility and new opportunities for underprivileged Southerners. For example, Congress passed the 1866 Southern Homestead Act, which was similar in purpose to the 1862 western Homestead Act. The Southern Homestead Act opened millions of acres of land in the Deep South for freed African Americans and loyal whites to have an opportunity to own lands at a low price; federal agencies managed these lands.[65]

Just as the Reconstruction Acts divided the South into military districts to remake the seceded states into loyal units of government, the federal government had already established the military Department of Utah and had discussed the potential of using arms to enforce federal and moral power. The same show of power was concurrently occurring in the West with installations like Fort Douglas and with the government's role in Indian affairs in Utah. Using the military to enforce the laws again revealed the increasing power of the national government over the local, a fact that did not escape the attention of those over whom power was exercised. Many in the South protested that republicanism had been replaced by despotism in the form of the Republican-led government in Washington.[66] The War Department, then, was playing an important role in implementing Reconstruction programs in the South by enforcing emancipation, feeding people, and ensuring freed peoples their franchise rights, while it was in position to aid in the enforcement of federal laws in the West. To a greater degree than white Mormons, Southerners revolted against outsider rule. Southern states had been sovereign entities prior to and during the war and were now being treated like territorial possessions. Believing that the central government overreached into local affairs, particularly because of the use of the military to support the cause of African American rights and the Freedmen's Bureau, the Southern response initially led to a stronger federal presence to impose control in the region.[67] Southerners retaliated with demonstrations of violence both against African Americans and government authority.

Congressional Republicans understood the power of legislation, but also understood that the means to enforce those laws required more, stronger personnel and proof that a plural marriage had taken place. It was a lesson they learned from the lack of enforcement of the Morrill Anti-Bigamy Act, but one they simultaneously struggled with in ensuring African American rights in the South. The passage of the Fourteenth Amendment established citizen rights and equal protection before the law for recently emancipated peoples, but safeguarding those rights and offering that protection was not so simple. It took more laws and the Fifteenth Amendment to attempt to provide for the people's rights. Emancipation forced the national government to extend citizenship rights to more Americans. Conversely, the activist central government debated numerous bills to deny citizenship rights to Mormon polygamists, to weaken the Latter-day Saint Church, and to strengthen federal officials and non-Mormons living in Utah.[68] These efforts demonstrated that the Bill of Rights had not and would not apply to all Americans despite the efforts to extend and protect African American liberties (which were, in and of themselves, paltry efforts after the initial surge of Reconstruction legislation).

In 1866 the House Committee on the Territories, led by Ohio congressman James M. Ashley, inquired about a bill to repeal the Utah Organic Act (the same suggestion the Democrat Stephen Douglas made nearly ten years earlier) because the people of Utah violated U.S. laws. This time instead of violations of federal Indian laws, Mormons had transgressed by sustaining "the abominable system of polygamy, and the numbers who practice it." The Morrill law against polygamy was not being enforced, and, in the judgment of congressional Republicans "this great and remaining barbarism of our age and country should be swept (like its twin system—slavery) from the territories of the republic . . . means adequate to that end should be adopted."[69] Criticizing the abhorrent polygamous structure of the Mormon family provoked Washington lawmakers to again turn to legislation as a tool of state power.

Utahns made another petition for statehood in 1867, when a territorial convention requested repeal of the Morrill Act and admission to the Union. Instead of granting that appeal, Congress soon redoubled its efforts at passing new legislation to more strongly enforce federal laws on marriage. Additionally, in 1867 Congress established a law to end peonage and Indian slavery in New Mexico, and authorities began to enforce this change in a centuries-old colonial custom with the goal to transform the Southwest into a proper part of the United States.[70] The writing on the wall became even clearer: the federal government was going to transform western peoples not through local sovereignty and choice but through the enforcement of its laws.

In 1869 Aaron H. Cragin, a Republican senator from New Hampshire, and Shelby Cullom, the new chair of the House Committee on the Territories and a Republican from Illinois, introduced legislation to bolster the enforcement of antipolygamy legislation and to bring any vestige of Mormon influence over civil affairs to an end. Neither of these proposals became law. However, describing them will demonstrate the potential for federal reconstruction efforts in Utah. The Cragin bill would have made it unlawful for the church or any of its officers or members to perform marriages and declared that "criminal cases" arising under the 1862 Morrill Anti-Bigamy Act "shall be heard, tried and determined by the district courts of said Territory of Utah, *without a jury.*" Furthermore, Cragin called for the denial of portions of the Bill of Rights to Utah's citizens, primarily the right to a trial by jury and freedom of religion. Had it become law, the measure would have given Utah's territorial governor financial control over the LDS Church as well as the power to appoint all territorial officers, including land agents, and it would have forbidden the territorial legislature to assemble, thereby assigning all legislative powers to the governor.

The Cullom bill was similar, although it would have outlawed not just plural marriages but also cohabitation. It also prohibited anyone believing in polygamy from serving on a grand or petit jury in Utah. A grand jury in Utah, it was believed, would not indict anyone accused of violating the laws preventing polygamy. According to Michigan congressman Austin Blair, it was "a most singular oversight that when Congress passed the law in 1862 against polygamy it left the execution of the law against polygamy in the hands of the polygamists themselves."[71] In the late 1860s and early 1870s Congress moved to rectify this mistake. Cullom further demanded the disenfranchisement of all practicing polygamists and restricted them from holding political office, going so far as to revoke citizenship from those practitioners. Finally, Cullom wanted to use the army to enforce federal law and to allow an additional forty thousand men to enlist in Utah for this purpose.

These proposals were not enacted, but many of the measures they proposed, Congress ultimately adopted. These bills also highlight the federal government's potential to control and remake a place and people. As one opponent of the Cullom bill said, "This country is to-day passing away from the theory of being supported by the hearts of the people, and it is becoming a mere Government of coercion, and this bill (Cullom) is a suggestion of it."[72] The national government had been exercising coercive influence with some early success in the South, but some legislators appear to have been wary of the slippery slope of continued intervention.

In the South, the government intervention ensured rights, but in the West, these bills would eliminate rights. In the 1870s the Republican Congress pushed forward more strong-armed legislation enacting a series of Enforcement Acts to counteract terrorist violence in the South and to nationalize black rights and enfranchisement. The violence itself was surely a backlash against congressional intervention and what that represented: black equality. Military aid and enforcement waned, however, and could not keep up with those Southerners intent on restricting equality. Verbal and rhetorical protests turned into vicious action in the former Confederacy, and while troops fought the good fight for a decade, in 1877 newly elected president Rutherford B. Hayes removed federal troops from the South. He did so after a contested election led Republicans to strike a deal with Southern Democrats to seat Hayes for the promise to withdraw federal troops and end Reconstruction in the South. Hayes made good on that promise and in so doing forsook the defense of black rights and equality.[73]

Though Reconstruction had begun auspiciously in providing African Americans greater inclusion into the political community, the goal of inclusiveness was ultimately elusive for blacks as well as other racial, cultural, and religious groups such as American Indians, Mormons, and Chinese. As historian Elliott West has stated, "The greater the political inclusion, the greater the apparent need for cultural exclusion—and the greater the need to tighten what it has meant to be American."[74] Just as Southerners, when left to their own devices, would not obey and enforce federal laws supporting African American rights, Mormons did not obey or enforce the marriage law in their territory. More federal legislation replete with greater authority over the lands, properties, and religious practices of this group was needed to meet the challenge of prosecution. The rights of religious practice and equal protections were being contested in the nation.

Federal Power and Plural Marriage

While federal power abated in the South, in the 1870s and 1880s it was more vigorously employed in Utah and the West. During these decades, the Mormon practice of polygamy came under fire from all three branches of the federal government. In 1872 President Ulysses S. Grant called upon Congress in his State of the Union address to enact a law that would "secure peace, the equality of all citizens before the law, and the ultimate extinguishment of polygamy."[75] But, the federal government was still handicapped in Utah because of the population differential greatly favoring Mormons as well as the number of Mormons operating in positions of authority in the territory, particularly in the legal system. Less than two years after President Grant's plea, Congress passed the Poland Act, which altered and redefined judicial processes in the territory and interjected greater national authority into those processes. Republican Luke Poland, who had succeeded Justin Morrill in Vermont's second district, explained that his proposal would "put the legal machinery in motion in that Territory."[76] Under the Poland Act probate courts were restricted to matters of estates and guardianship while all civil, chancery, and criminal cases were now under the exclusive jurisdiction of federal courts. In other words, Mormon crimes could no longer skirt around the system by going to probate courts and had to instead be heard by a presidentially appointed federal judge at the district courts. The Poland Act also reformed jury selection. Federal representatives now had an equal share in selecting the grand and petit jurors, a significant move away from all authority being vested in a local (usually Mormon) judge.[77]

This measure was hailed for its remarkable "moderation when compared with previous bills," but some national legislators feared that it gave national authorities too much power and removed from the local population an opportunity for self-rule.[78] Before the act passed, Congress debated a particular line in the proposed bill that would have allowed U.S. authorities to remove from a jury any person who practiced plural marriage or "believe[d] in the rightfulness of the same" in any case involving adultery, bigamy, or polygamy.[79] Nebraska Republican Lorenzo Crounse argued against the Poland Act as a whole, and in that provision in particular, out of sheer desire to prevent a precedent that would allow federal officials "to oppress people of other Territories." "Congress should not," Crounse passionately enunciated, "and I say cannot in consistency with the principles underlying our institutions, enact laws which will thrust upon that people a set of Government officials responsible to no one except the Government here at Washington." Crounse wanted Congress to act more cautiously, stating that the overextension of national influence "would be indeed a dangerous step for us to take."[80] Though federal authority in the territories was no longer questioned, some in Congress continued to fear the precedent set by an overuse of power. More moderate voices like Crounse surely played a role in the lengthy and uneven processes of applying the federal mandate in Utah.

George Q. Cannon, the nonvoting congressional delegate from Utah Territory, also implored lawmakers to vote against the passage of the Poland Act. Cannon argued that all territories had disputes with U.S. authorities under the territorial system because they had not consented in the selection of their representatives. In language that mirrored long-standing arguments of territorial westerners against federal appointees, Cannon articulated, "No people can live under a territorial form of government without irritation arising between the people ... and the officers in whose appointment they have no voice."[81]

Americans had long wanted a role in their representation in government; the territorial system had already removed some measure of their self-government, and Cannon wanted to restore the promise of American republican government to Utah and the territories. Southern Democrats also opposed the antipolygamy legislation on the grounds that it violated local will.[82] Finally, the Utah delegate declared, "The only difference between Utah and the other Territories is that her people, having an unpopular religion, afford her enemies a better chance to talk against them."[83] The religious prejudice found in the Poland Act, Cannon asserted, was utterly "dangerous and subversive of all republican government."[84] Despite Cannon's pleas and Crounse's arguments the Poland Act was signed into law on June 23, 1874. Proposals for further anti-Mormon legislation largely stopped between 1874 and 1882, a period that saw diminished Republican power in Congress, but that also produced a Democratic Party that did not defend local rights in the West after Southern Democrats came out victorious in the battle against Reconstruction in the South.[85] Party machinations did not stop government officials from using the weight of the federal judicial system against Mormons.

In 1878 Mormon polygamist George Reynolds, who had broken federal marriage laws by being married to multiple women at the same time and had been convicted in lower courts, took his case to the United States Supreme Court arguing that his religion required him to marry more than one woman.[86] The Reynolds case tested the limits of religious liberty, the Bill of Rights' free exercise of religion, and federal power. Supreme Court Chief Justice Morrison R. Waite delivered the court's first ruling that interpreted with specificity the meaning of the free exercise provision of the First Amendment: religion did not protect local religious practice and difference in domestic relations at the expense of the law. Waite declared, "Laws are made for the government of actions and while they cannot interfere with mere religious belief and opinions, they may with practices."[87] Boiling it down to its essence, legal historian Sarah Barringer Gordon has stated that the *Reynolds* decision confirmed that "Mormon polygamists had no constitutional right to engage in a form of marriage directly prohibited by Congress."[88] National law prohibited a man from being married to more than one woman at a time, and religious belief could not be put into action to supersede that law. According to this definition, Mormons were not free to exercise or physically act on their religious belief in plural marriage but could still believe in it. The laws and the judicial branch's upholding of those laws made it clear that the government was more forcefully using its supremacy to exterminate the Mormons' religious marriage practice.

Governing Utah according to local popular will had never seemed so distant. The general government, both through legislative and judicial action, not to mention the continuing military presence in the territory, was extending its power over individual actions and family relationships. The question had clearly moved out of the realm of whether the government could or ought to interfere with local or religious relations of peoples of the territories, which had been the crux of pre–Civil War popular sovereignty debates, and into the realm of how much force the national government should use to enforce the laws.[89]

The third branch of the federal government, the executive, had long played a vital role in the application of power in Utah and over the territories. The president had exercised key appointment powers for territorial offices, and in 1857 the president sent the army to Utah to install national sovereignty and to develop infrastructure there. In the late 1870s and early 1880s, presidents used their influence to further the campaign against Mormon religious practice.

In the wake of the *Reynolds* Supreme Court decision, President Rutherford B. Hayes urged Congress to amend antipolygamy legislation and to put more power into punishing plural marriage. On December 1, 1879, in his third annual message, Hayes stated that the nation would not approve of Utah advancing to sovereign statehood while a "very considerable number uphold a practice which is condemned as a crime by the laws of all civilized communities throughout the world." To "firmly and effectively" execute marriage laws, the president advocated for the withdrawal or withholding of the rights and privileges of citizenship of "those who violate or oppose the enforcement of the law on this subject."[90] Hayes again called for severe measures against Mormon polygamy, telling Congress the very next year that "the sanctity of marriage and the family relation are the corner stone of our American society and civilization" and that the nation needed to "reestablish the interests and principles which polygamy and Mormonism have imperiled."[91] Recalling an argument from the 1850s discussion of Utah and hearkening back to foundational documents on federal authority over the territories, the president promoted greater control over Utah's government "analogous to the provisional government established for the territory northwest of the Ohio by the ordinance of 1787."[92] Finally, Hayes recommended "that the right to vote, hold office, and sit on juries in the Territory of Utah be confined to those who neither practice nor uphold polygamy."[93] The president's comment unveiled designs to push toward the disenfranchisement of Mormons.

The rhetoric of the next two presidents—James Garfield and Chester A. Arthur—took up the mantle left by Hayes. Garfield reminded Americans in his inaugural address that "the Territories of the United States are subject to the direct legislative authority of Congress, and hence the General Government is responsible for any violation of the Constitution in any of them. It is therefore a reproach to the Government that in the most populous of the Territories the constitutional guaranty is not enjoyed by the people and the authority of Congress is set at naught. The Mormon Church not only offends the moral sense of manhood by sanctioning polygamy, but prevents the administration of justice through ordinary instrumentalities of law." No ecclesiastical organization, Garfield declared, could destroy "family relations and endanger social order" or be permitted in any form "to usurp in the smallest degree the functions and powers of the National Government."[94]

After Garfield was assassinated, Chester A. Arthur also spoke out against polygamy. He strongly encouraged Congress to pass forceful, resolute legislation requiring women to testify against men in polygamy cases and mandating the filing of a certificate for all marriages taking place in Utah. Such measures, the president believed, would destroy "this barbarous system."[95] Within four months of Arthur's 1881 annual message, Congress passed yet another series of amendments to federal marriage laws known as the Edmunds Act. Introduced by George F. Edmunds, a senator from Vermont, the act prohibited plural marriage and unlawful cohabitation, removing the need for law enforcers to prove a marital union. It also disenfranchised convicted polygamists or cohabitants and made them ineligible to hold political office. Under this legislation, Mormon polygamists could no longer serve on a jury in cases involving plural marriage or cohabitation. The Edmunds Act also reinforced the Morrill Act, the Poland Act, and the ruling in *Reynolds* by preventing those who believed in plural marriage from serving on juries, even if they did not practice polygamy; another step in the move toward disenfranchising believing Mormons. Finally, the 1882 legislation created a new federal bureaucracy in Utah, known as the Utah Commission, which directed elections in the territory and ensured that polygamists would be disqualified from holding office. Under the 1882 Edmunds Act, the Utah Commission not only prevented polygamists from holding office, it also prohibited them from voting by initiating an oath that each voter had to take certifying that he or she did not practice polygamy.[96]

According to Grover Cleveland's 1885 message to Congress, laws enacted for the "suppression of polygamy" had been "energetically and faithfully executed during the past year, with measurably good results."[97] The president continued, "A number of convictions have been secured for unlawful cohabitation, and in some cases pleas of guilty have been entered and a slight punishment imposed, upon a promise by the accused that they would not again offend against the law, nor advise, counsel, aid, or abet in any way its violation by others."[98] Cleveland lauded reports that indicated fewer plural marriages were taking place in Utah and that no one elected to offices in the territory had been found guilty of practicing polygamy or cohabitation. He went on the offensive against the continuing Mormon belief in the "doctrine of polygamous marriages." Belief in this doctrine, and federal efforts to legislate belief, Cleveland asserted, put Mormons at odds with the United States; the religion continued to place religious belief (and practice) above local and national law. Returning to the constitutional principle requiring a republican form of government, the president decried Mormon belief that was protected by republicanism but that simultaneously "set at naught that obligation of absolute obedience to the law of the land which lies at the foundation of republican institutions."[99] Cleveland may have been sensing that Mormon resolve to resist federal authority was weakening. Now was the time to break their spirit and finally eradicate this last element holding the Mormons of Utah back from being considered fully devoted to the United States. "There should be no relaxation in the firm but just execution of the law now in operation," Cleveland proclaimed, "and I should be glad to approve such further discreet legislation as will rid the country of this blot upon its fair fame."[100]

Presidential clout extended to foreign diplomacy as well. Dating back to Rutherford B. Hayes, presidential administrations made anti-Mormon immigration part of their foreign policy rhetoric. Hayes's secretary of state, William Evarts, complained that "the annual statistics of immigration into the United States show that large numbers of immigrants come to our shores every year from the various countries of Europe, for the avowed purpose of joining the Mormon community at Salt Lake, in the Territory of Utah." "The ignorant classes" of Europe, Evarts argued, buoyed up the Mormon polygamy structure. Calling the Mormons perpetual criminal offenders, the secretary of state requested that European governments "check the organization of these criminal enterprises . . . [and] prevent the departure of those proposing to come hither as violators of the law."[101] Evarts received responses from several nations, including Italy, England, France, and Norway. The response from England suggested that the government on the island would take it under consideration and use its influence to notify and caution its citizens about the American law and "against being deceived by Mormonite emissaries."[102]

The overall campaign to cease Mormon immigration from European countries to the United States was largely unsuccessful and caused some debate about freedoms and rights.[103] Grover Cleveland's 1885 annual presidential message made the foreign policy connection more direct, combining it with other federal efforts to end the Mormon belief and practice of plural marriage.[104] "Since the people upholding polygamy in our Territories are reenforced by immigration from other lands," Cleveland pronounced, "I recommend that a law be passed to prevent the importation of Mormons into the country."[105] The president stated that incoming Mormons were already criminals because of their belief in polygamy.[106] President Cleveland's desire to seal America's borders from Mormons, in the same era that saw the United States excluding Chinese peoples from immigrating to the country, demonstrates the disdain the United States government had for Mormon plural marriage.

The final piece of legislation that ultimately ushered in the demise of mainstream polygamy in Utah was the 1887 Edmunds-Tucker Act, a draconian measure that, among its many tenets, required plural wives to testify against their husbands and disincorporated the Latter-day Saint Church. The act also disenfranchised the territory's women; suffrage had been granted to Utah women in 1870. In addition, the Edmunds-Tucker Act made all judges in the territory federal appointees, allowed the government to confiscate church real estate that was not directly used for religious purposes and valued over $50,000, and dissolved the LDS Church's fund to aid Mormon immigration to the United States.[107] Though direct presidential foreign policy to prevent Mormon immigration did not materialize, the provision of the Edmunds-Tucker Act forbidding the funding of immigration significantly halted Mormon efforts, slowing the immigration of people with "criminal character," and ultimately producing the results that earlier presidential administrations had sought. With presidential appointees running the entirety of the judicial system in Utah, and with more authority to enforce the laws, Mormon violators of the law were imprisoned in greater numbers and church members' property seized.

Federal legislation and enforcement, judicial rulings, and presidential directives culminated in the imprisonment of church leaders, the confiscation of property holdings, and the slowing of Mormon immigration. The Supreme Court upheld the Edmunds-Tucker Act's provision to seize the church's property in a decision made in *The Late Corporation of the Church of Jesus Christ of Latter-day Saints v. United States*.[108] Just over four months after the Supreme Court's ruling, LDS leader Wilford Woodruff wrote the following in his journal: "I have arrived at a point in the History of my life as the President of the Church of Jesus Christ of Latter Day Saints where I am under the necessity of acting for the Temporal Salvation of the Church. The United States Government has taken a Stand & passed Laws to destroy the Latter day Saints upon the Subject of polygamy or Patriarchal order of Marriage."[109] Belief in the practicality of plural marriage had abated.

Woodruff also wrote that after prayer he felt inspired to issue a proclamation, which has become known as the Manifesto, discontinuing the teaching and, eventually, the practice of plural marriage among Latter-day Saints. "Inasmuch as laws have been enacted by Congress forbidding plural marriages, which laws have been pronounced constitutional by the court of last resort," Woodruff declared, "I hereby declare my intention to submit to those laws, and to use my influence with the members of the Church over which I preside to have them do likewise."[110] Wilford Woodruff had only arrived at this point after decades of struggle and a final acknowledgment that the LDS Church was distinct from civil government in theory and practice and that it was the future destiny of the church "to aid in the maintenance and perpetuity" of American political, cultural, and economic institutions.[111] Mormons had finally conformed to these norms and acquiesced to federal authority; they now could be accepted into the nation, but not on their terms.

Conclusion

The Civil War and reconstruction eras produced turbulent times in the United States. Legal rights were created for African Americans (although not long protected) even as other racial and religious minority groups, primarily those in the West, had their rights rescinded or restricted. Historian Richard White has stated, "The West itself served as the kindergarten of the American state" as "the federal government controlled the governments of the territories and withheld from their citizens rights and privileges held by American citizens elsewhere."[112] The general government asserted its authority in the West and South with mixed results. Indeed, in Utah, the government tested its power in the 1850s and then, in the wake of the Civil War with federal supremacy assured, slowly increased efforts to enforce its will on the territory over the next thirty years. The Utah example demonstrates that federal power, and the application thereof, was a process—and an uneven one at that. In Utah, it was long and slow, but ultimately resulted in Mormon conformity.

Latter-day Saints eventually obeyed the laws of the land more quickly and soundly than white Southerners, who collectively considered laws to ensure African American rights detrimental to their economic and political livelihoods.[113] Southerners violently resisted the muscular federal presence in the South, leading to the withdrawal of federal authority and the weakening of Washington's resolve to stand up to domestic terrorism and combat racial discrimination.[114] The white majority's violent resistance came at the expense of the rights and lives of a racial minority group that the federal government was no longer willing to help or protect. Reconstruction in the South began auspiciously and ended tragically. In the same era that saw Washington's resolve to uphold equal protection withering in the South, the government redoubled its efforts to willingly exert its power over racial and religious minorities in the West to enforce white, Protestant majority norms and American institutions. Mormons also resisted what they considered to be religious discrimination, but they eventually succumbed to the increasingly strong federal presence in the West.

The long-term implementation of national authority in Utah was among the most successful campaigns of the larger reconstruction era. In the processes of the government's project of applying power in the West, it took decades to end the despised practice of polygamy. But in the end, the question of federal power over popular will was settled, and the results of the process endured. The Woodruff declaration on marriage remains part of the LDS Church's canon, while the government's foray into marriage legislation eventually made it the arbiter of accepted forms of marriage and family in the nation. Beyond that, the failure of the government to protect the rights of freed blacks created a host of systemic racist issues that continue to haunt American society. Meanwhile, the enduring presence and authority of the federal government, particularly in economic, legal, and land matters, does not go unnoticed by present-day westerners.

Notes

1. See, for example, Eric Foner, *Reconstruction: America's Unfinished Revolution, 1863–1877* (New York: W. W. Norton, 1988); Eric Foner, *A Short History of Reconstruction* (New York: Harper and Row, 1990), 196; and Richard White, *The Republic for Which It Stands: The United States during Reconstruction and the Gilded Age, 1865–1896* (New York: Oxford University Press, 2017).

2. See Michael F. Holt, *The Fate of Their Country: Politicians, Slavery Extension, and the Coming of the Civil War* (New York: Hill and Wang, 2004); Brent M. Rogers, *Unpopular Sovereignty: Mormons and the Federal Management of Early Utah Territory* (Lincoln: University of Nebraska Press, 2017), introduction and chapter 1.

3. The Constitution authorized the acquisition of new territory and permitted the development of new states out of these lands if the people within those geopolitical boundaries operated a republican form of government. U.S. Const. art. IV, secs. 3, 4. For the founding generation and Americans that followed, republicanism meant a promise that a collection of self-governing communities would exercise their sovereignty to inhibit consolidated power and the threat of control by the few. Harry L. Watson, *Liberty and Power: The Politics of Jacksonian America* (New York: Hill and Wang, 1990), 6, 44.

4. William E. Gienapp, "The Crisis of American Democracy: The Political System and the Coming of the Civil War," in *Why the Civil War Came*, ed. Gabor S. Boritt (New York: Oxford University Press, 1996), 113.

5. Robert F. Berkhofer Jr., "The Northwest Ordinance and the Principle of Territorial Evolution" in *The American Territorial System*, ed. John Porter Bloom (Athens: Ohio University Press, 1973), 45; Peter S. Onuf, *Statehood and Union: A History of the Northwest Ordinance* (Bloomington: Indiana University Press, 1987), xiii.

6. John B. Floyd to James Buchanan, December 5, 1857, 3-4, in U.S. Congress, House of Representatives, Report of the Secretary of War in Message from the President of the United States, 35th Cong., 1st Sess. (1857), Exec. Doc. No. 2 (Washington, D.C.: Cornelius Wendell, 1857).

7. Richard White, *"It's Your Misfortune and None of My Own": A New History of the American West* (Norman: University of Oklahoma Press, 1991), 59.

8. For more, see Rogers, *Unpopular Sovereignty*, 11–19.

9. Howard R. Lamar, *The Far Southwest, 1846–1912: A Territorial History*, rev. ed. (Albuquerque: University of New Mexico, 2000), 75.

10. Memorial of the Members and Officers of the Legislative Assembly of the Territory of Utah, January 6, 1858, House Misc. Doc. No. 100, 35th Congress, 1st Sess., March 17, 1858.

11. "Remarks," *Deseret News*, September 23, 1857; Rogers, *Unpopular Sovereignty*, 10–11.

12. Holt, *The Fate of Their Country*, 20–22.

13. Wrapped up in this history of territorial expansion and management was the prevailing idea of the authority of individual states in the American federal project, better known as states' rights. For more on states' rights in the context of nineteenth-century American history and government, see, for example, Daniel Walker Howe, *What Hath God Wrought: The Transformation of America, 1815–1848* (New York: Oxford University Press, 2007); Sean Wilentz, *The Rise of American Democracy: Jefferson to Lincoln* (New York: Norton, 2005); Steven Hahn, *A Nation without Borders: The United States and Its World in an Age of Civil Wars, 1830–1910* (New York: Viking, 2016).

14. Kirk H. Porter and Donald Bruce Johnson, eds., *National Party Platforms* (Urbana: University of Illinois Press, 1966), 27; Nathaniel R. Ricks, "A Peculiar Place for the Peculiar Institution: Slavery and Sovereignty in Early Territorial Utah" (master's thesis, Brigham

Young University, August 2007); Tonya Reiter, "Redd Slave Histories: Family Race, and Sex in Pioneer Utah," *Utah Historical Quarterly* 85, no. 2 (Spring 2017): 108–26.

15. For more on the Republican Party's rhetorical arguments against popular sovereignty, see Rogers, *Unpopular Sovereignty*, 146–53, 169–75; John Mack Faragher, "The Frémonts: Agents of Empire, Legends of Liberty," in *Empire and Liberty: The Civil War and the West*, ed. Virginia Scharff (Oakland: University of California Press, 2015), 36–37.

16. Justin S. Morrill, "Utah Territory and its Laws," Appendix to the *Congressional Globe*, 34th Cong., 3rd Sess. (February 23, 1857), 285–87.

17. James Buchanan, *First Annual Message from the President of the United States to the Two Houses of Congress at the Commencement of the First Session of the Thirty-Fifth Congress* (Washington, D.C.: Cornelius Wendell, 1857).

18. Buchanan, *First Annual Message*.

19. Anonymous to John J. Crittenden, March 1, 1852, John J. Crittenden Correspondence 1851–1852, MS 8190 1, LDS Church History Library, Salt Lake City; Brent M. Rogers, "A 'Distinction between Mormons and Americans': Mormon Indian Missionaries, Federal Indian Policy, and the Utah War," *Utah Historical Quarterly* 82, no. 4 (Fall 2014): 250–71; Elliott West, "Reconstructing Race," *Western Historical Quarterly* 34, no. 1 (Spring 2003): 10–11.

20. William P. MacKinnon, *At Sword's Point, Part 1: A Documentary History of the Utah War to 1858* (Norman, Okla.: Arthur H. Clark, 2008), 117–19.

21. MacKinnon, *At Sword's Point*, 1:63–73.

22. Douglas argued that the "Mormon government" operated a nonrepublican form of government based on its peculiar institution of plural marriage and allegedly subversive alliances with Indian tribes. Congress, he believed, had the right to repeal the territory's organic act, remove it as a geopolitical entity, and assert national sovereignty over that jurisdiction. Douglas further asserted that the federal government could repeal the organic act because the Mormons disavowed their allegiance to the United States and they were "alien enemies and outlaws, unfit to exercise the right of self-government." The Illinois senator and chairperson of the Senate Committee on the Territories emphasized that Mormons were incapable of exercising popular sovereignty in the territory and that they only sought statehood to "protect them in their treason and crime, debauchery and infamy." Furthermore, he argued that to protect them in their "treasonable" and "bestial" practices by allowing them to govern themselves would be a disgrace to humanity and civilization and potentially fatal to American interests in the West. "Kansas—The Mormons—Slavery: Speech of Senator Douglas: Delivered at Springfield, Ill, 12 June 1857," *New York Times*, June 23, 1857. For more on Douglas and his Utah popular sovereignty rhetoric, see Rogers, *Unpopular Sovereignty*, 164–77.

23. "Lincoln's Springfield Speech," *Chicago Tribune*, June 29, 1857; "Reply to Senator Douglas: Speech of Hon. A. Lincoln, of Indiana," *New York Daily Times*, July 4, 1857.

24. Porter and Johnson, eds., *National Party Platforms*, 27.

25. "The Question of the Mormons," *Harper's Weekly*, July 4, 1857.

26. Rogers, *Unpopular Sovereignty*, 228–38.

27. Rogers, *Unpopular Sovereignty*, 238–63.

28. James F. Rusling, "Affairs in Utah and the Territories," June 17, 1868, U.S. Congress, House Misc. Doc, No. 153, 40th Cong., 2nd Sess., 25–27.

29. The text and subtext of speeches by Justin Smith Morrill, Stephen Douglas, Abraham Lincoln, Winfield Scott, and others connected federal action in Utah with disgust for the practice of plural marriage. See Rogers, *Unpopular Sovereignty*, 146–77. Visual images in newspapers also positioned the Utah War as a fight over polygamy. See, for example, "Brigham Young Mustering His Forces," *Harper's Weekly*, November 28, 1857; "Brigham Young's Preparations for the Defence of Utah—The Result," *Frank Leslie's Illustrated Newspaper*, December 19, 1857.

30. Heather Cox Richardson, *West from Appomattox: The Reconstruction of America after the Civil War* (New Haven, Conn.: Yale University Press, 2007), 14.

31. U.S. Congress, House of Representatives, "Territory of Nevada, [to Accompany Bill H.R. No. 567]," 35th Cong., 1st Sess. (May 12, 1858), H.R. Rep. No. 375.

32. Constitution of the State of Deseret, House of Representatives, 37th Cong., 2nd Sess., Mis. Doc. No. 78, p. 2.

33. Joshua Paddison, "Race, Religion, and Naturalization: How the West Shaped Citizenship Debates in the Reconstruction Congress," in *Civil War Wests: Testing the Limits of the United States*, edited by Adam Arenson and Andrew R. Graybill (Oakland: University of California Press, 2015), 190.

34. Heather Cox Richardson, *To Make Men Free: A History of the Republican Party* (New York: Basic Books, 2014), 36.

35. An Act to Secure Freedom to All Persons with the Territories of the United States, June 19, 1862, in *Statutes at Large, Treaties, and Proclamations of the United States of America*, vol. 12, ed. George P. Sanger (Boston: Little, Brown, 1863), 432.

36. Todd M. Kerstetter, *God's Country, Uncle Sam's Land: Faith and Conflict in the American West* (Urbana: University of Illinois Press, 2006), 75.

37. This became abundantly clear following the withdrawal of the soldiers from Camp Floyd and was reiterated again when federal officials discussed removing Connor's troops from Utah during the Civil War. See Governor Stephen S. Harding to General George Wright, February 16, 1863, in *The War of Rebellion: A Compilation of the Official Records of the Union and Confederate Armies*, edited by Daniel S. Lamont, George W. Davis, Leslie J. Perry, and Joseph W. Kirkley, ser. 1, vol. 50, pt. 2 (Washington, D.C.: Government Printing Office, 1897), 314–15.

38. Patrick Connor to Richard C. Drum, December 20, 1862, in Lamont et al., *War of Rebellion*, ser. 1, vol. 50, pt. 2, 256–57; James Duane Doty to General Wright, August 9, 1863, in Lamont et al., *War of Rebellion*, ser. 1, vol. 50, pt. 2, 583–84.

39. James W. Stillman, Orders, No. 1, August 6, 1862, in Lamont et al., *War of Rebellion*, ser. 1, vol. 50, pt. 2, 55.

40. Patrick Edward Connor to Richard C. Drum, February 19, 1863, in Lamont et al., *War of Rebellion*, ser. 1, vol. 50, pt. 2, 318–20.

41. Lincoln quoted in letter from T. B. H. Stenhouse to Brigham Young, June 7, 1863, found in Leonard J. Arrington and Davis Bitton, *The Mormon Experience: A History of the Latter-day Saints*, 2nd ed. (Urbana: University of Illinois Press, 1992), 170.

42. *Congressional Globe*, 37th Cong., 2nd Sess. (1862), 2507.

43. Richard Drum to Patrick Connor, July 16, 1864, in Lamont et al., *War of Rebellion*, ser. 1, vol. 50, pt. 2, 909–10.

44. E. J. Bennett, Report, July 2, 1866, in "The Condition of Utah," 26–27.

45. Norman McLeod, Report, June 15, 1866, in U.S. Congress, House Committee on the Territories Report, "The Condition of Utah," House of Representatives, Report No. 96, 39th Cong., 1st Sess., 19.

46. McLeod, "The Condition of Utah," 21.

47. Andrew Humphreys, Indian Agent, to William P. Dole, Commissioner of Indian Affairs, September 30, 1861, in *Report of the Commissioner of Indian Affairs, accompanying the Annual Report of the Secretary of the Interior, for the Year 1861* (Washington, D.C.: Government Printing Office, 1861), 140.

48. Humphreys to Dole, September 30, 1861, in Report of the Commissioner of Indian Affairs, 1861, p. 140; Dole, Report of the Commissioner of Indian Affairs, 1861, p. 21.

49. C. Joseph Genetin-Pilawa, *Crooked Paths to Allotment: The Fight Over Federal Indian Policy after the Civil War* (Chapel Hill: University of North Carolina Press, 2012), 26; Durwood Ball, "Liberty, Empire, and Civil War in the American West," in *Empire and Liberty: The Civil War and the West*, ed. Virginia Scharff (Oakland: University of California Press, 2015), 66; West, *The Last Indian War*, 319.

50. Dole, Report of the Commissioner of Indian Affairs (1861), 21.

51. Dole, Report of the Commissioner of Indian Affairs (1861), 21.

52. Doris Karren Burton, *A History of Uintah County: Scratching the Surface* (Salt Lake City: Utah State Historical Society and Uintah County Commission, 1996), 24; Fred A. Conetah, *A History of the Northern Ute People* (Salt Lake City: Uintah-Ouray Ute Tribe, printed by the University of Utah Printing Service, 1982), 78–79.

53. James Duane Doty to William P. Dole, September 12, 1862, in *Report of the Commissioner of Indian Affairs, accompanying the Annual Report of the Secretary of the Interior, for the Year 1862* (Washington, D.C.: Government Printing Office, 1861), 198–99, 202.

54. When it came to Indian affairs generally Dole advocated an intensified militarized policy to concentrate Indians on reservations. Later, during his presidency, Ulysses S. Grant likewise called for federal troops and officials to place all Indians on large reservations as the optimum method of protecting both white and Native interests. William P. Dole, Report of the Commissioner of Indian Affairs (1862), 32; Dole, Report of the Commissioner of Indian Affairs (1861), 21; Ball, "Liberty, Empire, and Civil War," 68; Richardson, *West from Appomattox*, 115.

55. Utes and other Native peoples would lose all sovereignty some six years later. An 1871 federal Indian Appropriations Act changed the legal status of Native national sovereignty. With this act, the federal government no longer recognized Natives as citizens of their own nations and ended their separate sovereign status, effectively making them wards of the federal state, thus legally dismantling their sovereignty and ability to make treaties and facilitating greater federal control over Native lands. Indian Appropriations Act, 25 U.S.C. 71, March 3, 1871.

56. Andrew Humphreys, Report, October 1, 1861, in Report of the Commissioner of Indian Affairs, 1861, 135–36; Burton, *History of Uintah County*, 24–25; Treaty with the Utah, Yampah Ute, Pah-Vant, Sanpete Ute, Tim-p-nogs, and Cum-nm-Bah Bands of the Utah Indians, June 8, 1865; Gustive O. Larson, "Uintah Dream: The Ute Treaty—Spanish Fork, 1865," *BYU Studies* 14, no. 3 (1974): 361–81.

57. John Alton Peterson, *Utah's Black Hawk War* (Salt Lake City: University of Utah Press, 1998), 2–5.

58. Peterson, *Utah's Black Hawk War*, 359.

59. Peterson, *Utah's Black Hawk War*, 2–5.

60. In a series of treaties with the Shoshones, Bannocks, and Goshutes in 1863 and with the Utes and Southern Paiutes in 1865, the federal government moved to extinguish Indian land claims in Utah and to confine all Indians on reservations, particularly on the Uintah Reservation. Burton, *History of Uintah County*, 84; *Report of the Commissioner of Indian Affairs, accompanying the Annual Report of the Secretary of the Interior, for the Year 1865* (Washington, D.C.: Government Printing Office, 1865), 149–52, 168–90.

61. Lamar, *Far Southwest*, 106–7.

62. See Forrest S. Cuch, ed., *A History of Utah's American Indians* (Salt Lake City: Utah State Division of Indian Affairs and Utah State Division of History, 2003), 44–57, 110–13, 140–45. See also Scott R. Christensen, *Sagwitch: Shoshone Chieftain, Mormon Elder, 1822–1887* (Logan: Utah State University Press, 1999); and Martha C. Knack, *Boundaries Between: The Southern Paiutes, 1775–1995* (Lincoln: University of Nebraska Press, 2004).

63. Elliott West, *The Last Indian War: The Nez Perce Story* (New York: Oxford University Press, 2009), 319.

64. "An Act to Provide for the More Efficient Government of the Rebel States," March 2, 1867, in *Statutes at Large*, vol. 14, ed. George P. Sanger (Boston: Little, Brown, 1868), 39th Cong., 2nd Sess., 428.

65. Warren Hoffnagle, "The Southern Homestead Act: Its Origins and Operation," *The Historian* 32, no. 4 (August 1970): 612–29; Paul Wallace Gates, "Federal Land Policy in the South, 1866–1888," *Journal of Southern History* 6, no. 3 (August 1940): 303–30.

66. White Southerners refusing to abide by laws or skirting around them forced Congress to pass coercive acts to protect African American rights, thereby giving the general government more power. See Richardson, *West from Appomattox*, 59.

67. Foner, *A Short History of Reconstruction*, 255.

68. Prior, "Civilization, Republic, Nation," 290; James M. Ashley, Report, "The Condition of Utah," 1.

69. Ashley, Report, "The Condition of Utah," 2.

70. Lamar, *Far Southwest*, 79, 114; see also William S. Kiser, *Borderlands of Slavery: The Struggle over Captivity and Peonage in the American Southwest* (Philadelphia: University of Pennsylvania Press, 2017).

71. Austin Blair of Michigan, *Congressional Globe*, 41st Cong., 2nd Sess. (1870), 2147.

72. Thomas F. Bayard of Delaware, *Congressional Globe*, 42nd Cong., 3rd Sess. (1873), 1813.

73. C. Vann Woodward, *Reunion and Reaction: The Compromise of 1877 and the End of Reconstruction* (Boston: Little, Brown, 1951).

74. West, *The Last Indian War*, 319.

75. *Congressional Globe*, 42nd Cong., 3rd Sess. (1872), 9.

76. Luke Poland of Vermont, *Congressional Record*, 43rd Cong., 1st Sess. (1874), 4467.

77. "An Act in Relation to Courts and Judicial Officers in the Territory of Utah," June 23, 1874, Sec. 4, 43rd Cong., 1st Sess., chap. 469, *Statutes at Large*, vol. 18, 253–55.

78. Luke Poland of Vermont, *Congressional Record*, 43rd Cong., 1st Sess. (1874), 4467.

79. Text of Poland Bill, Sec. 4, *Congressional Record*, 43rd Cong., 1st Sess. (1874), 4467.

80. Lorenzo Crounse of Nebraska, *Congressional Record*, 43rd Cong., 1st Sess. (1874), 4468.

81. George Q. Cannon of Utah, *Congressional Record*, 43rd Cong., 1st Sess. (1874), 4471.

82. Patrick Q. Mason, "Opposition to Polygamy in the Postbellum South," *Journal of Southern History* 76, no. 3 (August 2010): 541–78, 545.

83. George Q. Cannon of Utah, *Congressional Record*, 43rd Cong., 1st Sess. (1874), 4471.

84. George Q. Cannon, *Congressional Record*, 43rd Cong., 1st Sess. (1874), 4471.

85. See Patrick Q. Mason, *The Mormon Menace: Violence and Anti-Mormonism in the Postbellum South* (New York: Oxford University Press, 2011), chap. 5–6; Mason, "Opposition to Polygamy in the Postbellum South," 541–78.

86. For more on the details of the *Reynolds* case and its place in the reconstruction era, see Sarah Barringer Gordon, *The Mormon Question: Polygamy and Constitutional Conflict in Nineteenth-Century America* (Chapel Hill: University of North Carolina Press, 2002), 119–44.

87. *Reynolds v. United States*, 98 U.S. 145 (1879), 166.

88. Gordon, *The Mormon Question*, 130.

89. William Boyce of South Carolina, *Congressional Globe*, 33rd Cong., 1st Sess. (1854), 1110; Lawrence D. Branch of North Carolina, *Congressional Globe*, 36th Cong., 1st Sess. (1860), 1410; "The Law and the Mormons," *Harper's Weekly*, December 31, 1881, p. 891.

90. Rutherford B. Hayes, "Third Annual Message," December 1, 1879, online by Gerhard Peters and John T. Woolley, *The American Presidency Project*, http://www.presidency.ucsb.edu/ws/?pid=29520.

91. Rutherford B. Hayes, "Fourth Annual Message," December 6, 1880, online by Gerhard Peters and John T. Woolley, *The American Presidency Project*, http://www.presidency.ucsb.edu/ws/?pid=29521.

92. Hayes, "Fourth Annual Message," December 6, 1880.

93. Hayes, "Fourth Annual Message," December 6, 1880.

94. James A. Garfield, "Inaugural Address," March 4, 1881, online by Gerhard Peters and John T. Woolley, *The American Presidency Project*, http://www.presidency.ucsb.edu/ws/?pid=25823.

95. Chester A. Arthur, "First Annual Message," December 6, 1881, online by Gerhard Peters and John T. Woolley, *The American Presidency Project*, http://www.presidency.ucsb.edu/ws/?pid=29522.

96. Utah Commission, "The Edmunds Act: Reports of the Commission, Rules, Regulations and Decisions," (Salt Lake City: Tribune Printing and Publishing, 1883), 3–5; Amendment to 5350 U.S.C., in Compiled Laws of Utah, vol. 1 (Salt Lake City, Herbert Pembroke, 1888), 110–13.

97. The historian Kathryn Daynes has stated, "Between 1884 and 1895, over a thousand men were convicted of a crime relating to plural marriage." Kathryn M. Daynes, *More Wives than One: Transformation of the Mormon Marriage System, 1840–1910* (Urbana: University of Illinois Press, 2008), 175.

98. Grover Cleveland, "First Annual Message," December 8, 1885, online by Gerhard Peters and John T. Woolley, *The American Presidency Project*, http://www.presidency.ucsb.edu/ws/?pid=29526.

99. Cleveland, First Annual Message, December 8, 1885.

100. Cleveland, First Annual Message, December 8, 1885.

101. William M. Evarts, to the Diplomatic Officers of the United States, August 9, 1879, in *Papers relating to the Foreign Relations of the United States* (Washington: Government Printing Office, 1879), 11–12.

102. Lord Salisbury to W. J. Hoppin, September 5, 1879, in *Papers relating to the Foreign Relations of the United States* (Washington: Government Printing Office, 1879), 465.

103. "The Question of Mormon Rights," *New York Times*, August 13, 1879.

104. For a solid, more in-depth discussion of the end of plural marriage, see Christine Talbot, *A Foreign Kingdom: Mormons and Polygamy in American Political Culture, 1852–1890* (Urbana: University of Illinois Press, 2013), chapter 7; see also Gordon, *The Mormon Question*, particularly chapters 4 and 5.

105. Cleveland, First Annual Message, December 8, 1885.

106. "Curiosities of Immigration," *San Francisco Daily Evening Bulletin*, August 9, 1879.

107. *Statutes at Large*, chap. 397, 49th Cong., 2nd Sess. (March 3, 1887), vol. 24, p. 635–37.

108. *The Late Corporation of the Church of Jesus Christ of Latter-day Saints v. United States*, 136 U.S. 1 (1890).

109. Wilford Woodruff, Journal, September 25, 1890, in *Wilford Woodruff's Journal, Volume 9, 1 January 1889 to 2 September 1898*, ed. Scott G. Kenney (Midvale, Utah: Signature Books, 1985), 112–14.

110. "Official Declaration," *Deseret Evening News*, September 25, 1890.

111. Wilford Woodruff, George Q. Cannon, and Joseph F. Smith, "Official Declaration," December 12, 1889, in *Messages of the First Presidency of the Church of Jesus Christ of Latter-day Saints, 1833–1964*, ed. James R. Clark (Salt Lake City: Bookcraft, 1966), 3:184–87.

112. White, *"It's Your Misfortune and None of My Own,"* 58.

113. Mason, "Opposition to Polygamy in the Postbellum South," 545.

114. The excellent phrase "muscular federal presence" comes from West, *The Last Indian War*, xix.

= 5 =

"To Merge Them into More Wholesome Social Elements"

The Greater Reconstruction and Its Place in Utah

Brett D. Dowdle

While in Washington, D.C., in 1874, famed general William Tecumseh Sherman received a copy of a recently published book written by his friend and colleague Francis A. Walker. Walker had served as the Grant administration's commissioner of Indian affairs for two years, following which he had outlined his thoughts on the country's Indian policy in a volume titled *The Indian Question*. Hardly a generous assessment, Walker's treatise embodied the racialized thinking of the times, referring to American Indians as "savages" and "unruly children" in need of quieting.[1] Walker tried to provide answers to the question of how to prevent American Indians from interrupting the advancement of American progress across the continent. But perhaps more significantly, Walker asked what to do with American Indians when they ceased to be an obstacle to that progress.

Upon receiving Walker's book, Sherman replied in a letter that expressed his feelings regarding the "Indian problem" and his thoughts about its resolution. Although acknowledging no real answer, Sherman stated that the "Indians must assimilate to the white-man habits and thoughts." Unless they did so, "an irreconcilable conflict" would result, and be so significant as to preclude any leniency from the United States. Yet even assimilation seemed unlikely to the seasoned general. He compared the likelihood of Native assimilation to the probability of "the Leopard changing his spots."[2]

In explaining his belief in the near impossibility of assimilative change, Sherman likened American Indians to the Latter-day Saints, another group that he deemed to be incapable of becoming fully American. "Even the industrious Mormons," he wrote, "could not stay in Illinois" because of their differences from the larger American community. In Sherman's mind, a positive attribute like industriousness could not make Latter-day Saint beliefs palatable enough to warrant full inclusion within the body of nineteenth-century Americanism. For Sherman, only complete assimilation could justify a group's continuance. The differences between the Saints and Americans were sufficient to make Sherman doubt the longevity of the isolated Latter-day Saint settlement in the Great Basin. Conflict seemed inevitable, and he surmised that they would not be "permitted much longer to stay at Peace in the desert of Utah." Their continued residence within the borders of the United States would require either a complete cultural change among the Saints or a level of national tolerance for the community's distinctiveness. Both scenarios seemed unlikely to Sherman, who fully expected to see American forbearance dissipate into violence. Nineteenth-century America for him was simply not a place for pluralism or cultural distinctiveness.[3]

Returning to the topic at hand, Sherman surmised that just as America's patience was growing thin with the recalcitrant Saints, so it would with the American Indian populations. He believed that nominal peace would be insufficient, as white Americans would charge every theft, murder, or other crime on the frontier to their account. Unchecked, these circumstances would ultimately mature into a complete and bloody "Frontier War," a notion that conveniently disregarded the already bloody state of warfare existing between white settlers and American Indians. In Sherman's mind, complete assimilation alone could prevent such circumstances and remove this burden of constant warfare from the West. But even this "peaceful solution," according to Sherman, could only come "through military force."[4]

Sherman's letter is illustrative of the larger ideology and cultural forces that moved the United States during the second half of the nineteenth century. In calling for the complete assimilation of both American Indians and Latter-day Saints, if necessary by force, Sherman perfectly articulated the dominant American ethos of the time concerning the place of American Indians and minorities within the body of American citizenship. Far from being seen as vital threads in the tapestry of the American republic, distinctiveness and pluralism were interpreted to be dangerous to and even destructive of the notion of Americanism. Indeed, Sherman's America demanded assimilation and conformity. Significantly the word "Union" functioned as one of the most popular synonyms for the United States during this period. Those who opposed or complicated that "Union" were in rebellion and in need of social, cultural, economic, and political correction.

Yet even as Sherman drew connections between American Indians and the Saints, he likewise drew distinctions between the two groups, distinguishing the Saints by describing them as industrious. Accordingly, as Natalia Molina has aptly argued, the similarities in the racial scripts that white Protestant Americans projected onto American Indians and minority groups did not equate to an exact uniformity of experiences. Although the Saints were frequently compared to the nation's racial minorities, such comparisons did not preclude the Saints from benefitting from their trappings of potential whiteness.[5] In nineteenth-century America, some groups were deemed more capable of assimilation than others.

To be certain, Americans like Sherman had reason to want unity and unanimity during the period. At the time Sherman wrote his letter, the nation was only ten years removed from a civil war that was attributable to the significant distinctions between the North and the South. In terms of national losses, disunion had cost the combined Northern and Southern states more than eight billion dollars, to say nothing of the more than 600,000 lives. By 1874 the pull for reconciliation and reunion was so strong that many Americans were beginning to grow weary of Southern Reconstruction.[6] Union had thus become one of the dominant themes of postbellum America by the time Sherman wrote to Walker in 1874.

Sherman's letter, however, clearly demonstrated that union came at a heavy price. Groups that diverged from core concepts of Americanism found themselves disenfranchised and threatened within the United States. Just as Sherman did with American Indians and the Saints, the country judged those who defied the basic precepts of white Protestant Americanism to be incapable of full citizenship; in short, they were beyond the American pale.[7] Such judgments called for groups to either accept assimilative reconstruction or face forced removal. In nineteenth-century America, there was no middle ground between these two alternatives. Under such policies and their reformulated concepts of Americanism, many groups within the United States found themselves reconstructed to one extent or another in what Elliott West has referred to as "the Greater Reconstruction."[8] Within the West, American Indians, Chinese immigrants, Catholics, and Latter-day Saints experienced a barrage of reconstructive efforts, each aimed at bringing their recipients more fully in line with the new strictures of a unified American ideal.

During this time period, the federal government engaged in a multifaceted effort to reshape these groups and assimilate their populations into the larger

FIGURE 5.1. "Uncle Sam's Troublesome Bed Fellows."
San Francisco Illustrated Wasp, February 8, 1879.

body of white Protestant Americanism. To achieve this end, the government utilized military campaigns, railroads and economic programs, schools, social institutions, legislation, and legal entities such as prisons as means of reconstruction. These efforts attacked virtually all of these groups in an effort to undermine the distinctive practices and beliefs that distinguished them from the broader American populace.

Latter-day Saints and the Other Americans

Sherman's comparison between the Saints and American Indians was far from uncommon. In conceptualizing the nineteenth-century Latter-day Saint community, Americans of the period frequently drew a likeness between the Saints and other groups of ethnic and religious minorities. Far from complementary, these observations often served as verbal and visual justifications for reconstructing both Latter-day Saints and their fellow minority groups. Through the mediums of both political cartoons and pejorative epithets, Americans portrayed the Saints as a dangerous curse to American republicanism, and equated them variously to secessionists, Catholics, Muslims, American Indians, and Chinese immigrants. By conflating race and religion, such sentiments demonstrated the convoluted categorizations that motivated the Greater Reconstruction and shaped the emerging notions of American citizenship.[9]

Even before the Civil War, Americans were comparing Latter-day Saints and Southerners, the most notable linkage being polygamy and slavery as the "twin relics of barbarism." During the secession crisis, newspapers had carried the correlation further, suggesting that if the Southern states seceded, Utah would "certainly" join them in declaring independence.[10] The comparison continued to hold weight after the war. Having spent time in Utah following the Civil War, Brigadier General James F. Rusling wrote to his superiors about "the real condition of affairs in Utah." Rusling stated, "It is the same as it was [in the] South before the war. 'Peculiar institutions,' whether slavery or polygamy breed the same results, whether in South Carolina or Utah."[11] Despite considering Utah to be "the best governed Territory of any," New York Republican congressman George A. Bagley believed it was "too much like the South," to merit inclusion in the Union.[12] Even the Saints felt they had been "treated a good deal as the South had been," making a clear comparison between the federal policies in Utah and the reconstructive policies in the South.[13]

Some Americans highlighted similarities between the Saints and the country's other outsiders, including racial, ethnic, and religious minorities. In its February 8, 1879, issue the *San Francisco Illustrated Wasp* published a political cartoon titled "Uncle Sam's Troublesome Bed Fellows" (figure 5.1).[14] The cartoon depicted the personification of the nation sharing a bed with an American Indian, a freedman, and an Irishman, and having expelled a Chinese immigrant and a polygamist. For this cartoonist in 1879, the continuing relationship with these minorities meant troubles for the United States. After nearly thirty years of invectives and antipolygamy legislation aimed at the Saints, the cartoon suggested that the nation had determined to excise the Utah problem, or at least kick them first out of bed, followed by the Chinese immigrant.[15] While the American Indian, freedman, and Irish immigrant remained in bed, the cartoon implied these groups also were troublesome additions to the nation, and might, in due time, be subjected to the same treatment as the Chinese immigrant and the polygamist.

Similarly, Thomas Nast's circa 1880s cartoon titled "Religious Liberty Is Guaranteed, But Can We Allow Foreign Reptiles to Crawl All Over US?" (figure 5.2) highlighted comparisons between Latter-day Saints and Catholics, suggesting that both posed significant dangers to American democracy. The cartoon showed a Catholic alligator and a Latter-day Saint snapping turtle crawling on top of the United States capitol building, with the phrase "At the Very Feet of Liberty"

FIGURE 5.2. Thomas Nast, "Religious Liberty is Guaranteed, But Can We Allow Foreign Reptiles to Crawl All Over US?," 1860–1902. *Library of Congress, Prints & Photographs Division, LC-USZ62-50658.*

written on the pinnacle. Although Nast makes clear that the Catholic alligator was clearly more dangerous to the nation than Utah's tabernacle-shaped turtle, both entities were reptilian in nature. Paying homage to the First Amendment, Nast acknowledged that religious liberty was, indeed, "guaranteed," but that such liberties also needed to be limited to prevent "foreign reptiles" from crawling "all over" the nation and the privileges it offered. Implied in Nast's criticisms was the idea that immigrants who lacked an understanding of the democratic government populated both the Latter-day Saint and Catholic congregations. Each was governed by hierarchical ecclesiastical structures that challenged the more egalitarian and democratic models of American Christianity. Religious freedom in America thus had denominational limits and was best entrusted only to Protestant faiths with a democratic makeup.

By comparing Latter-day Saints to secessionists, freedmen, American Indians, Chinese immigrants, and Catholics, politicians and the press created a justification by which the Saints might also be subjected to reconstructive politics. From the perspective of most national leaders, none of these groups, including the Saints, measured up to the perceived requirements for inclusion in nineteenth-century America. Those falling beyond the boundaries of this American pale became the subjects of government actions, each with the intention of "merg[ing] them into the more wholesome social elements," meaning, of course, that they should be assimilated into the dominant culture of white American Protestantism.[16]

Southern Reconstruction

To grasp the significance of reconstruction in the West, it is vital to understand how reconstruction functioned in the South. Although often overshadowed by the war that preceded it, few periods of American history have been as dynamic and formative as the Reconstruction era. Traditionally, the term "reconstruction" has referred specifically to the twelve years directly following the Civil War, 1865 to 1877, a period in which three critical amendments were added to the Constitution and several other bills were passed that made more than simple overtures toward civil rights for the freedmen population. Growing out of the ashes of the Civil War, this Southern Reconstruction attempted to recalibrate American society and eradicate Southern slavery that had threatened to turn the entire nation into a "slaveholding republic."[17]

Southern Reconstruction was a complex mixture of policies that aimed both to punitively punish the South for the Civil War and to provide freedmen with a measure of the social, political, and economic assistance they would need in moving forward as citizens of the United States. Amending the Constitution, Southern Reconstruction made slavery an illegal practice, guaranteed citizenship and its attendant rights to those born within the confines of the nation, and established voting rights for African American males.[18] Further, supportive Northerners helped to establish schools to educate African American children, in accordance with one of the most frequent requests of the freedmen.[19] Others suggested land reform measures that would provide freedmen with some of the farmland and implements that were necessary for success in their new economic circumstances.[20] Legislation allowed the army to remain stationed in the South, attempting to protect the freedmen from the newly fashioned Ku Klux Klan and its terrorizing of the African American citizenry.[21] Finally, the Fifteenth Amendment provided former slaves with an opportunity to vote and to hold public office, thus giving them a hand in the government. Under such provisions freedmen served not only in local and state positions, but also in the chambers of the House of Representatives and the United States Senate.[22] In many regards, therefore, Southern Reconstruction was motivated by the noblest of aims and represented an effort to extend the full rights of American citizenship to those who had built the nation and its economy through their uncompensated labor.

In spite of the nobleness of these ideals, reconstructive ideology manifested itself in less altruistic ways. These less admirable aspects consisted of more than just the stated concerns of the white Southern hegemony that resisted its own loss of power.[23] Rather, they revealed the extent to which reconstruction politics empowered certain classes of Americans while ignoring or even disenfranchising others. The legislative powers that pushed to bring the postbellum South into line with the North were susceptible to misuse. Indeed, the same powers that attempted to transform the culture and behavior of Southern whites could mandate changes in other peoples, who, like Southern whites, held to their own peculiar institutions and cultures. For many, the strong arm of American reconstruction seemed to dramatically overstep constitutional boundaries. For other groups, Southern Reconstruction failed to go far enough, leaving some of the critical questions regarding America to be addressed by future generations. Finally, critics saw the late stage of Southern Reconstruction as a period that was more marked by scandal and political overreach than it was by expanded rights and freedoms.

The effort to educate freedmen is one area where this overreach is evident. As the historian Steven Hahn notes, prior to emancipation, even antebellum abolitionists had not been entirely comfortable with some aspects of African American culture. Patronizingly, they had instructed free blacks to "be industrious, let no hour pass unemployed . . . be virtuous . . . use no bad language . . . in a word be good Christians and good citizens, that all reproach may be taken from you."[24] Such attitudes carried over into the educational efforts in the post–Civil War South. Although generally admirable, the very schools that were established to assist freedmen were also used as tools of black reconstruction. Their purposes were to inculcate white Protestant ideals and culture into the newly freed populace. Specifically, Northern Protestants hoped to use the schools to reconstruct black worship so that it would conform more readily to white Protestant ideals. Hence, although black schools provided a needed service within the South, they also operated according to reconstructionist patterns that assumed the white Protestant culture of the North was superior to the culture constructions of other races and peoples. Furthermore, such efforts demonstrated that in some regards, Southern Reconstruction focused on freedmen as well as Southern whites.[25]

Women, and especially those who were suffragists, likewise had reasons to push back against Southern Reconstruction. Despite having devoted themselves to the abolitionist cause for the better part of two decades, the rights of women were left out of the critical conversations and amendments of reconstruction. In their appeals to have the franchise extended to women as well as freed*men*, suffragists were told simply that "Reconstruction was 'the negro's hour,'" and women would have to continue to wait for the full rights of American citizenship.[26] For white Protestant Americans, "male-headed households" remained "the sine qua non of social stability," and the paragon of the American system of governance.[27] After thirty years of struggle, female leaders like Susan B. Anthony and Elizabeth Cady Stanton felt a deep sense of betrayal at such explanations.[28]

Beyond the discussion of which groups were the victims and which beneficiaries, some Americans criticized the politics of the period as being rife with corruption. Although intended as a measure to combat Andrew Johnson's efforts to disrupt Southern Reconstruction in 1867, the Tenure of Office Act also demonstrated Congress's willingness to increase its own political power through legislation. Passed to protect the position of Secretary of War Edwin Stanton, the bill represented a dramatic overreach of legislative power by stripping Johnson of the ability to make changes within his own cabinet without congressional approval.[29] Charges of corruption, however, went well beyond the political infighting of the Republicans over Southern Reconstruction. Indeed, Mark Twain's 1874 labeling of the period as "The Gilded Age" was not without reason.[30] For Twain and other Americans, reconstruction-era politics were often marked by dubious policies that enriched politicians and businessmen at the expense of the nation. In the midst of Southern Reconstruction, these schemes extended to the highest national levels, including the Ulysses S. Grant administration. Such corruption cast doubts upon the federal government and contributed to a downturn in support for reconstruction in the South.[31]

Each of these complaints highlighted the complexity that marked Southern Reconstruction in particular, and the Greater Reconstruction era in general. By the early 1870s, a strong push for national reconciliation attempted to downplay or just ignore the racial aspects of the war and confounded the efforts of some Republican politicians to facilitate racial equality. With the rise of reconciliation, the "Dunning School," named for the historian William Dunning, helped to entrench a negative narrative of reconstruction that gained great acceptance by the early twentieth century. Dunning argued that reconstruction had been perpetrated by an antagonistic coalition of freedmen, radical republican congressmen, the army detachments that remained in the South, the so-called Northern carpetbaggers who went to the South after the war, and the Southern scalawags who cooperated with them.³² For the Dunning school, these groups imposed a kind of demagogic rule upon the South that inhibited progress and limited the freedoms of white Southerners throughout reconstruction.

Not until the 1950s did C. Vann Woodward and others launch an effort to revise the "Dunning School" narrative.³³ Building on these efforts, Eric Foner's *Reconstruction: America's Unfinished Revolution* (1988) created a new interpretation for Southern Reconstruction that defied all of Dunning's earlier assumptions.³⁴ Rather than an unprincipled imposition of Northern power, Foner argues that Southern Reconstruction was the nation's "first attempt to live up to the noble professions of [its] political creed."³⁵ Whereas the "Dunning School" had described Southern Reconstruction as a period of radical and dangerous politics whose failure was something to be cheered, Foner lamented this failure holding that it was an unfinished revolution.

Along with Foner, other historians have demonstrated that the failure of Southern Reconstruction was an unquestioned tragedy, caused, at least in part, by the national ideology of racism.³⁶ Although some were hopeful for racial justice and equal rights, many Northerners held to deeply entrenched racial views that allowed them to abandon Southern Reconstruction when it failed to meet their political, economic, or religious needs. Racism, however, was not solely visible in the dissolution of Southern Reconstruction. It was this very concept that motivated the national reconstructive efforts that extended westward as well as southward.

Recently, historians of the American West have reexamined the government's actions. They see the antebellum and postbellum United States as a nation that ran from east to west, as well as from north to south, which provides new insights into the Civil War era. As Elliott West has noted, race remains at the center of these discussions, but this expanded view of reconstruction illustrates the fact that the nation's racial problems were far more complex than the black-white binary that has traditionally dominated the American narrative.³⁷

While other historians have contributed to our understanding of this process, Heather Cox Richardson, along with Elliott West, has perhaps made the most important contributions to this field, highlighting its importance to the larger national historiography.³⁸ Richardson suggests that the West in particular was crucial to this postwar restructuring, as it represented the country's "region of inexhaustible resources."³⁹ Beyond providing the natural bounty that powered America's postwar growth, the West seemed to personify the individualist mentality of the national transformation. The quest for wealth and national prestige helped to create a nation governed by "middle-class individualism" that was united by commerce and laissez-faire capitalism rather than equality and civil rights.[40]

Like Richardson, Elliott West argues that the American West is critical to understanding reconstruction. Although focusing specifically on the Nez Perce War of 1877, West's book asserts that this was an era of "Greater Reconstruction," embracing the nation as a whole, rather than just a period of localized Southern Reconstruction. For West, this broader reconstruction "essentially remade the nation," creating policies that reverberated throughout the country and that have "rippled ahead to the present day."[41] West argues that this Greater Reconstruction addressed three main questions concerning the nation's unity in geographic terms, the federal government's sovereignty over states and territories, and the nature of American citizenship. Federal initiatives strived to determine who could and could not be citizens, and what those citizens could and could not believe and do.[42]

Taken together, these recent additions to the historical scholarship reveal a reconstruction that was complex, multifaceted, and diverse. Reconstruction ideology and policy could be and were applied in various ways and locations, and amongst differing groups of people. Indeed, in many regards, the whole of America was reconstructed, with no single group remaining untouched by the period's dramatic changes.

The Why of Western Reconstruction

Throughout the nineteenth century, Americans had considered the West to be a location of opportunity. Speaking to such expectations, Frederick Jackson Turner's famous frontier thesis at the end of that century voiced a long-standing American conception of the West as a place that embodied the American democratic experience.[43] For Turner and others, it was at the "meeting point between savagery and civilization" where democratic ideals would not only be protected from degradation but also enhanced.[44] The West beckoned as a vast region of untapped wealth and opportunities.[45] By the time of the postbellum period, this myth of the West had become such an encompassing and compelling narrative that the nation began a desperate attempt to protect at least a modicum of this ideal. Such desires led to the creation and exploration of America's first national park at Yellowstone in the 1870s, the efforts to preserve the dwindling buffalo population, and the dramatic successes of Buffalo Bill's Wild West Show.[46] In the minds of the American public, the Old West and that critical "meeting point between savagery and civilization" were disappearing amid the technological and economic advancements of America's industrial revolution.

As much as Americans wanted the West to be a place of unbounded opportunities, however, many also spoke of the western frontier with a foreboding sense of concern. For example, some in the federal government had viewed the region with skepticism and caution since the earliest days of the nation's founding.[47] Before it became the region of manifest destiny, some Americans maintained a sense of trepidation about both the inhabitability and governability of the West. Furthermore, being disconnected from the nation at large, the West seemed to embody lawless chaos at least as much as it represented economic opportunity and democratic hope.

With each new expansion of America's western territories, the potential problems of the West heightened. Nowhere was this more evident than with the 1848 Treaty of Guadalupe Hidalgo, which dramatically expanded the length and breadth of the United States to include what is now California, Nevada, and Utah, as well as large portions of Arizona, Wyoming, Colorado, and New Mexico. The expansion brought with it access to immense resources of arable land, navigable waterways, and mineral wealth, all capable of transforming the United States into an international economic power. Coupled with the expansion into Oregon, the Treaty of Guadalupe Hidalgo transformed the United States into a nation that stretched between the Atlantic and Pacific Oceans.

While the American net gain from the treaty was immeasurable, the increased landholdings also presented the nation and particularly the federal government with unforeseen challenges. Significantly, the treaty dramatically transformed the ethnic, racial, and religious makeup of the nation. In addition to adding thousands of Tejanos, Nuevo Mexicanos, and Californios to the populace, the treaty situated thousands of American Indians within the American borders. The treaty mandated that the people who lived in the newly acquired lands should be "incorporated into the Union of the United States, and be admitted at the proper time (to be judged by the Congress of the United States) to the enjoyment of all the rights of citizens of the United States, according to the principles of the Constitution." The rights of these new citizens were specifically to be "maintained and protected in the free enjoyment of their liberty and property, and secured in the free exercise of their religion without restriction."[48] These stipulations granted automatic citizenship to all those who had formerly been citizens of Mexico, but did not apply to American Indians. Instead the treaty called for the United States to subdue the American Indian tribes along the Mexican border.[49]

The population increase not only complicated the ethnic and racial demographics of the United States, but also the religious complexity of the country, with most of the new populations diverging strongly from the Protestant-dominated society east of the Mississippi. Although the presence of Protestants grew with each new pioneering expedition, the region in 1848 boasted a strong Catholic population, numerous American Indian religions, and a growing Latter-day Saint settlement. In subsequent decades, Buddhism and Hinduism, along with several other Asian faiths, gained greater visibility. Indeed, Elliott West contends that during the 1850s, "no nation on earth had a region with so rich an ethnic stew as the American West."[50] Accordingly, in contrast to the assumptions of manifest destiny, the prevalence of these other faiths seemingly threatened the white Protestant nation's designs for the West.

Beyond the important racial and religious aspects, the vast new lands created additional challenges. The massive rush to California's gold fields soon after the transfer of Mexican lands to the United States quickly demonstrated both the breadth of these new territories and the difficulties of travel and communication across such a vast region. Successive rushes to Oregon, Colorado, Montana, and Nevada would each provide additional evidence about the lack of national infrastructure in the West.

Finally, and perhaps most importantly, the expansion of western territories intensified the already virulent national debate over slavery.[51] This extension of American landholdings, most of which fell well north of the areas traditionally reserved for slaveholding, increased apprehensions among Southerners about the longevity of their peculiar institution. Efforts to protect slavery resulted in debates over popular sovereignty, filibustering expeditions throughout Latin America, fugitive slave codes, and outbursts of violence.[52] For their part, Northerners began pressing for measures supporting free soil, free labor, and free men in order to keep the newly acquired territories free from slavery.[53] The West accordingly became a region of political combat where both Northerners and Southerners hoped to expand their own power.

A Reconstructive Plan for the West

The West was not merely a flash point for Northern and Southern causes. Importantly, for the national government, the region represented a significant opportunity to expand its own power. The litany of problems created by the new western territories provided the government with a blank canvas on which to sketch out new laws for territories that would ultimately influence the entire nation. With most of the western areas not ready for statehood and full incorporation within the union, the West offered the government the ability to implement laws and policies that would have been deemed dramatic overreaches of federal power within established states. The West, as Richard White has argued, became "the kindergarten of the American state," functioning as a place where the federal government could "[grow] in power and influence."[54]

A demonstration of this federal power involved granting and withholding statehood as a means of furthering white Protestant Americanism in the West. Whereas California, with its rich gold fields and dramatic population surge, gained almost immediate statehood following the Treaty of Guadalupe Hidalgo, other regions became incorporated as territories. That status allowed for federal control of those regions for an indefinite period of time. Such was the case with the region that came to be known as Utah. Contemporary with California's petition, the Latter-day Saint settlement in the Great Basin had applied for admittance to the Union by 1849 as a state under the name of Deseret. Latter-day Saint leaders well recognized the importance of statehood, which provided the promise of full citizenship and incorporation within the federal government, including two senators and proportional representation in the House of Representatives. Perhaps of even greater importance, statehood brought with it a state government and high levels of local sovereignty, limiting the federal reach into the area. While California was admitted under the auspices of the Compromise of 1850, the Saints' settlement of Deseret was granted only territorial status and was renamed Utah.[55] Similarly, the well-established region of New Mexico was denied statehood and became a territory.

The formation of Utah and New Mexico as territories rather than as states was both significant and calculated. In terms of racial and religious demographics, the two territories posed challenges for the governance of a white Protestant nation. In 1850 both regions likely boasted nearly as many American Indians as American citizens. In addition, both territories were religiously distinctive. A growing Latter-day Saint population, for which the United States had long manifested complex feelings of pity, suspicion, and antipathy, populated Utah's valleys. Similarly, the Catholic Nuevo Mexicanos inhabited New Mexico. Although the government deemed these former Mexicans to be white citizens in accordance with the Treaty of Guadalupe Hidalgo, in reality they were treated largely as nonwhite, non-Protestant foreigners. Expansion had, therefore, "triggered an American race crisis," with the West becoming an epicenter of the new challenges.[56]

By establishing Utah and New Mexico as territories, the federal government claimed the right to control each location and its non-Protestant populations. With that control, Congress was free to enact strict laws and implement reconstructive policies that neither populace would have passed by vote. The limited democracy in the two territories was part of a purposeful effort to remove by legislation and administration perceived un-American cultural behaviors. As such, the government withheld statehood, awaiting sufficient Americanization in each location.

Although western reconstruction did affect territorial governance in New Mexico and Utah, its true purposes were aimed at specific groups that were not characterized as being white, Protestant, and American. Catholics, American Indians, Chinese immigrants, and Latter-day Saints specifically failed to live up to these requirements. Accordingly, in various ways, these groups became the targets of policy makers and legislation throughout the latter half of the nineteenth century.

In stating that the government worked to reconstruct these groups, however, one should by no means assume that they were either passive participants or recipients. Similar to the postbellum white Southerners, and later Jim Crow–era African Americans, each of these groups found their own ways to push back against federal reconstructive policies. Whether it was through open warfare, economic resistance, constructing independent schools, creating paper families, willfully accepting prison sentences, or simply continuing to speak their own native languages, America's reconstructed peoples consistently manifested a doggedness in the face of assimilative mandates. Even when diminished size and strength forced measures of acceptance, each group staged their own private revolutions against federal assaults upon their community's cultural distinctiveness. As such, despite the ideologies that declared them to be un-American, through their opposition to such policies, each added to the tradition of resolve and independent spirit that Americans had claimed to distinguish the country since its revolutionary founding.

Reconstructing Catholic Americans

David Emmons has explained that "true Americanism" was founded not only on "ethnicity or color," but also upon Protestantism, with the wages of whiteness being tied as intricately to conversion as they were to color.[57] Accordingly, in the minds of the nation's reconstructionists, race and religion were frequently conflated, with non-Protestantism often defining the religion of those who fell outside the borders of the American pale. In this regard, America's Catholic populations were frequently the recipients of nineteenth-century reconstructive measures.

Throughout the 1840s, the country received a heavy influx of Catholic immigration from Ireland, leading to a growth of nativist feeling. This growth built upon the already strong anti-Catholic sentiment that pervaded the United States. Manifesting their anti-Catholicism, several states passed strict laws regarding Sabbath activities and alcoholic consumption.[58] Politically, the new emigrants tended to gravitate toward the Democratic Party, which was generally far less concerned with "waging cultural warfare over matters of schooling, drinking, workplace demeanor, and forms of entertainment" than were the Whigs. The allegiance of Catholic immigrants gave Democrats significant electoral advantages in the nation's urban centers, where the new citizens tended to congregate.[59]

Even more significantly, the U.S.-Mexican War became a kind of crusade against Catholicism. As one historian has suggested, the war "revealed the universality of a peculiarly American anti-Catholicism" that informed "nearly every major argument for or against the war."[60] The outcome of the war and the Treaty of Guadalupe Hidalgo added a substantial Catholic population to the United States who, by treaty, were legal citizens, but in reality constituted a racial and religious minority.

The arguments leading up to the Civil War cemented the place of American Catholics as a problematic group. As the antislavery rhetoric grew more strident in the years preceding the Civil War, some Americans drew connections between slavery and Catholicism, claiming that the two went "hand in hand in their diabolical works of inhumanity and desolation."[61] Such statements established in antebellum minds that the coming reconstruction would be not only a Christian reconstruction, but specifically a Protestant reconstruction.

Following the Civil War, as non-Protestant minorities, American Catholics were subjected to special policies. Public schools in the West and throughout the nation included Bible instruction from the King James Version as a critical part of their curriculum. Catholics saw such measures as an assault upon their religion and an undisguised effort to evangelize their children with the use of public funds.[62] In response, they turned to parochial schools, where they could ensure that their children would not be proselytized to other faiths. Justifying their actions, anti-Catholics charged that the Catholics had demonstrated "open sympathy for the Confederate cause" during the Civil War.[63] Northern anti-Catholics believed that public schools were critical to the safety of the nation, in that they would help to Americanize Catholic children, thus ensuring that they would become productive citizens in American society.

In the Southwest, both Arizona and New Mexico maintained large Catholic populations that alarmed American officials. Admitted to the United States as a part of the Treaty of Guadalupe Hidalgo, the region that encompassed New Mexico and later Arizona posed challenges not only due to their Latino and Indian populations, but also due to the strong Catholic presence that stretched back to the 1500s. As New Mexico attempted to establish public schools, it became clear that members of the Catholic clergy formed the majority of the teaching force. As such, American officials doubted the extent to which these schools were "secular, public, or [even] American."[64] Such circumstances led Republicans to conclude that the region's Catholics were not sufficiently Americanized by the late 1890s, fearing that statehood would result in "a Spanish-American government."[65]

Overall, Catholics created a problem for reconstruction-minded Americans. Whether by immigration or treaty, they generally held status as citizens of the United States. Accordingly, the reconstructive aims of the nation were often focused on public institutions, such as schools. In the Southwest, the government used the elusive status of statehood as a means of limiting the power of the Catholic Church in America.

Reconstructing American Indians

While Catholics and other groups were the recipients of reconstructive policies, no group in the West was more consistently victimized by these policies than the American Indian populations. As white settlers expanded further and further west, the question of how to handle the "Indian problem" became more pressing. White desires for additional arable lands, water, gold, and other resources created continual conflict with Native peoples who inhabited those lands. In California, the newcomers carried out a genocidal decimation of the indigenous populations.[66] Whereas many western settlers advocated either annihilation or strict segregation, reform-minded Americans viewed the Native groups as "culturally retrograde," but capable of being civilized through literacy, Christianity, and agrarianism; in short, through the processes of cultural assimilation and Americanization.[67]

It must be acknowledged that Native peoples were members of independent tribes and Native nations. As such, they were the only group that was formally excluded from the benefits of the Fourteenth Amendment.[68] Hence, they were distinct from the other reconstructed groups in the West, which means it is inaccurate to speak of them as reconstructed peoples. This difference, however, did not preclude other Americans from viewing the various Indian tribes as peoples in need of reconstruction. Although some Americans feared that the Indian "will neither reconstruct nor exterminate," others believed it was the right and duty to impose reconstructive measures upon Native peoples.[69] Interpreting the Fourteenth Amendment differently, Arkansas's *Daily Republican* declared unequivocally that American Indians were citizens of the United States and should therefore abide by the laws that governed other citizens. The editorial stated that the time had come "when it is the obvious duty of Congress ... to reconstruct the Indian relations in harmony with the principles extended to other territories."[70] The *Weekly Arizona Miner* similarly bemoaned the supposed additional rights that "the noble red man" enjoyed "to swing around the circle, and do as he pleases." The paper hoped for congressional committees to be "appointed to reconstruct him" with troops being sent "to overawe and force him to obey the laws of God and man."[71] Accordingly, while white Protestant Americans saw differences in the Native peoples, they nevertheless viewed them through the lens of reconstruction.

Between 1848 and 1877, the army forcefully attempted to subjugate Native peoples. Indeed, in the language of one early editorialist, some Americans hoped to "reconstruct the red miscreants" at the point of a bayonet.[72] The U.S. Army played a critical role in removing American Indians from desired lands, imposing treaties, and regulating Native lives on the reservations. Resisting these efforts toward compulsion, Native groups resoundingly pushed back against this armed reconstruction during the 1860s, leading Colorado governor John Evans to conclude that "the tribes of the plains are nearly all combined in this terrible war," with violent repercussions stretching from the Canadian border to Texas.[73] Armed forces responded to this pushback with greater strength, resulting in massacres at locations like Sand Creek, carried out by Colorado volunteers, and on the Bear River in present-day Idaho where a group of California volunteers led the attack.[74] Despite years of cooperation and friendly relationships with the government, even the Nez Perce became the object of militaristic reconstruction, prompting a prolonged campaign by the U.S. Army and a march of more than a thousand miles to enforce compliance with the nation's demands.[75] Many aspects of military reconstruction, and particularly the Sand Creek Massacre, drew public outcry, as Protestant Northerners denounced the excessive use of force rather than attempts at peace.[76]

Through the means of military compulsion, indigenous tribes across the nation were forcibly confined to reservations throughout the West, with these locations becoming the not-so-tame compromise between annihilation and acceptance. Francis Prucha has noted that from the beginning these reserves were designed to ensure "that the Indians should be made as comfortable on, and uncomfortable off, their reservations as it was in the power of the Government to make them."[77] Reservations accordingly became locations where the government intended to carry out a "peace policy" initiated with the presidency of Ulysses S. Grant that would move American Indians toward assimilation. In 1873 Secretary of Interior Columbus Delano highlighted the five aims of this policy. First, the government would continue its efforts to situate Native groups on reservations where they "could be kept from contact with frontier settlements and could be taught the arts of agriculture and other pursuits of civilization." Second, authorities would punish those who rebelled against the reservations in order to teach subservience to the federal government. Third, they would paternalistically govern the supplies sold on the reservations to ensure that the funds appropriated for the reservations were not squandered. Fourth, they would utilize religious organizations to distribute goods among the Indians. And finally, they would use those same organizations to establish churches and schools that would help to Christianize the American Indians, thus preparing them for the responsibilities of American citizenship.[78]

Corresponding with these initiatives, the government launched other efforts beyond the borders of the reservations that were aimed at eliminating any reasons why American Indians would want to leave their confines. Throughout the 1860s and 1870s, the government abetted a massive effort to eradicate the buffalo population, which was crucial to the autonomy and survival of the plains Indians.[79] The expansion of railroads throughout the West, together with an increased public demand for buffalo-derived products, and a growth of national interest in hunting for sport contributed to the near extinction of the species.[80]

While the government hoped to keep recalcitrant Indians confined, the ultimate aim was to move the country's indigenous peoples toward a renunciation of Nativeness and an eventual acceptance of assimilation. Nonetheless, reservations segregated American Indians from the broader national population, complicating this goal. The 1887 Dawes Severalty Act attempted to accelerate assimilation by breaking up reservations and enforcing privatized landownership among American Indians.[81] The act divided the reservations into parcels that were to consist of one hundred and sixty acres for individual Native families, although in actuality the acreage allotments varied from family to family. Those who accepted their allotment "separate and apart from any tribe of Indians therein," and "adopted the habits of a civilized life," were granted citizenship with "all the rights, privileges, and immunities of such citizens."[82] By dividing reservation lands, the government hoped to lessen or eliminate the tribal influence, thereby establishing loyalty only to the United States.

Similarly, Native reconstruction also included efforts to Protestantize and Americanize Indian children through educational means. Most notably the establishment of the Carlisle Indian School in 1879 furthered the efforts of reform-minded Christians to establish a series of boarding schools throughout the nation aimed at helping Native children to transition from Indianness toward Americanness.[83] Richard H. Pratt, founder of the Carlisle school, openly admitted that such institutions aimed to "kill the Indian" within the child, "and save the man." He thoroughly believed that "all the Indian there is in the race should be dead," and education was the "civil" means of accomplishing that end.[84] Far from a matter of parental choice, attendance at boarding schools was often mandatory, with some children being forcibly removed from their homes.[85] Once there, students were subjected to rules regarding their grooming, conduct, and speech, all designed to replace Native culture with white Americanism.[86] Furthermore, education at the schools included a steady inculcation of Protestantism with the aim of undermining indigenous religious beliefs and practices.[87]

Reconstructing Chinese Immigrants

Like American Indians, Chinese immigrants were "doubly marked as inferior," owing to the fact that they were both racial others and generally non-Christians. Indeed, as the historian Joshua Paddison noted, "Firmly located outside both whiteness and Christianity in the public imagination, Indians and the Chinese both tested the limits of national belonging like no other groups." These likenesses resulted in each population being marginalized within the United States.[88] The two peoples, however, were not entirely comparable in the minds of white Americans. Unlike the Indians who appeared to be caught in the throes of inevitable declension and threatened extinction, by the 1860s the Chinese appeared to be arriving in the West in ever-greater numbers that threatened America's Protestantized manifest destiny.[89] The growing Chinese presence in the West was all the more complicated by the fact that it was occurring during the height of China's "century of humiliation," a 110-year span (1839–1949) in which the long-venerated Chinese empire seemed to crumble under the growth of European power in the Pacific.[90] Such events caused Americans and others to see the Chinese as a weakened people, with the immigrants to America being "hopelessly pagan coolies, without families or morals, the diametrical opposite of the free Christian, wage-laboring, married men."[91]

Despite these perceptions, Chinese immigrants were vital to the growth and development of the American West during the 1860s. In particular, they played a critical role in the construction of the transcontinental railroad. Because they could be employed at wages significantly less than white workers, Chinese immigrants became the major portion of the workforce for the Central Pacific Railroad Company.[92] For reconstruction-era Protestant Americans, the continuous arrival of Chinese immigrants became a perplexing challenge. As with many other minority groups, white Americans relied upon Chinese immigrants to construct the West, but also hoped to deny them the full rights of citizenship, particularly those accorded through the Fourteenth Amendment.[93]

Consistent with other reconstructive measures, efforts toward Chinese Americans included a strong component of evangelization. Throughout the 1860s and 1870s, several Protestant groups reached out to immigrants with schools, boarding houses, and missions, all hoping to convert the new population to Protestant Americanism. Additionally, churches wrote, translated, and distributed missionary pamphlets among the immigrant communities.[94] Christian reformers hoped that these efforts would lead to conversion and then perhaps to full citizenship.[95]

As railroad construction was completed and the nation slipped into a depression following the Panic of 1873, the apparent advantages that led Americans to accept immigrant labor gave way to deeper anti-Chinese sentiments. These attitudes resulted in efforts to curb the arrival of Chinese immigrants in the United States. The 1882 Chinese Exclusion Act explained that "the coming of Chinese laborers to this country endanger[ed] the good order" of various places within the nation. The act accordingly suspended legal Chinese immigration to the United States for a minimum of ten years. Immigrants who violated this law were subject to a term of imprisonment "not exceeding one year." Those laborers already residing in the country were to have their names "entered in registry-books" that kept a detailed record of "the name, age, occupation, last place of residence, physical marks or peculiarities, and all facts necessary for the identification of each of such Chinese laborers." A further provision offered free transportation of any Chinese Americans who wished to "leave the United States by water." Finally, the law specified that it applied to both "skilled and unskilled laborers," with a particular application to any Chinese immigrants "employed in mining."[96] In California, such exclusive measures extended to the schools, which prohibited attendance even by the wealthiest of Chinese families during the 1870s.[97]

Significantly, by the 1882 passage of the Chinese Exclusion Act, Americans had come to the conclusion that Chinese immigrants were incapable of Americanization. Through such measures, Americans deemed the West's growing Chinese population to be "racially unworthy of participation in American society."[98] Accordingly, the Greater Reconstruction had its limits. The combination of racial distinction and non-Christian faith meant that some populations could only be "solved" by exclusion and not incorporation through reconstructive policy.

Reconstructing Utah

Like the American Indian tribes and other racial and ethnic minorities, the Saints found themselves targets of sustained efforts toward reconstruction from 1856 to 1890. By the time they arrived in Utah in 1847, the Latter-day Saint community had already been compelled to vacate settlements in Ohio, Missouri, and Illinois, the latter two exits under force. Yet troubles followed the Saints because of their unique social, religious, economic, and political beliefs. Following the first three removals and the assassination of the faith's founder, Joseph Smith, the Latter-day Saints had determined to entirely vacate the United States, seeking refuge and political independence within the northernmost borders of Mexico.[99] Within two years of leaving Illinois, however, Mexico ceded the Saints' isolated refuge in the deserts of the Great Basin to the United States. Three years after that cession, credible reports of polygamy would begin to turn Utah into a religious and ideological battleground regarding the boundaries and meanings of American citizenship.[100]

Following the official report and the subsequent Latter-day Saint acknowledgement of the territory's polygamous practices, Utah became the subject of sustained reconstructive efforts.[101] As with the attempts to reshape American Indians, the exertions to reconstruct Utah were multifaceted and varied in their application. The backbone of this reconstruction was legislative in nature. Throughout the 1860s, 1870s, and 1880s, Congress debated and passed a number of bills that were aimed at stamping out polygamy.[102] The most notable of these acts were the 1862 Morrill Anti-Bigamy Act, the 1874 Poland Act, the 1882 Edmunds Act, and the 1887 Edmunds-Tucker Act. Working in conjunction with each other, these bills progressively increased the penalties for polygamous marriages, while narrowing the range of rights afforded to Saints who engaged in the practice. Although generally in favor of the antipolygamy legislation, the editors of the *New York Tribune* drew connections between these laws and Southern Reconstruction, briefly worrying that Utah's Latter-day Saint settlers would be "crushed or driven out" of the territory with their own version of "carpet-baggers reveling in the plunder of their property."[103] These bills were, for the Saints, similar to what the Dawes Allotment Act was for American Indians and what the Chinese Exclusion Act was for Chinese immigrants—narrowly directed pieces of legislation designed to legislate away the faith's most distinctive practices. Although these measures formed the mainstay of the government's efforts, they were hardly the only means of reconstruction within the territory.

Antedating the onslaught of legislation against polygamy, the attempt to reshape Utah focused on federal appointments and military power. Throughout the 1850s, many of Utah's federal officials used their positions to effect changes in the territory.[104] Such efforts led to frequent clashes with the Utah community, and ultimately to the 1857–58 Utah War, wherein U.S. President James Buchanan sent a detachment of the army to install a new governor in the territory.[105] Although significant open hostilities never ignited between the Latter-day Saint community and the army, the military presence in Utah served as a tangible threat of what awaited the territory if the Saints resisted federal laws too vigorously.[106] In the view of Latter-day Saint officials, Utah was subjected to a militaristic reconstruction that, at points, was akin to what awaited for the South during its reconstruction.

With the outbreak of the Civil War pushing Utah and the Saints to the background, military officials and federal appointees pushed ahead in reconstructing Utah even without a sizable army for enforcement. Brigadier General Patrick Edward Connor accused the Saints of pro-Confederate sympathies and requested additional troops to fight them. Connor's requests were denied, however, compelling him to pursue other reconstructive actions.[107] These measures functioned alongside the pieces of antipolygamy legislation. In this way, between 1860 and 1890 the government relied on both economic and educational measures to reinforce its Utah-directed legislative acts.

Both government officials and American businessmen encouraged mining and railroad development in Utah, believing that the free hand of commerce would undercut the cultural distinctiveness of Utah. Commanding Utah's army post throughout the course of the Civil War, Connor concluded that discovering gold, silver, and minerals in Utah was "of the highest importance" because it would induce a substantial non-Mormon immigration to the territory. Connor accordingly believed that mining successes represented "the only sure means of settling peaceably the Mormon question."[108] In addition, Ohio congressman Robert C. Schenck advocated "the advance of railroads and the progress of the tide of immigration" that would ultimately prove "more effectual than all the enactments of Congress" in bringing an end to polygamy.[109] Such proposals paralleled the construction of the railroad and the destruction of the buffalo in pacifying American Indians and showed a commitment to not allow the Saints independence from the larger national economy.

Similarly, government officials and others championed educational measures that would lessen the faith's influence upon Utah's children. In 1870 Republican William F. Prosser of Tennessee bemoaned the fact that of all the bills offered by the House and the Senate "to reconstruct the chronic troubles in Utah," not one had yet proposed to educate the children.[110] For Prosser, federally supported education was the surest path to reforming the Saints. With hearty support from the territory's federal appointees, as well as their own eastern parishioners, Protestant denominations began establishing schools throughout Utah, each with the aim of offering free education to Latter-day Saint children in exchange for proselytizing these young people. Through such efforts, Protestant educators in Utah felt they were "putting our clutches to [Young's] very throat," and, as a result, to the whole community.[111] Being made aware of these efforts, William Seward was cheered by the prospects, reportedly commenting that "the church and schools undertaken by the Episcopalian Church would do more to solve the Utah problem than the army and Congress of the United States combined."[112] These missionary schools followed in some ways the pattern of the Indian Boarding Schools, the freedmen's schools in the postbellum South, and the educational measures aimed at Catholic children throughout nineteenth-century America.

Differences persisted in how reconstructive efforts were applied to various groups. Yet, these initiatives demonstrated that throughout the latter half of the nineteenth century, the United States had begun a process of national reconstruction. These efforts provided an ideological reformulation of the very notion of Americanism and the stipulations that accompanied American citizenship. In addition to increasing the power of the federal government in the West, these activities allowed the government to regulate, reform, and even exclude specific groups. Through these undertakings, the government redefined the fundamental notions of American citizenship and dramatically increased its own power.

Beyond the Pale of Human Sympathy

Eric Foner and other scholars have ably demonstrated the tragic results that arose from the failure of Southern Reconstruction. Unfinished by 1877, Southern Reconstruction left a litany of unsettled problems that continue to plague the nation down to the present. At the same time, the successes of reconstructionist policies in the West provided another detrimental legacy for the nation. By seeking to create a uniform definition of American citizenship, the Greater Reconstruction of the West fundamentally influenced the ways that nineteenth-century Americans thought about the nation's racial, ethnic, and religious minorities. Rather than viewing those minorities as important threads in the tapestry of American citizenship, the Greater Reconstruction called for a kind of uniformity that eschewed a plurality of races, cultures, ideas, and religions.

A study of Utah during the period from 1856 to 1890 helps to illuminate both the extent of these reconstructionist policies and the multifaceted ways in which they were implemented throughout the West. Although many of the details of Utah's reconstruction were peculiar to the Latter-day Saints, the modes and methods of these actions found important similarities in the other reconstructions. In the eyes of many nineteenth-century Americans even before the Civil War, the faith was "as despotic, dangerous, and damnable" an organization "as has ever been known to exist in any country." If properly reported to the nation, the affairs in Utah would "startle the conservative people of the States, and create a clamor" that would "not be readily quelled."[113] For such citizens, many of the differences within the Latter-day Saint community amounted to "open and undisguised *treason*" against the United States. Such observations provided "*proof positive*" that the Saints were an uncivilized and un-American community, which was "*beyond the pale of human sympathy*." Only the hard hand of the government could reform such a people.[114] In the view of the nation, government intervention and "the correction of outrage" were necessary to protect those who met the period's full criteria for citizens of the United States.[115]

Other minorities such as indigenous Natives, Chinese immigrants, and Hispanic Catholics joined the Saints "*beyond the pale of human sympathy*." Observers like William Tecumseh Sherman and Thomas Nast saw dangers for the nation in the ways these groups differed from mainstream Americanism. To preserve union after the Civil War, nineteenth-century Americans felt it essential to reform and reconstruct outsiders like the Saints, justifying the abuses against these peoples in the name of "merg[ing] them into the more wholesome social elements" of the nation and thus preserving the nation under the auspices of white Protestant Christianity.[116] Such was the nation's purpose with its Greater Reconstruction.

Notes

1. Francis A. Walker, *The Indian Question* (Boston: James R. Osgood, 1874), 8.
2. William Tecumseh Sherman to Francis Amasa Walker, August 20, 1874, L. Tom Perry Special Collections, Harold B. Lee Library, Brigham Young University, Provo,

Utah (hereafter Special Collections, BYU). My thanks to Jeffrey D. Mahas for pointing me to this source.

3. Sherman to Walker, August 20, 1874, Special Collections, BYU.

4. Sherman to Walker, August 20, 1874, Special Collections, BYU.

5. Natalia Molina, *How Race is Made in America: Immigration, Citizenship, and the Historical Power of Racial Scripts* (Berkeley: University of California Press, 2014), 6–11.

6. David W. Blight, *Race and Reunion: The Civil War in American Memory* (Cambridge, Mass.: Belknap Press, 2001).

7. David M. Emmons, *Beyond the American Pale: The Irish in the West, 1845–1910* (Norman: University of Oklahoma Press, 2010).

8. Elliott West, *The Last Indian War: The Nez Perce Story* (New York: Oxford University Press, 2009), xx.

9. For a discussion of how Latter-day Saints were racialized in the nineteenth century, see W. Paul Reeve, *Religion of a Different Color: Race and the Mormon Struggle for Whiteness* (New York: Oxford University Press, 2015).

10. "News from Washington," *New York Herald*, December 5, 1860, p. 10, column 1.

11. U.S. Congress, *Congressional Globe*, 41st Cong., 2nd Sess. (1870), 3580.

12. George Q. Cannon, Diary, January 11, 1877, accessed February 27, 2017, https://www.churchhistorianspress.org/george-q-cannon/1870s/1877/01-1877.

13. George Q. Cannon, Diary, January 2, 1877, accessed February 27, 2017, https://www.churchhistorianspress.org/george-q-cannon/1870s/1877/01-1877.

14. "Uncle Sam's Troublesome Bed Fellows," *San Francisco Illustrated Wasp* 3, no. 2 (February 8, 1879): 441.

15. Reeve, *Religion of a Different Color*, 238–39.

16. *Speech of John A. McClernand of Illinois, on Polygamy in Utah: Delivered in the House of Representatives, April 3, 1860*, LDS Church History Library, Salt Lake City, Utah; Stephen A. Douglas, *Remarks of the Hon. Stephen A. Douglas, on Kansas, Utah, and the Dred Scott Decision: Delivered at Springfield, Illinois, June 12th 1857* (Chicago: Daily Times Book and Job Office, 1857), 12–13.

17. Don E. Fehrenbacher, *The Slaveholding Republic: An Account of the United States Government's Relations to Slavery* (New York: Oxford University Press, 2002).

18. Eric Foner, *Reconstruction: America's Unfinished Revolution, 1863–1877* (1988; repr., New York: History Book Club, 2005), 66, 253–61, 446–49.

19. Foner, *Reconstruction*, 96–102.

20. Foner, *Reconstruction*, 70–71.

21. Foner, *Reconstruction*, 440.

22. Foner, *Reconstruction*, 360–64.

23. Foner, *Reconstruction*, 17, 425–44.

24. Quoted in Steven Hahn, *A Nation without Borders: The United States and Its World in an Age of Civil Wars, 1830–1910* (New York: Viking Press, 2016), 71.

25. Foner, *Reconstruction*, 147.

26. Foner, *Reconstruction*, 255.

27. Hahn, *A Nation without Borders*, 312.

28. Foner, *Reconstruction*, 25, 255–56.

29. Foner, *Reconstruction*, 333.

30. Mark Twain and Charles Dudley Warner, *The Gilded Age, A Tale of To-Day* (Hartford, Conn.: American Publishing, 1874).

31. Foner, *Reconstruction*, 486–88.

32. William A. Dunning, *Reconstruction, Political and Economic: 1865–1877* (1907; repr., New York: Harper and Row, 1962), 1.

33. C. Vann Woodward, *Reunion and Reaction: The Compromise of 1877 and the End of Reconstruction* (1951; repr., New York: Oxford University Press, 1966); C. Vann Woodward, *The Strange Career of Jim Crow* (New York: Oxford University Press, 1955).

34. Foner, *Reconstruction*.

35. Foner, *Reconstruction*, xxvii.

36. Edward J. Blum, *Reforging the White Republic: Race, Religion, and American Nationalism, 1865–1898* (Baton Rouge: Louisiana State University Press, 2005); Blight, *Race and Reunion*; Heather Cox Richardson, *The Death of Reconstruction: Race, Labor, and Politics in the Post-Civil War North, 1865–1901* (Cambridge, Mass.: Harvard University Press, 2001).

37. West, "Reconstructing Race," 7–26.

38. Importantly, Howard Lamar's *The Far Southwest* suggested that reconstructive processes were taking place in the West, but remained relatively limited in its discussion of those processes. Similarly, Ronald W. Walker's *Wayward Saints*, Sarah Gordon's *The Mormon Question*, and Gaines Foster's *Moral Reconstruction* made passing references to reconstruction with regard to Utah. Eugene Berwanger's *The West and Reconstruction* was the first book to seriously consider how reconstruction played out in the West. He was particularly interested in the ways that western newspapers and politicians spoke of Southern Reconstruction, but his idea suggested important venues for additional research. Lamar, *The Far Southwest*, 113, 223, 318–19, 353; Ronald W. Walker, *Wayward Saints: The Social and Religious Protests of the Godbeites Against Brigham Young* (1998; repr., Salt Lake City: University of Utah Press, 2009), 215; Sarah Barringer Gordon, *The Mormon Question: Polygamy and Constitutional Conflict in Nineteenth-Century America* (Chapel Hill: University of North Carolina Press, 2002), 14; Gaines M. Foster, *Moral Reconstruction: Christian Lobbyists and the Federal Legislation of Morality, 1865–1920* (Chapel Hill: University of North Carolina Press, 2002); Eugene H. Berwanger, *The West and Reconstruction* (Urbana: University of Illinois Press, 1981).

39. Richardson, *West from Appomattox*, 37.

40. Richardson, *West from Appomattox*, 343, 346.

41. West, *Last Indian War*, xx.

42. West, *Last Indian War*, xx-xxi.

43. David M. Wrobel, *The End of American Exceptionalism: Frontier Anxiety from the Old West to the New Deal* (Lawrence: University of Kansas Press, 1993), 32–36.

44. Frederick Jackson Turner, "The Significance of the Frontier in American History," in *The Frontier in American History* (New York: Holt, 1921), 3.

45. Henry Nash Smith, *Virgin Land: The American West as Symbol and Myth* (Cambridge, Mass.: Harvard University Press, 1950).

46. Karl Jacoby, *Crimes Against Nature: Squatters, Poachers, Thieves, and the Hidden History of American Conservation* (Berkeley: University of California Press, 2001), 84–89; Joy S. Kasson, *Buffalo Bill's Wild West: Celebrity, Memory, and Popular History* (New York: Hill and Wang, 2000); West, *The Last Indian War*, 214–18.

47. Peter J. Kastor, *William Clark's World: Describing America in an Age of Unknowns* (New Haven, Conn.: Yale University Press, 2011), 173–75.

48. Treaty of Guadalupe Hidalgo, February 2, 1848, Article IX, accessed May 4, 2017, http://www.loc.gov/rr/hispanic/ghtreaty/.

49. Brian DeLay, *War of a Thousand Deserts: Indian Raids and the U.S.-Mexican War* (New Haven, Conn.: Yale University Press, 2008).

50. Elliott West, "Reconstructing Race," *Western Historical Quarterly* 34, no. 1 (Spring 2003): 8.

51. David M. Potter, *The Impending Crisis, 1848–1861* (New York: Harper and Row, 1976).

52. Walter Johnson, *River of Dark Dreams: Slavery and Empire in the Cotton Kingdom* (Cambridge, Mass.: Belknap Press, 2013).

53. Eric Foner, *Free Soil, Free Labor, Free Men: The Ideology of the Republican Party Before the Civil War* (1970; repr., New York: Oxford University Press, 1995); Jonathan H. Earle, *Jacksonian Democracy and the Politics of Free Soil, 1824–1854* (Chapel Hill: University of North Carolina Press, 2004).

54. Richard White, *"It's Your Misfortune and None of My Own": A History of the American West* (Norman: University of Oklahoma Press, 1991), 58.

55. Utah was organized as a slave territory with a slave code prior to the Civil War. Christopher B. Rich Jr., "The True Policy for Utah: Servitude, Slavery, and 'An Act in Relation to Service,'" *Utah Historical Quarterly* 80, no. 1 (Winter 2012): 54–74.

56. West, "Reconstructing Race," 8.

57. Emmons, *Beyond the American Pale*, 6.

58. Kyle G. Volk, *Moral Minorities and the Making of American Democracy* (New York: Oxford University Press, 2014), 37–45.

59. Hahn, *A Nation without Borders*, 171–72, 469.

60. John C. Pinheiro, *Missionaries of Republicanism: A Religious History of the Mexican-American War* (New York: Oxford University Press, 2014), 1.

61. Emmons, *Beyond the American Pale*, 55–56.

62. Ward M. McAfee, *Religion, Race, and Reconstruction: The Public School in the Politics of the 1870s* (Albany: State University of New York Press, 1998), 3.

63. McAfee, *Religion, Race, and Reconstruction*, 29.

64. Howard R. Lamar, *The Far Southwest, 1846–1912: A Territorial History* (1966; rev. ed., Albuquerque: University of New Mexico Press, 2000), 144.

65. Lamar, *The Far Southwest*, 164.

66. Albert L. Hurtado, *Indian Survival on the California Frontier* (New Haven, Conn.: Yale University Press, 1988), 100–192; Robert F. Heizer, ed., *The Destruction of California Indians* (Lincoln, Neb.: Bison Books, 1993); West, "Reconstructing Race," 13.

67. Hahn, *A Nation without Borders*, 280.

68. Stephen Kantrowitz, "'Not Quite Constitutionalized': The Meanings of 'Civilization' and the Limits of Native American Citizenship," in *The World the Civil War Made*, edited by Gregory P. Downs and Kate Masur (Chapel Hill: University of North Carolina Press, 2015), 89.

69. "The Squaw as a Chambermaid," *Inter Ocean* (Chicago, Ill.), September 14, 1876, p. 4, column 2.

70. "The Revenue Troubles in the Indian Territory," *Daily Republican* (Little Rock, Ark.), February 25, 1870, p. 2, column 1.

71. "The Indian Question," *Weekly Arizona Miner* (Prescott, Ariz.), April 30, 1870, p. 2, column 1.

72. "From Southern Arizona," *Weekly Arizona Miner* (Prescott, Ariz.), July 9, 1870, p. 2, column 3.

73. John Evans to William Dole, quoted in Hahn, *A Nation without Borders*, 283.

74. Hahn, *A Nation without Borders*, 283; Elliott West, *The Contested Plains: Indians, Goldseekers, and the Rush to Colorado* (Lawrence: University of Kansas Press, 1998), 297–307; Brigham D. Madsen, *The Shoshoni Frontier and the Bear River Massacre* (Salt Lake City: University of Utah Press, 1985).

75. West, *Last Indian War*, xvii, 169–300.

76. Francis Paul Prucha, *The Great Father: The United States Government and the American Indians, Abridged Edition* (Lincoln: University of Nebraska Press, 1986), 153.

77. Prucha, *The Great Father*, 167.

78. Prucha, *The Great Father*, 153.

79. Prucha, *The Great Father*, 179–80.

80. The 1873 establishment of Yellowstone National Park included provisions to protect the bison herds within the park, but even these measures functioned to limit the autonomy of American Indian peoples by prohibiting them from hunting within the park. William Cronon, *Nature's Metropolis: Chicago and the Great West* (New York: W. W. Norton, 1991), 215–18; Jacoby, *Crimes Against Nature*, 83–90.

81. Prucha, *The Great Father*, 226–27.

82. "An Act to Provide for the Allotment of Lands in Severalty to Indians on the Various Reservations, and to Extend the Protection of the Laws of the United States and the Territories Over the Indians, and for Other Purposes," *U.S. Statutes at Large* 24 (1887): 390.

83. David Wallace Adams, *Education for Extinction: American Indians and the Boarding School Experience, 1875–1928* (Lawrence: Kansas University Press, 1995).

84. Richard H. Pratt, "The Advantages of Mingling Indians with Whites," *Americanizing the American Indians: Writings by the "Friends of the Indian," 1880–1900* (Cambridge, Mass.: Harvard University Press, 1973), 260–71.

85. Margaret D. Jacobs, *White Mother to a Dark Race: Settler Colonialism, Maternalism, and the Removal of Indigenous Children in the American West and Australia, 1880–1940* (Lincoln: University of Nebraska Press, 2009).

86. Adams, *Education for Extinction*, 101–12.

87. Adams, *Education for Extinction*, 166–70.

88. Joshua Paddison, *American Heathens: Religion, Race, and Reconstruction in California* (Berkeley: University of California Press, 2012), 3, 123.

89. Paddison, *American Heathens*, 4.

90. Alison Adcock Kaufman, "The 'Century of Humiliation,' Then and Now: Chinese Perceptions of the International Order," *Pacific Focus: Inha Journal of International Studies* 25, no. 1 (April 2010): 4–5.

91. Paddison, *American Heathens*, 49.

92. Richard White, *Railroaded: The Transcontinentals and the Making of Modern America* (New York: W. W. Norton, 2011), 30.

93. D. Michael Bottoms, *An Aristocracy of Color: Race and Reconstruction in California and the West, 1850–1890* (Norman: University of Oklahoma Press, 2013), 167.

94. Paddison, *American Heathens*, 35.

95. Paddison, *American Heathens*, 36–37.

96. "An Act to Execute Certain Treaty Stipulations Relating to Chinese," *U.S. Statutes at Large* 24 (1882): 58–61.

97. Bottoms, *An Aristocracy of Color*, 126–35.

98. Bottoms, *An Aristocracy of Color*, 167.

99. Thomas Ford to Brigham Young, April 8, 1845, in "Council of Fifty Minutes, April 15, 1845," in *Council of Fifty Minutes, March 1844–January 1846*, edited by Matthew J. Grow et al., vol. 1 of the Administrative Records series of *The Joseph Smith Papers*, edited by Ronald K. Esplin, Matthew J. Grow, and Matthew C. Godfrey (Salt Lake City: Church Historian's Press, 2016), 428–29; "Council of Fifty Minutes, March 18, 1845," in Grow et al., *Council of Fifty Minutes*, 328–29.

100. Ronald W. Walker, "The Affair of the 'Runaways': Utah's First Encounter with the Federal Officers," *Journal of Mormon History* 39, no. 4 (Fall 2013): 1–43; Matthew J. Grow and Ronald W. Walker, "The People are 'Hogaffed or Humbugged': The 1851–52 National Reaction to Utah's 'Runaway' Officers," *Journal of Mormon History* 40, no. 1 (Winter 2014): 1–52.

101. See Gordon, *The Mormon Question*; Gustive O. Larson, *The "Americanization" of Utah for Statehood* (San Marino, Calif.: Henry E. Huntington Library and Art Gallery, 1971).

102. The preeminent work on these legislative acts is Gordon, *The Mormon Question*.

103. "More Reconstruction," *New York Tribune*, June 4, 1874, p. 4, columns 3–4.

104. Walker, "The Affair of the 'Runaways,'" 1–43; Grow and Walker, "The People are 'Hogaffed or Humbugged,'" 1–52; Ronald W. Walker, "'Proud as a Peacock and Ignorant as a Jackass': William W. Drummond's Unusual Career with the Mormons," *Journal of Mormon History* 42, no. 3 (July 2016): 1–34; Ronald W. Walker, "The Tintic War of 1856: A Study of Several Conflicts," *Journal of Mormon History* 42, no. 3 (July 2016): 35–68.

105. William P. MacKinnon, *At Sword's Point, Part 1: A Documentary History of the Utah War to 1858* (Norman, Okla.: Arthur H. Clark, 2008); William P. MacKinnon, *At Sword's Point, Part 2: A Documentary History of the Utah War, 1858–1859* (Norman, Okla.: Arthur H. Clark, 2016).

106. Although the Utah War contained no major battles, its connection to the Mountain Meadows Massacre and the murder of more than 120 emigrants from Arkansas and

Missouri precludes any notion that the war was bloodless. Although the massacre was not formally a part of the Utah War, it is impossible to comprehend the event outside the context of the Utah War and its militaristic and violent rhetoric. The principal histories of the massacre are Juanita Brooks, *The Mountain Meadows Massacre*, 2nd ed. (Norman: University of Oklahoma Press, 1962); Will Bagley, *Blood of the Prophets: Brigham Young and the Massacre at Mountain Meadows* (Norman: University of Oklahoma Press, 2002); Ronald W. Walker, Richard E. Turley Jr., and Glen M. Leonard, *Massacre at Mountain Meadows* (New York: Oxford University Press, 2008). While the authors debate the extent to which the massacre can be considered a military engagement of the Utah War, they all place the event squarely within the broader context of the Utah War.

107. Brigham D. Madsen, *Glory Hunter: A Biography of Patrick Edward Connor* (Salt Lake City: University of Utah Press, 1990), 66–67.

108. Patrick Edward Connor to Richard C. Drum, October 26, 1863, in *Utah and the American Civil War: The Written Record*, ed. Kenneth L. Alford (Norman, Okla.: Arthur H. Clark, 2017), 339.

109. "House of Representatives," *New York Tribune*, March 23, 1870, p. 8, column 2; George Q. Cannon to Brigham Young, March 23, 1870, Brigham Young Office Files, CR 1234 1, reel 51, box 38, folder 12, LDS Church History Library, Salt Lake City.

110. U.S. Congress, *Congressional Globe*, 41st Cong., 2nd Sess. (1870), 761.

111. Daniel S. Tuttle to Harriet Tuttle, July 10, 1867, in Daniel S. Tuttle, *Reminiscences of a Missionary Bishop* (New York: Thomas Whittaker, 1906), 114.

112. Thomas W. Haskins to Mrs. Haskins, December 10, 1891, in Tuttle, *Reminiscences of a Missionary Bishop*, 365.

113. W. M. F. Magraw to Franklin Pierce, October 3, 1856, U.S. Department of State, Miscellaneous Letters of the Department of State, 1789–1906, NARA RG 59 2, M179, frame 64–66 (hereinafter cited as Misc. Letters).

114. N. W. Green to James Buchanan, August 4, 1857, Misc. Letters, frame 642. Emphasis in original.

115. Magraw to Pierce, October 3, 1856, Misc. Letters, NARA.

116. *Speech of John A. McClernand of Illinois, on Polygamy in Utah*, 12–13.

= 6 =

The Case for Containing Reconstruction

Rethinking and Remeasuring

Rachel St. John

In 1865 Judge John Perkins Jr. set out for Mexico. A Confederate congressman and author of Louisiana's secession ordinance, Perkins had devoted himself to the defense of slavery and the creation of a republic that would ensure its persistence. In the face of emancipation and the defeat of the Confederacy, he opted to relocate to Mexico rather than submit to Union authority. As Reconstruction proceeded in his home state of Louisiana, Perkins worked as a colonization agent, attempting to recruit former Confederates to settle in the new colony of Carlota west of Veracruz.[1]

Twenty years later in 1885, Miles Park Romney also sought refuge in Mexico. A prominent member of the Church of Jesus Christ of Latter-day Saints and the husband of five wives, Romney moved from Arizona to southern Utah and then to northern Mexico to escape prosecution under federal antipolygamy laws. As one of his sons recalled years later, Romney and other "harassed religionists" had chosen "to flee to a foreign land" to "escape the searching eye of the ever-vigilant United States marshal who was always on the alert to bring the polygamist to judgment."[2]

In many of the essays in this volume the authors have emphasized Mormons' position as an oppressed religious minority and have compared their treatment to that of other groups that have been constructed as racial minorities. There is certainly value in doing so, as these essays clearly show. But in this essay I position

Mormons a bit differently—as members of a church that operated at various times in the nineteenth century as a semiautonomous state and that had a contentious and at times antagonistic relationship with the U.S. federal government. Thinking about Mormons in this way leads me to a different Reconstruction-era comparison—Confederates.

An awareness of the state- and nation-building dimensions of nineteenth-century Mormonism makes it difficult not to see comparisons with the Confederacy. Both sought self-rule and pursued independent governance. In doing so, both argued that they were not treasonous, but rather the true heirs of the American Revolution and defenders of the U.S. Constitution. Federal officials rejected these claims in both cases. And the federal government mustered its military, legislative, and police powers to subordinate both groups to federal authority and to assert the principle of federal supremacy over local rule. In both cases, the story of political subordination was tied up with moral questions. Both Mormons and Confederates embraced practices that, as Christine Talbot reminds us in her essay, the Republican Party deemed barbaric.[3] And, although by the mid-nineteenth century those practices were out of step with most of the western world with which Confederates and Mormons culturally identified, slavery and polygamy became cornerstones of Confederate and Mormon societies. As a result, both groups faced condemnation from moral reformers and eventually became the focus of government assaults on these peculiar institutions.

Also like the Confederacy, Mormons went to war with the United States. In 1857 President James Buchanan dispatched federal troops to impose federal authority on the Mormons, much as Lincoln would do four years later in the face of Southern secession. Of course, that is about where the similarities between those two conflicts end. The Utah War produced very little bloodshed. Federal officials and LDS leaders ultimately managed to negotiate a compromise in which Mormons recognized federal authority while maintaining a significant degree of control over the Utah Territory. Moreover, polygamy, although a central piece of the context surrounding the conflict between Mormons and the U.S. government, was not at stake in the Utah War. As a result, in 1858 Mormon recognition of U.S. authority was not—yet—contingent on abandoning the principle of plural marriage. The initial decoupling of subordination to federal authority and the abandonment of polygamy allowed for a less violent but more attenuated process in which the federal government sought to reconstruct Mormon society. As Brent Rogers notes in his essay, the application of federal authority in Utah was a "long, slow process" that played out over thirty years.[4]

By contrast, in the South, the Civil War marked the abrupt, bloody end of both slavery and Southern sovereignty. The imposition of federal power was even more jarring for white Southern elites who, in addition to celebrating states' rights, had long enjoyed disproportionate power over federal affairs.[5] Within a relatively short period, they lost control of the federal government, lost a devastating war, lost their defining social and economic institution, and lost self-rule.

Meanwhile, the Mormons were able to retain their "peculiar institution," for a time at least. The remaining "relic of barbarism" persisted for three decades as a thorn in the side of Republicans who were committed to moral reform and cultural conformity. Beginning with the Morrill Anti-Bigamy Act of 1862, Congress enacted a series of ever more punitive laws in an attempt to stamp out polygamy.

However, despite the divergent timelines, ultimately, the federal government demanded the abandonment of both slavery and polygamy as a sign of subordination and as a condition of political incorporation into the Union. Southerners had to accept the Thirteenth, Fourteenth, and Fifteenth Amendments. Mormons had to phase out polygamy. Significantly, once they did so, the federal government allowed both groups to join the nation. Despite the violence and animosity produced by the struggles over sovereignty, slavery, and polygamy, by the beginning of the twentieth century both Mormons and former Confederates enjoyed the privileges of other white Americans.

Of course, in the midst of their struggles with the federal government, members of neither group could clearly imagine that eventual endpoint (a lot of suffering and death might have been avoided if they had). By starting with refugees, I intentionally brought you into the middle of the story—when U.S. authority was on the brink of being secured. These two stories of American exiles in Mexico provide a window into a shared history of the assertion of U.S. federal power—and resistance to it—that linked Mormons and former Confederates in the nineteenth century. In the second half of the nineteenth century, both groups faced a newly empowered federal government intent on limiting the autonomy of their local governments and on eradicating the peculiar institutions—slavery and polygamy—that had come to define their societies in the minds of reform-minded Americans.

In the South, the federal government's effort to reconstruct state governments and create a post-emancipation society was known as Reconstruction. In the West, the federal government's effort to suppress the autonomy and influence of the LDS Church and eradicate polygamy was known as . . . well, I don't really know that there was a term for it. But it was not called Reconstruction.

It was this simple fact, underscored by reading Patrick Mason's paper—and particularly his comments about the anachronism and analytical slipperiness of extending the term "Reconstruction" to the Utah Expedition—that made me scrap my initial draft of this essay and go back to the drawing board.[6] I had originally set out to argue that we should think of Mormons and former Confederates as being subjected to a shared—and prolonged—process of federal Reconstruction. In doing so, I was, like many of the essayists, riffing on Elliott West's idea of a "Greater Reconstruction" and on Sarah Barringer Gordon's formulation of a "second Reconstruction."[7]

It is worth noting that these are just two variations—and in my opinion two particularly useful variations—on what is a much broader theme in the historiography of Reconstruction in the past two decades. Reconstruction seems to be getting bigger and bigger all the time. The term was once fairly narrowly defined in terms of region, time period, and policy. Spanning a period from midway through the Civil War until the Bargain of 1877, "Reconstruction" once meant the official federal program to create a post-emancipation society and reconstruct new state governments in the postbellum South. However, in the past few decades, historians have dramatically expanded their conception of "Reconstruction," emphasizing the connections between the aims and effects of the official program of Reconstruction and a much broader transformation in how federal power and ideas and laws regarding citizenship, suffrage, race, and freedom changed across the United States in the mid-to-late nineteenth century.

Scholars have adopted a more expansive take on the chronology of Reconstruction. Elliott West places its starting point in the 1840s—well before secession and the deconstruction of the nation. Angela Pulley Hudson's essay in this volume—perhaps only at the urging of the editors and primarily to be provocative—draws the timeline even further back to the Trail of Tears and Mormon persecutions in the Midwest. Steven Hahn, on the other hand, has extended the period of Reconstruction forward. First, in *A Nation under Our Feet*, he demonstrated that the 1877 stopping point was somewhat arbitrary when thinking about the experience of African Americans in the South. More recently, in *A Nation without Borders*, he has argued for the benefits of considering the period between 1890 and 1920 as a period defined by a series of "reconstructions."[8]

At the same time, historians have stretched the geographic space of Reconstruction. They have shown how the newly empowered federal government imposed its authority on people in the North and West, as well as the South. They have emphasized how the rethinking of the relationship between race, citizenship, and suffrage extended beyond the community of freed people to include Asian and European immigrants, Native people, and American citizens of Mexican descent.[9]

Reconstruction now often seems less a specific government program or even a distinct period (or "era" in the language of the conference title), and more a term that encompasses a whole series of state- and nation-building activities carried out by federal officials over decades (if not the entire century). This point was driven home to me when I set out to cover the topic in a single eighty-minute lecture in my lower-division U.S. history survey. I was initially somewhat chagrined to realize that within the constraints of a ten-week quarter and a class title that promised the students the "History of the United States to 1877," I needed to scale my ambitions back to the period of official Reconstruction and keep my sights focused pretty narrowly on the South. What had happened to my aspirations of including Joshua Paddison's and Michael Bottoms's insights about the connections between the redefinition of citizenship and racial exclusion in California? Why had I failed to incorporate Amy Dru Stanley's incisive analysis of the implications of freedom of contract for women? How could I possibly skip over the work of Elliott West and others on the assaults on Native autonomy? And, geez, couldn't I even squeeze in something from the paper I was simultaneously writing on Mormons and Reconstruction?[10]

Initially, I wrote this off as a teaching problem. Of course, we can never fit everything in. But that doesn't answer the question of why, when faced with eighty minutes to devote to Reconstruction, I, a western historian at heart, decided to more or less entirely jettison the West (not to mention Northern labor and gender and a great many more topics). I hadn't done this in earlier lectures. It was no less difficult to winnow the Civil War down to eighty minutes, and yet I simply could not ignore the Dakota Uprising and its violent suppression by the U.S. Army. When faced with the need to choose, I had opted for the narrower and more historically specific version of Reconstruction over the broader, more conceptual one. And I think this was a good choice.

I want to make the case for containing Reconstruction. That is, to reserve the term "Reconstruction" to apply to the federal government's effort to reestablish Southern state governments and reincorporate them into the Union and to create a post-emancipation society and economy during the period between 1863 and 1877. In calling for this narrow and more historically specific version of Reconstruction, I am in no way rejecting the critical insights of the histories of the varied configurations of greater, longer, or broader or multiple, national, or transnational reconstructions. To the contrary, I argue that the scope—in time and space—of the U.S. federal government's efforts to expand its power, impose its authority, redefine citizenship, establish racial and gender hierarchies, and enshrine the principles of free labor and freedom of contract in the capitalist economy is simply too great to try to contain under the umbrella of Reconstruction.

The recent attempts to expand our conceptions of Reconstruction have been both persuasive and productive. They have forced us to acknowledge the context within which the reconstruction of the South took form and to connect Reconstruction policies to a broader set of historical processes that shaped the United States (and the world). By expanding on the connections and detailing how other regions experienced "Reconstruction," recent histories have added significantly to our understanding of how Americans redefined citizenship and how the federal government developed and deployed a state apparatus that allowed it to assert greater authority over the entire nation. The experiences of Mormons during a broadly defined era of Reconstruction, as the essays in this volume have shown, further illuminate the range of the federal government's activities and how religion limited Mormons' ability to access their full rights as U.S. citizens.

However, using the term "Reconstruction" to make sense of these processes seems to me to be problematic. First, it lacks historical grounding. Reconstruction meant something specific to nineteenth-century Americans. By using the term broadly in hopes of illuminating its wider implications and connections to larger processes, historians have also begun to change its definition in ways that would make it unrecognizable to the people who crafted and experienced the policies of Reconstruction. Moreover, it seems important to recognize that in naming Reconstruction, nineteenth-century Americans marked it as exceptional and finite. That they did not apply this term more openly—to other projects that historians now consider part of a broader history of Reconstruction—matters.

Second, as Patrick Mason notes in his essay, the broad application of Reconstruction can lead to anachronisms. Southern Reconstruction was in essence a postwar program—made necessary by secession, war, and emancipation; justified, as Gregory Downs has recently emphasized, as part of a continuation of war powers; and made possible by, as Eric Foner has shown, a federal state that had expanded dramatically in power and personnel.[11] Applying the term to antebellum events obscures all of these critical developments.

Moreover, Reconstruction is largely about the creation of a post-emancipation society and about the fundamental redefinition of citizenship in the Fourteenth and Fifteenth Amendments. As Angela Pulley Hudson emphasized in our conference discussions, much of the state's prewar activity, especially the conquest of Native lands and removal, was intimately tied to the expansion of slavery.[12] I worry about a history of Reconstruction in which the abolition of chattel slavery is incidental. Similarly, it is essential that we do not lose sight of how Reconstruction changed the meaning of citizenship. Emancipation and the expansion of citizenship were, as John Mack Faragher underscored in his commentary during the conference, good things.[13] It is, of course, true that they fell short and were unrealized in many ways. But historians generally emphasize that their greatest shortcomings were products of the failures of Reconstruction, rather than its intended goals. I fear that in our pursuit of expansive Reconstruction we are in danger of inadvertently collapsing Reconstruction and the Redeemer governments that facilitated its fall into a single state project. In the context of Mormon history, for instance, it seems significant that the federal government's most concentrated assaults on Mormon autonomy occurred outside the period of official Reconstruction. The first occurred before the Civil War began in the late 1850s, and the second came after the collapse of Reconstruction in the 1880s.

Third, "Reconstruction" does not seem to be a very apt descriptor of the processes that unfolded outside the South. In the South, the "re" part of Reconstruction was clear; these were states that had been established and incorporated into the Union. It was secession and war that made it necessary to do so again. (Here I'm building on Patrick Mason's related, but slightly different, comment about Mormon "construction" as opposed to "(re)construction."[14]) In contrast to the South, most of the West was, at least in the eyes of the federal government, unconstructed. By imposing the "re," we risk naturalizing federal authority over western lands and people. "Reconstruction" was a word deliberately chosen to suggest not the making of state power but the radical and comprehensive remaking of that power to reflect the post-emancipation order. For the most part, western lands and peoples, including the Mormon emigrants who had relocated to the Great Basin and attempted to establish a semi-independent religious and political community, were not being reconstructed, but rather conquered and incorporated.

Fourth, given how powerful the themes of Reconstruction history are, the application of the term to other places and people risks forcing divergent processes of conquest, incorporation, and assimilation into a Southern framework. Angela Pulley Hudson makes a similar point with her emphasis on the importance of foregrounding settler colonialism.[15] It is certainly the case, as Brett Dowdle emphasizes in his article, that some specific actors, ideas, and policies associated with

Reconstruction did travel west.[16] But for the most part, U.S. officials recognized that the South, freed people, and former Confederates posed a different set of problems than the West, American Indians, and Mormons. They sought to impose their authority over both regions and shared strategies and personnel between the two, but they did not constitute a single government program. Perhaps the best evidence of this is that while Southern Reconstruction ended in 1877, federal intervention in the West continued uninterrupted. In fact, as I noted above, it was only after the cessation of official Reconstruction that the federal government concentrated its efforts to outlaw polygamy and bring the Mormon church to heel.

Finally, as a westerner and western historian, as well as a historian who works on transnational borderlands, I can't help but feel like some of the appeal of bringing the West into Reconstruction lies in the promise of making the West part of an exceptionalist narrative of the United States that centers on the Civil War. Making connections between the East and the West helps us better understand both regions, as well as the nation to which they both belong, but I remain skeptical of attempts to do so that rely on subsuming the West within eastern frameworks and narratives. Moreover, we should not lose sight of how the policies and ideologies associated with controlling labor, expanding state power, and redefining citizenship and racial hierarchies crossed not only regional, but national boundaries.

All these issues lead me to think that "Reconstruction" is both too historically specific and insufficiently broad to effectively encompass the diverse and far-reaching processes of state formation, nation building, colonization, and subordination of racial and religious minority groups that shaped North America in the nineteenth century. We need a more capacious umbrella. I welcome suggestions for a catchy phrase or single word. But in the absence of a creative catchall, I propose that we talk about the expansion of state power, the definition of citizenship, and, borrowing again from Patrick Mason's essay, disciplining.[17]

Focusing on these large processes would allow us, as Elliott West urged in "Reconstructing Race," to think about race—and other processes—on a continental level. However, rather than stretching an essentially Southern phenomenon to cover the country, Southern Reconstruction would become just a chapter in this national story. Letting Reconstruction just be Reconstruction allows for greater attention to variations across time, region, group, and situation. It seems particularly critical to avoid the potential trap of making the Southern experience the normative vision of "Reconstruction" against which other state projects were measured because of the variability of government policies.

Over the course of the nineteenth century, the federal government developed divergent policies to apply to different people and places. In the decades following the establishment of constitutional guarantees to birthright citizenship and universal male suffrage, U.S. officials proved remarkably adept at developing new ways to maintain racial hierarchies. Following a brief moment of political access and opportunity during Reconstruction, Southern politicians, with the support of federal courts and Northern noninterference, created a violent regime that disenfranchised African Americans and denied them civil rights and economic opportunity. Meanwhile, westerners and federal officials took a different tack in dealing with Chinese people. Faced with the guarantee of birthright citizenship, they gradually constructed a new immigration restriction regime meant to deny Chinese immigrants legal access to the United States. In the Southwest, Anglo Americans developed a series of strategies to limit the political and economic participation of people of Mexican descent. And finally, even as the U.S. government continued to dispossess Native people and demand assimilation, a series of court rulings excluded Indians from the benefits of birthright citizenship entirely.

It was also in the second half of the nineteenth century that the federal government became more strategic in distinguishing between different forms of U.S. territory. By admitting some territories as states, while keeping others under territorial control (or in the case of the unreconstructed South, military occupation), Congress asserted federal authority and ensured that some Americans had more rights than others. This inequality was even more apparent on Indian reservations and in unincorporated island possessions.

It was the assertion of federal authority from which both John Perkins Jr. and Miles P. Romney sought refuge in Mexico. Other groups, it is worth noting, also sought to elude the federal government this way—the Lakota bands that crossed into Canada; the Nez Perce, who hoped to do the same, but were stopped short of the border; and African Americans who looked to Liberia in the face of the decline of Reconstruction, the rise of white paramilitary groups, and the unfulfilled promises of freedom, citizenship, and suffrage.[18]

Thinking about this more diverse array of refugees returns us to the essential argument that Elliott West made in "Reconstructing Race"—we must think about a continental story of race, as he emphasized, but also, I would underscore, of state formation, nation-building, conquest, and struggles over sovereignty. I may not agree that we should think of this history as "Greater Reconstruction," but it is without a doubt the greater and, again borrowing from Elliott West, the "longer, grimmer, but more interesting" story of which Reconstruction was a part.[19]

Notes

1. Biographical Note, John Perkins Papers, Southern Historical Collection, Special Collections, Lewis Round Wilson Library, University of North Carolina, Chapel Hill; Andrew Rolle, *The Lost Cause: The Confederate Exodus to Mexico* (Norman: University of Oklahoma Press, 1965), 91.

2. Thomas Cottam Romney, *The Mormon Colonies in Mexico* (1938; repr., Salt Lake City: University of Utah Press, 2005), 267.

3. Christine Talbot, "Constructing a National Marital and Sexual Culture: Reconsidering the 'Twin Relics of Barbarism,'" herein.

4. Brent M. Rogers, "The Application of Federal Power in Utah Territory," herein, 43.

5. For a recent book making this point, see Matthew Karp, *This Vast Southern Empire: Slaveholders at the Helm of American Foreign Policy* (Cambridge: Harvard University Press, 2016).

6. Patrick Q. Mason, "Disciplinary Democracy: Mormon Violence and the Construction of the Modern American State," herein, especially the first three paragraphs.

7. Elliott West, "Reconstructing Race," *Western Historical Quarterly* 34, no. 1 (Spring 2003): 6–26; Sarah Barringer Gordon, *The Mormon Question*, 14.

8. West, "Reconstructing Race"; Angela Pulley Hudson, "There Is No Mormon Trail of Tears: Roots, Removals, and Reconstructions," herein; Steven Hahn, *A Nation without Borders: The United States and Its World in an Age of Civil Wars, 1830–1910* (New York: Penguin, 2016), 7; Steven Hahn, *A Nation under Our Feet* (Cambridge: Harvard University Press, 2003).

9. West, "Reconstructing Race"; Elliott West, *The Last Indian War: The Nez Perce Story* (New York: Oxford, 2009); Eric Foner, *Reconstruction: America's Unfinished Revolution, 1863–1877* (New York: Harper and Row, 1988); Amy Dru Stanley, *From Bondage to Contract: Wage Labor, Marriage, and the Market in the Age of Slave Emancipation* (New York, Cambridge University Press, 1998); Heather Cox Richardson, *West from Appomattox: The Reconstruction of America after the Civil War* (New Haven, Conn.: Yale University Press, 2007); Richard White, *The Republic for Which It Stands: The United States during Reconstruction and the Gilded Age, 1865–1896* (New York: Oxford University Press, 2017); Joshua Paddison, *American Heathens: Religion, Race, and Reconstruction in California* (Berkeley: University of California Press, 2012); D. Michael Bottoms, *An Aristocracy of Color: Race and Reconstruction in California and the West, 1850–1890* (Norman: University of Oklahoma Press, 2013); Stacey L. Smith, *Freedom's Frontier: California and the Struggle over Unfree Labor, Emancipation, and Reconstruction* (Chapel Hill: University of North Carolina Press, 2013); Adam Arenson and Andrew R. Graybill, eds., *Civil War Wests: Testing the Limits of the United States* (Berkeley: University of California Press, 2015); Virginia Scharff, ed., *Empire and Liberty: The Civil War and the West* (Berkeley: University of California Press, 2015).

10. Paddison, *American Heathens*; Bottoms, *An Aristocracy of Color*; Stanley, *From Bondage to Contract*; West, "Reconstructing Race"; Elliott West, *The Last Indian War*.

11. Gregory Downs, *After Appomattox*; Foner, *Reconstruction*.

12. Angela Pulley Hudson, comments made during "The Era of Reconstruction in Mormon America, a Working Conference for a Collaborative Book," sponsored by the Charles Redd Center for Western Studies, Brigham Young University, Provo, Utah, June 15–16, 2017.

13. John Mack Faragher, comments made during "The Era of Reconstruction in Mormon America, a Working Conference for a Collaborative Book," sponsored by the Charles Redd Center for Western Studies, Brigham Young University, Provo, Utah, June 15–16, 2017.

14. Mason, "Disciplinary Democracy," 4.

15. Hudson, "There Is No Mormon Trail of Tears."

16. Brett Dowdle, "'To Merge Them into More Wholesome Social Elements': The Greater Reconstruction and Its Place in Utah," herein.

17. Mason, "Disciplinary Democracy."

18. Robert Marshall Utley, *The Lance and the Shield: The Life and Times of Sitting Bull* (New York: Ballantine Books, 1994); West, *The Last Indian War*; Steven Hahn, *A Nation under Our Feet*, 317–63.

19. Elliott West, "A Longer, Grimmer, but More Interesting Story," in *Trails: Toward a New Western History*, Patricia Nelson Limerick, Clyde A. Milner II, Charles E. Rankin, eds. (Lawrence: University of Kansas Press, 1991), 103.

PART III
Aftermaths

Interlude 3

Reckoning with Lost Causes

Brian Q. Cannon

The essays in this section incisively explore why Mormons, unlike Southerners, do not possess a vibrant Lost Cause tradition, despite their history of forced accommodation to American norms. The authors identify several factors that prevented strong Lost Cause sentiments from taking root in Mormon country. Eric Eliason indicates that most Mormons were New Englanders, midwesterners, and English immigrants who lacked the hotheaded, Scots-Irish honor culture that animated former Confederates following the Civil War. Moreover, a Lost Cause mentality that glorified polygamy and civil disobedience would be counterproductive for modern Mormonism. Jared Farmer points to the fact that few Mormons died at the hands of oppressors; as Eric Eliason observes, the Mormon military heritage is "meager," consisting of a few battles with state militia and mobs in Missouri and Illinois. Armed Mormons burned military supply trains and torched Fort Bridger during the Utah War of 1857–58 but fought no battles with the troops. Clyde Milner points out that although Mormons were compelled to abandon significant elements of their religion late in the nineteenth century, rather than commemorating what was lost, Mormons fruitfully focused on celebrating their shared western heritage of pioneering.

The lack of a robust, enduring persecution complex is well demonstrated in these essays, a lack that is especially remarkable given the malice that first-generation

Mormons nursed toward their persecutors. In the 1850s Mormons chafed under the memory of mobbing and murder at the hands of state militias and elected officials in Missouri and Illinois. The assassination of Joseph Smith, his brother Hyrum, and Apostles David Patten and Parley Pratt, along with the murder, rape, and maiming of dozens of Mormon men, women, and children in Missouri fomented resentment. The chilling rhetoric preserved in the minutes of a Sunday meeting on the Mormon frontier illuminates the depth of their animosity. On Sunday, May 14, 1854, John Lott preached, "We suffered from damned Sectarians in Mo., driven, robbed, and murdered. I hope to see the day when the blood of martyrs will be avenged, and these damnable rebels make restitution, or the children suffer for the wickedness of their fathers." James Lewis followed Lott to the pulpit and vowed, "My Brother Benjamin was killed [in] Missouri, and I am alive to avenge his blood when the Lord will."[1] Just three years later some of the congregants who listened to these tirades took revenge at Mountain Meadows.

In territorial Utah, hostilities between United States soldiers and the Mormons galvanized additional resentment and defiance. After Brigham Young announced in 1857 that much of the American army was marching to Utah to suppress the Latter-day Saints, Apostle Heber C. Kimball laid down the gauntlet: "Send 2,500 troops here, our brethren, to make a desolation of this people! God Almighty helping me, I will fight until there is not a drop of blood in my veins. Good God! I have enough wives to whip out the United States."[2] Calmer heads prevailed and peace was preserved, but tales of individual soldiers who abused civilians during the subsequent military occupation of Utah accentuated many Mormons' contempt for federal troops. Mormon grievances stemming from the Utah War were ephemeral, though; the troops committed no wholesale depredations and within a short time Mormons reframed the war's outcome as a victory for the Saints. In 1861, shortly after the army was withdrawn to fight the Civil War, Apostle George A. Smith crowed, "The army has been withdrawn from our country, and they have gone away, in a manner acknowledging their defeat. To be sure, many of the officers went away saying, 'We will come by-and-by and wipe you out.' But as God would have it, they are employed in paying such compliments to each other as they had designed to inflict upon us."[3] As a result of the Utah War, the governorship was taken from Brigham Young and conferred upon Alfred Cumming, but as Young quipped nearly a decade later, "I believe that Governor Cumming came to the conclusion that he was Governor of the Territory as domain; but that Brigham Young was governor of the people. They have to acknowledge this, no matter whom they may send here." In short, Young boasted, "James Buchanan did all he could do, and when he found he could do nothing, he sent a pardon here."[4] In 1879 Apostle Franklin Richards boasted that the army came to Utah to suppress polygamy. Instead, once they were stationed in Utah at Camp Floyd they discovered that they "were dependent upon polygamists for their subsistence, [and] the prestige of the campaign dwindled down to what was commonly known as the 'contractor's war on the Treasury,'" a war that enriched Mormon farmers, laborers, and merchants.[5]

In the 1880s the federal government's disfranchisement of all women in the territory and the prosecution and imprisonment of Mormon polygamous husbands again aroused a sense of righteous indignation and moral outrage. George Washington Bean scornfully derided the authorities who hounded and imprisoned Mormon fathers and husbands as "official wolves." Casting herself as an innocent victim oppressed by corrupt judges and legislators, Flora Robertson Brimhall recalled, "The laws of the land were against plural marriage. I, being the second wife, had to live in seclusion under an assumed name... Our perplexities seemed to multiply, and there were thorns continually in our pathway. This was due in large measure to the spirit of persecution abroad in the land."[6]

Resentment arising from the cumulative weight of persecution crystalized in an oath of vengeance the faithful recited for a time in their temples. Apostate Mormon August Lundstrom recalled the substance of the oath: "We and each of us solemnly covenant and promise that we shall ask God to avenge the blood of Joseph Smith upon this nation." David Cannon, a regionally prominent Latter-day Saint, confirmed the gist of Lundstrom's claim; temple worshippers implored God "to avenge the blood of the prophets and righteous men that has been shed, etc."[7]

Federal lawmakers, marshals, and Congress placed church president Wilford Woodruff in an untenable situation by banning polygamy, disincorporating the church, seizing church property, imprisoning ecclesiastical leaders, and disfranchising women and polygamous men. Woodruff was "under the necessity," he concluded, "of acting for the temporal salvation of the church" by advising members to obey the law and desist from polygamy. Some Mormons welcomed Woodruff's announcement, known as the Manifesto. Wrote James Jepson, "When the Manifesto was signed I felt very much relieved, for in my own heart I really never wanted two wives at one time." But Woodruff's Manifesto provoked shell shock and "psychic pain," as Farmer observes, among many who had sacrificed intensely to practice their religion. "Many of the Saints" surrounding Joseph Dean in the Salt Lake Tabernacle when the Manifesto was first read from the pulpit "seemed stunned and confused and hardly knew how to vote, feeling that if they endorsed it they would be voting against one of the most sacred and important principles of their religion." Dean saw no hands raised that day in opposition to Woodruff's Manifesto, but "many of the saints refrained from voting either way." Particularly plural wives were unmoored by the announcement that seemed to relegate them to physical, financial, and religious limbo as relics of an outmoded practice. "A great many of the sisters weeped silently, and seemed to feel worse than the brethren," recalled Dean. Lorena Eugenia Washburn Larson explained why the news was particularly onerous for plural wives. "My feelings were passed [sic] description," she recalled. "I fancied I would see myself and my children, and many other splendid women and their children turned adrift . . . I sank down on our bedding and wished in my anguish that the earth would open and take me and my children in." Many Mormons blamed the United States for forcing Woodruff's hand and pronounced a pox on the nation. Edward Stevenson shed "a tear for Zion and 2 tears for the American Nation[.] [D]readful is it, for this Great Nation to fall upon Jesus Rock. . . . for they who fall upon it shall be broken and I prophecy [sic] it shall be so with this Nation and Zion will be built upon its ruins." Likewise Joseph Robinson decreed, "Let the responsibility lie with the government."[8]

As Milner observes, it would have been natural in the 1890s for these raw resentments to have calcified into intractable alienation and mourning for a lost way of life, but this did not occur. One mitigating factor, as Eliason mentions, was Christian idealism. "However much we may feel aggrieved at the acts of men towards us, we should not pray for their condemnation. Let us confess our own sins and pray that we may be forgiven for them, and leave other sinners to the Lord, who has said that judgements are His, and He will repay," the church's First Presidency advised shortly before Christmas in 1890, at a time when church members were "menaced with a total deprivation of our rights as freemen and citizens."[9]

Another factor that tempered Mormon resistance and counternarratives in the 1890s was the fact that federal authorities had not yet restored their civil rights or church property, and Mormons' only bargaining chip was compliance with federal demands. Over a year after the Manifesto had been announced, the church's First Presidency petitioned President Benjamin Harrison for amnesty and restoration of their rights, likening themselves to ex-Confederates following the Civil War. They reasoned, "When the men of the South, who were in rebellion against the Government in 1865 threw down their arms and asked for recognition along the old lines of citizenship, the Government hastened to grant their prayer. To be at peace with the Governor and in harmony with their fellow citizens who were not of their faith and to share in the confidence of the Government and people, our people have voluntarily put aside something which all their lives they have believed to be a sacred principle. Have they not the right to ask for such clemency as comes when the claims of both law and justice have been fully liquidated?"[10]

More than a year passed before President Harrison pardoned the Mormons in 1893. Three more years passed before Utah's admission as a state restored the right to vote for Mormon women and conferred the perquisites of self-rule: Mormon majorities in the legislative and the executive branches, and full-fledged representation in the nation's capital.

As they had done following the Utah War, Mormons managed to preserve their sense of autonomy in the face of acquiescing to federal authority over the matter of polygamy, telling themselves that their cause was not lost at all. As Joseph Christenson wrote, "We only layed [polygamy] by for a time," expecting that in the future national sentiment would change and the practice would be revived. In the short term, many men including church presidents continued to cohabit with their plural wives, while law enforcement officials looked the other way; others surreptitiously contracted additional plural marriages, most commonly in Mexico. Over two hundred plural marriages were performed by church leaders between 1890 and 1904. Summoned before the Senate Committee on Privileges and Elections to answer for those marriages, church president Joseph F. Smith made clear that no amount of legislation could alter his belief that polygamy was divinely ordained. Woodruff's Manifesto "did not change our belief at all," he insisted. When asked if he "continued to believe that plural marriages were right," Smith stated, "I believe that the principle is as correct a principle to-day as it was then [prior to the Manifesto]." Discredited before the Senate, Smith was persuaded by monogamous apostle Reed Smoot, whose seat in the Senate weighed in the balance, to issue a Second Manifesto in 1904 threatening all who entered future plural marriages with excommunication.[11]

While Smith and many of his generation clung fiercely to polygamy, many of their children and almost all of their grandchildren adopted a "progressive version of Mormonism," as Farmer notes. Unlike the progeny of unreconstructed Southerners, the posterity of Mormon polygamists had little to gain economically or socially from restoring the old order. A generation or two removed from the prosecution of polygamists and eager to breach the cultural barriers that defined Mormons as inferior, they made their peace with mainstream American culture, finding it in their interests culturally and socially. As one of their number, Stanford-educated journalist Isaac Russell, observed two decades following the Woodruff Manifesto, "New generations have largely gained control [in Utah], and to goad them on the old polygamy matter is a good deal like goading the South on slavery might have been along about 1870 or 1875. They are supersensitive because they are striving by every possible means to work away from the old issue" even though "they have not turned on the old men and women who were in polygamy before 1890."[12]

As Stephen Taysom has shown, the near-erasure of polygamy from popular Mormon theology was facilitated by monogamous apostle James E. Talmage, a geologist with a PhD from Wesleyan University, who creatively redefined a key term in the Mormon lexicon, celestial marriage, as monogamous temple marriage rather than polygamous unions. Ignoring the weight of theological evidence, he argued in print in 1901, a decade before his call to the apostleship, that polygamy "was an incident—never an essential" component of Mormonism. In 1930 Talmage prepared for church publication a distillation of "scriptures of general and enduring value" from the canonized revelations of Joseph Smith and his successors, omitting entirely Joseph Smith's revelation on polygamy. When Fundamentalist, polygamous splinter groups accused the church of suppressing its founder's teachings, church president Heber J. Grant withdrew Talmage's work from circulation.[13]

The modern institutional church acknowledges but does not celebrate its polygamous past or its history of civil disobedience. As Milner concludes, unlike white Southerners, Mormons have not cultivated "a heritage of hatred." Even the assassination of its founding prophet is memorialized by volunteer missionaries at Carthage Jail in Illinois in ways that emphasize peace and reconciliation rather than bloodshed and recrimination.[14] As Farmer keenly observes, though, "politicized stories of governmental tyranny" do circulate unofficially "in contemporary Mormonism," and not only among fringe groups. Moreover, Mormon scholars and activists are increasingly rediscovering and celebrating their polygamous foremothers, finding inspiration in the political independence, professional advancement, and economic self-reliance that polygamy afforded. In this manner Mormons continue to find ways to remember their own past.

Notes

1. Thomas D. Brown, "Journal of the Southern Indian Mission," May 14, 1854, quoted in Juanita Brooks, *The Mountain Meadows Massacre* (Norman: University of Oklahoma Press, 1991), 33.

2. Heber C. Kimball, August 4, 1857, *Journal of Discourses* (Liverpool: Latter-day Saints Book Depot, 1855–1886), 5:95. (Hereafter, the *Journal of Discourses* will be cited as *JD* with appropriate volume and pages following.)

3. George A. Smith, September 10, 1861, *JD* 9:112.

4. Brigham Young, February 10, 1867, *JD*, 11:323–24.

5. F. D. Richards, October 6, 1879, *JD*, 20:311.

6. George Washington Bean, "Journals, Including Account Book, Diary, Biographical Sketch and Book of Family History," p. 320, SCM 252, Item 4, L. Tom Perry Special Collections (hereafter LTPSC), Harold B. Lee Library, Brigham Young University, Provo, Utah; Flora Robertson Brimhall, Autobiography, pp. 3–4, MSS 458, LTPSC.

7. Testimony of August W. Lundstrom, *Proceedings before the Committee on Privileges and Elections of the United States Senate in the Matter of the Protests Against the Right of Hon. Reed Smoot, a Senator from the State of Utah, to Hold His Seat* (Washington, D.C.: Government Printing Office, 1906), 2:153; David John Buerger, "The Development of the Mormon Temple Endowment Ceremony" 34 (Spring/Summer 2001): 103.

8. Wilford Woodruff diary, quoted in Thomas G. Alexander, *Things of Heaven and Earth: The Life and Times of Wilford Woodruff, a Mormon Prophet* (Salt Lake City: Signature Books, 1993), 266; James Jepson Jr., *Memories and Experiences of James Jepson, Jr.* (privately published, 1944), LTPSC; Joseph H. Dean, Journal, October 6, 1890, LDS Church History Library (hereafter CHL), Salt Lake City; Lorena Eugenia Washburn Larsen, Autobiographical Writings, MS 9775, CHL; Edward Stevenson, Diaries and Reminiscences, October 6, 1890, MS 4806, CHL; Joseph Lee Robinson, Journal, October 6, 1890, MS 7042, CHL.

9. "First Presidency to the Presidents of Stakes & Their Counselors," quoted in Rudger Clawson Diary, Dec. 22, 1890, Clawson Papers, Marriott Library, University of Utah.

10. "Petition for Amnesty," quoted in B. Carmon Hardy, *Doing the Works of Abraham: Mormon Polygamy, Its Origin, Practice, and Demise* (Norman, Okla.: Arthur H. Clark, 2007), 358.

11. Joseph Christenson, Journals and Autobiographical Writings, MSS 6088, CHL; B. Carmon Hardy, *Solemn Covenant: The Mormon Polygamous Passage* (Urbana: University of Illinois Press, 1992); "Joseph F. Smoot Testimony before the Senate Committee on Privileges and Elections," quoted in Michael Harold Paulos, "Under the Gun at the Smoot Hearings: Joseph F. Smith's Testimony," *Journal of Mormon History* 34 (Fall 2008): 201, 205.

12. Isaac K. Russell to National Board of Censorship, January 24[?], 1912, box 4, folder 16, Scott G. Kenney Collection, LTPSC.

13. Stephen C. Taysom, "A Uniform and Common Recollection: Joseph Smith's Legacy, Polygamy, and the Creation of Mormon Public Memory, 1852–2002," *Dialogue: A Journal of Mormon Thought* 35 (Fall 2002): 132–34; Newell G. Bringhurst, "Section 132 of the LDS Doctrine and Covenants: Its Complex Contents and Controversial Legacy," in *The Persistence of Polygamy: Joseph Smith and the Origins of Mormon Polygamy*, edited by Newell G. Bringhurst and Craig L. Foster (Independence, Mo.: John Whitmer Books, 2010), 83–84.

14. Brian Q. Cannon, "'Long Shall His Blood . . . Stain Illinois': Carthage Jail in Mormon Memory," *Mormon Historical Studies* 10 (Spring 2009): 1–20.

═ 7 ═

Why Don't Mormons Have a Lost Cause?

Clyde A. Milner II

In the summer of 2002, my wife, Carol O'Connor, and I moved from Logan, Utah, to Jonesboro, Arkansas. We had spent a combined fifty-one years as members of the history faculty at Utah State University (twenty-six years for me and twenty-five years for Carol). Now we were joining the faculty at Arkansas State University, where I had agreed to direct a new PhD program in Heritage Studies. Central to heritage studies is the public representation and collective memory of the past. If you wish, you may consider "heritage studies" to be an expansive form of "public history" influenced by various forms of cultural studies, most especially in my case, folklore.

I grew up in Chapel Hill, North Carolina, but I had not lived in the South since 1971, and I had never lived in Arkansas. What amazed me right away as I settled into my new community, located fifty miles west of the Mississippi River, was the continuing recognition not only of the Civil War, but most especially the public interpretation of that war advocated most openly by white Southerners. I soon discovered that Jonesboro had a Southern Confederate Heritage Park, complete with flags and stone markers that had been dedicated not in the 1890s, but in 1997, only five years before I came to town.[1] Located next to a McDonald's and not far from one of the town's two Walmart stores, the park cannot be idly ignored. On August 2, 2012, as part of Arkansas's participation in the Civil War

Sesquicentennial, the Sons of Confederate Veterans (SCV) dedicated a cannon in memory of the one Confederate soldier who died in the Battle of Jonesboro, an event where seven Union soldiers were killed. Not the same as the massive losses at Gettysburg, it can be noted. Ray Jones, the SCV division commander said at the dedication, that the purpose was not to glorify war, but to honor "the fallen soldiers we lost in the war and that's the whole purpose of the Sons of Confederate Veterans to keep the memory alive of our brave Confederate soldiers." As reported online, a small crowd stood quietly and then joined at the end in singing "Dixie." Nearly three years later, in late June 2015, when renewed protests over displays of the Confederate flag surged, a convoy of trucks and motorcycles traveled out of Jonesboro to neighboring towns displaying the rebel banner and stickers reading "heritage not hate." Spreading the message that the flag was a "symbol of history," one female participant opined, "Men died for that flag just like they died for the American flag. . . . If they can take our heritage and that flag from them soldiers that did die for it, what are they going to do next? Are they going to take down the American flag too?"[2]

Scholars who have examined the public memory of the Civil War—and an extensive number of studies have done so[3]—would not be surprised by what I found in Jonesboro. The representation of the Confederacy across the South with battle reenactments, marble statues, and the ubiquitous "Stars and Bars" of the rebel flag demonstrates what is known as the "Lost Cause"—the dominant collective memory of the war for white Southern families. Simply put, what I, and many other observers, have noticed is that the Lost Cause is not lost in the South. If not overtly stated, what the Lost Cause represents captures one or more of what the historian Caroline E. Janney considers the six tenets of this public ideology.

> "(1) Secession, not slavery, caused the Civil War.
> (2) African Americans were 'faithful slaves,' loyal to their masters and the Confederate cause and unprepared for the responsibilities of freedom.
> (3) The Confederacy was defeated militarily only because of the Union's overwhelming advantages in men and resources.
> (4) Confederate soldiers were heroic and saintly.
> (5) The most heroic and saintly of all Confederates, perhaps of all Americans, was Robert E. Lee.
> (6) Southern women were loyal to the Confederate cause and sanctified by the sacrifice of their loved ones."

As Janney states, and other scholars would no doubt agree, "The historical consensus, however, presents a picture that is far more complicated, one in which some tenets of the Lost Cause are obviously false and some are at least partly true."[4] Perhaps this easily found and undying Lost Cause is part of what the South's most revered novelist, William Faulkner, meant for us to contemplate when he wrote, "The past is never dead. It's not even past."[5]

The question that frames this essay, "Why don't Mormons have a Lost Cause?" did not come to me quickly as I settled down in Jonesboro, Arkansas. I did want my PhD students to understand the public memory of the Civil War, which led me to assign, right away, David Blight's magnificent book, *Race and Reunion: The Civil War in American Memory*, published in 2001. It's a book I used each year in the introductory doctoral seminar for heritage studies. Blight made me think about some parallels in western history and memory. We could look at the Texas Revolution and remember the Alamo, for example, or consider the Great Sioux War and contemplate the legend of Custer at the Little Bighorn. And we would learn that just as black Southerners are outraged by most of the Lost Cause mythology, Lakotas and Texas-Mexicans feel equally upset about tales of heroic defeat that vilify the victors. But I had not focused on the saga of the Latter-day Saints in the Great Basin until I started looking at pioneer memory, public celebration, and nationalistic narratives in the West. That brought me to an examination of Pioneer Day in Utah and a chance to read the work of Eric Eliason. In his 1997 essay, "Pioneers and Recapitulation in Mormon Popular Historical Expression," Eliason considers the "martyrological potential" for remembering resistance to the imposition of federal power during the era of reconstruction in Mormon America. He asserts that "to celebrate resistance now would be to memorialize *a lost cause* [italics added by me] that is embarrassing to many modern Mormons—a struggle for a principle [i.e. plural marriage] that the LDS Church now vehemently opposes."[6]

I do not disagree with this conclusion, but I do wonder why Latter-day Saints, if they had a Lost Cause, could not use some of the same tricks of memory that white Southerners have used. After all, if the Lost Cause eliminates slavery as the reason for the Civil War, could not Mormons say that religious freedom or, yes, "states' rights" and not polygamy, brought on resistance to federal actions against the Latter-day Saints? Indeed, all six of Caroline Janney's tenets might work nicely in this creative exercise. Consider the final two: Robert E. Lee as heroic saintly figure and the loyalty of Southern women to the Confederate cause. Latter-day Saints erected many statues of Brigham Young (with and without a beard) and even named a major university after him. And we do know about the loyalty of many Mormon women to the religious principle of plural marriage.

So why didn't Latter-day Saints end up like Latter-day Southerners? Why aren't Mormons lost in their own Lost Cause? As a historian, following Eric Eliason's lead, I would say that if the equivalent of a Latter-day Lost Cause were to take root in the collective memory of Mormons, it should have happened by the end of the 1890s. In that decade, the historian David Blight tells us that the Lost Cause had become well established across the South and had greatly shaped the story of national reunion in its representation of white supremacy.[7] And in that decade with the Latter-day Saints, a church Manifesto ended the sanctioning of plural marriage, the trials of federal reconstruction ceased, and statehood finally came to Utah. But Mormons did not emerge from the 1890s as defiantly unreconstructed rebels. Instead, they affirmed a distinctly patriotic mainstream national identity that highlighted another narrative, their trek to the far West's Great Basin as pioneers.

The formal celebration of this pioneer status by westering Mormons began in 1849, only two years after their arrival in the valley of the Great Salt Lake. The initial "Pioneer Day" had an inclusive character. Numerous visitors attended; many were on their way to the California gold fields. Two of these argonauts, each from Massachusetts, recorded their impressions. One had been invited to the celebration by Parley P. Pratt, a member of the church's Council of the Twelve Apostles. Each observer estimated that some five thousand people gathered in what one described as "a kind of shed supported by a great number of posts." It was a large bowery near the site where the new LDS Temple would be constructed. Speakers included Brigham Young and other church leaders. These speeches seemed "inflammatory" with "threats against their enemies in Missouri" according to one of the Massachusetts men. The other reported, "Both the prophets & elders speeches were rantings malignant & hostile to our government & administration & people in the West." Brigham Young was not ready to make nice (if he ever was), but the Mormons were prepared to serve a great meal after two hours of hard talk. Pies, cakes, puddings, and other fine fare pleased the visitors so much that one considered it "one of the best dinners we had enjoyed for many a day" and the other felt "altogether this has been one of the happiest days of my journey."[8]

Mormon women provided more detailed accounts of the first Pioneer Day celebration. Their letters and diaries revealed their important labor in the preparations. Perhaps most dramatic among these efforts was a flag sown by at least two, and possibly three, of Brigham Young's wives. This mammoth sixty-foot-long "Flag of Deseret" flew from a "liberty pole" 104 feet tall. What did this flag represent? As one of the wives, Augusta Cobb, explained, "Brother Brigham" had brought the material for the project and "The standard is to be raised on the 24 of this month and we expect to proclaim our Independence." Yet, this proclamation did not mean secession from the United States. It fit within a tradition of raising liberty poles to embrace the ideals of the American Revolution. The historian Laurel Thatcher Ulrich noted "the impulses that animated the new holiday" included aspects of the Fourth of July as well as a "First Thanksgiving." She also recognized "the decorous, almost genteel quality of the arrangements, which contrasted not only with the raucous atmosphere of July 4 celebrations elsewhere, but with the commercialized parades emerging in Eastern cities."[9]

The first Pioneer Day expressed social, religious, and even geographic alienation from the United States, but it did not produce a call for political independence. In fact, three days after the July 24 celebration, Almon Babbitt, the State of Deseret's purported delegate to the U.S. Congress, departed Salt Lake City carrying a petition for statehood. The historian John G. Turner observed that Brigham Young established Deseret "to present the United States with a *fait accompli*, much as Americans in California established a state government later in 1849 . . . to bypass territorial status." Brigham Young wanted Mormons to govern themselves in their own state within the United States.[10] Efforts to gain statehood would continue for decades as would the annual Pioneer Day celebrations. Obviously, establishing a new Mormon holiday proved more readily successful than creating a new Mormon state.

Steven L. Olsen, a senior scholar in the LDS Church History Department, has asserted in his writings, "In the second half of the nineteenth century, Pioneer Day was one of the most important public expressions of Mormon identity. Although Salt Lake City hosted the main event, tens of thousands of Latter-day Saints in towns throughout the western United States participated in their own parades, devotionals, feasts, sporting events, dances, and excursions."[11] The extraordinary compilation of newspaper clippings and other documents contained in the daily record of the Journal History of the LDS Church contain an abundance of accounts of Pioneer Day that support Olsen's contention.[12] The festivities are not limited to Salt Lake City, and indeed during years when Pioneer Day had modest, restrained recognition in that metropolis, the celebrations continued in smaller communities. In fact, Salt Lake City did not have a major Pioneer Day from 1856 to 1862. The first two years of that span saw Brigham Young host a huge picnic for Pioneer Day at Silver Lake up Big Cottonwood Canyon. At the second gathering in 1857, news arrived that the U.S. Army, commanded by Albert Sidney Johnston, was marching on Utah. The imminent threat from federal troops readily disrupted the tenth anniversary of the arrival of the Mormon pioneers.[13] What followed in the next four decades could have made Latter-day Saints a bitter, alienated people. The remnant of Johnston's army eventually left in 1861 with the coming of the Civil War, but after that bloody conflagration, the attentions of national reconstruction focused first on the South, then on western Indians, and with little delay on the Latter-day Saints. Yet, Mormons did not give up their annual celebration of Pioneer Day or turn it into an unrepentant expression of rebellion against federal oppression.

Mormons continued to see themselves as heroic pioneers and not as unreconstructed rebels. Indeed, by the 1890s the Latter-day Saints had begun to assert their place in mainstream American culture, as demonstrated in Reid L. Neilson's study *Exhibiting Mormonism*, which looks at the Utah exhibits and Mormon participation in the 1893 Chicago World's Fair.[14] At that grand event, Frederick Jackson Turner proclaimed the significance of the frontier in American history while announcing that the frontier had closed. Whatever the historical validity of his analysis, Turner did capture the large nationalistic desire to explain American exceptionalism by viewing the frontier experience as formative. Put simply, pioneers were important because they defined American history and character, even though for Turner the pioneer era on the frontier had ended. In Turnerian terms, being pioneers meant being part of the essential mainstream of American history. But Mormons did not need Frederick Jackson Turner to tell them that pioneers were important. They had been celebrating that significance since at least 1849. Indeed, two major events had helped both expand and solidify the "pioneer identity" of Latter-day Saints in the American West. First was the tragically foolhardy, yet heroic story of the handcart companies that trekked to the Great Basin Kingdom especially in the fateful year of 1856. And then, the driving of the "golden spike" at Promontory Summit meant that Mormons had a neatly focused chronology for their western pioneer era, beginning in 1847 and ending with the completion of the transcontinental railroad in 1869. Not surprisingly, pulling handcarts and driving golden spikes became part of the annual Pioneer Day celebration.[15]

In the July 24, 1880, festivities, the enfolding of Mormon history into American history seemed highly evident. That year marked the fiftieth anniversary of the founding of the church. The semiannual general conference in April had recognized this "Jubilee Year," but as historian Steven L. Olsen observed, "its principal observance was on 24 July."[16] The non-Mormon governor of Utah Territory, Eli H. Murray, had insisted on a Fourth of July event to which no Mormons were invited. Perhaps to upstage the governor, but also to demonstrate the importance of marking the church's half-century, a massive celebration took place on July 24 in Salt Lake City. Federal officials, including the governor, were invited but none formally attended. Nonetheless, if in the city, they could not have missed the spectacle. The day began with a procession three miles in length. At the front rode the surviving members of Brigham Young's original 1847 pioneer band in five wagons. Representations from trades, education, arts, agriculture, and manufacturing showed the people's progress, whereas the Pilgrim Fathers, the Pony Express, and the completion of the transcontinental telegraph demonstrated historical connections. Fifteen thousand people attended services at the Tabernacle and heard orations of the pioneer saga plus an accounting by Orson Pratt of the church's mission work, which concluded with representatives from twenty-five countries dressed in native garb presented to the audience.[17]

The religious scholar Stephen C. Taysom has traced what he considers continuity and reconstitution in Mormon history. He does not see overt ruptures in belief and behavior even with major events such as the Manifesto ending the official practice of plural marriage. Mormons had set a pattern where they could "accommodate the increased pressure and reformulate the boundaries and the narrative" of their collective identity.[18] It seems that Taysom's "continuity and reconstitution" happened as well with the narrative of the Mormon pioneers. The saga became effectively entwined with both the history of the LDS Church and the history of the American West. By 1897, with the fiftieth jubilee for the Mormon pioneers, this interweaving seemed complete.

The event had grand aspirations. On January 8, 1896, four days after President Grover Cleveland signed the proclamation of statehood for Utah, the new state's governor, Heber Manning Wells, in his first message to the new state's legislature, advocated an appropriately monumental celebration. By early April a commission had been appointed that advocated "the biggest celebration in the country since the 1893 World's Fair and the largest event yet to be seen west of the Mississippi."[19] One day would not be enough. What became officially designated as the "Utah Pioneer Jubilee" extended from July 20 to July 25. More than 100,000 people came to Salt Lake City, where they could view five massive parades, concerts, plays, baseball games, horse races, a rodeo (termed a "cowboy tournament"), and much more. A specially constructed "Hall of Relics" displayed pioneer artifacts, and on the first day a still incomplete pioneer monument was unveiled, crowned with a statue of Brigham Young, a likeness first displayed at the 1893 Chicago World's Fair.[20]

Early on, the commission, which had expanded from ten to fifteen members, resolved the issue of who would be the pioneers commemorated for the semicentennial. Anyone who arrived in Salt Lake Valley in 1847 now had this recognition. On the first day of the jubilee, these pioneers from 1847 attended a special ceremony at the Tabernacle, where they received an impressive gold badge created by Tiffany and Company of New York City. The individual name of the honored pioneer was inscribed on the back of the badge. The imagery on the front comfortably melded Mormon elements with western history. Brigham Young's portrait appeared in the center of each badge surrounded by the words "Utah Semi-Centennial Pioneer Jubilee." This lettering was blue enamel except for those survivors of Brigham Young's original company, whose pins had white lettering. At the top corner outside these letters appeared the beehive seal of the new state of Utah. The other three corners displayed a covered wagon, a pony express rider, and a locomotive. Railroad companies provided free transportation to Salt Lake City for any of the 1847 pioneers. A total of 663 appeared at the jubilee and received their badges. They participated in both the opening-day parade on July 20 and the final parade on July 24 and could attend all official events for free. Many also took part in the public memorial service on Sunday, July 25 that honored deceased pioneers.[21]

The speakers on that occasion placed the pioneers, living and dead, in the center of both Mormon and western history. As reported in the *Deseret News*, the major speaker, Joseph F. Smith of the church's First Presidency, stressed not only the leadership of Brigham Young in bringing the first pioneer band to Utah, but also the prediction of Joseph Smith about establishing the church in "the midst of the Rocky Mountains." Then he surmised, "The Pioneers, and those who followed them, were also blessed of the Lord in their arduous undertaking; and now Utah, after passing through persecution and suffering, caused by misunderstanding and misrepresentation, has emerged from privations, toils, travails and sufferings of early days, and has come up into the light and liberty and glory of a sovereign State in the great American Union. She is surrounded by other commonwealths whose beginnings grew out of the root planted here by the hand of the Pioneers."[22]

Joseph F. Smith grandly claimed primacy for Utah among western states. Fifty years on, with many of the first arrivals still alive to hear his words, the explanation of the past had become one of both religious and national triumph. The Mormon pioneers were important to the church and the Union. This story highlighted a celebration of religious identity that fused with a national narrative of western pioneering. Yet, this patriotic identity did not guarantee an end to anti-Mormon attitudes and images across the United States. Indeed, looking at popular representations of Utah Mormons and Southern Confederates well into the twentieth century, the white Southern rebels had the more readily positive image.

Not only David Blight, but also many other historians have grappled with the post–Civil War narratives of reconciliation and reunion that overwhelmed the counternarratives of emancipation and racial justice.[23] The acceptance of the "Lost Cause" in popular representation of the war and its aftermath became well established by the start of the twentieth century. As the historian Karen L. Cox explains, Confederate celebrations in the South expanded in the 1890s, supported by the United Confederate Veterans, the Sons of Confederate Veterans, and most especially by the United Daughters of the Confederacy (UDC). Founded in 1894, the UDC insisted on a pro-Southern interpretation of the Civil War. Aside from building heroic monuments and supporting romanticized reconciliation literature, these women fiercely monitored public schools to see that the proper version of the Southern past was taught. Also at both northern and southern colleges, with an eye toward training future teachers, the UDC sponsored scholarships to study and preserve Confederate history. Cox concludes that by the outbreak of World War I, "National reconciliation had been achieved effectively . . . on the Daughters' terms. The North had accepted the Lost Cause narrative as fact, which was an essential element of reunion."[24]

National reconciliation for the Latter-day Saints did not come as readily. The Daughters of the Utah Pioneers (DUP), first organized in April 1901, had idealistic intentions similar to the United Daughters of the Confederacy. They too sponsored monuments, publications, and events. For their fellow Mormons, the DUP provided an effective organization to perpetuate as its constitution stated, "the names and achievements of the men, women, and children" who founded Utah.[25] Yet, these women had little impact on changing national popular assumptions about Mormons. Indeed, by the time of World War I, when Lost Cause ideology may have reached its zenith in terms of national acceptance, Latter-day Saints still faced familiar attitudes about polygamy and patriarchy. The best indication of this ongoing conundrum may be seen with two major Hollywood silent films of that time. The first, *The Birth of a Nation*, released in early March 1915, retains great notoriety as cinematic art in support of white supremacy. The second, *A*

Mormon Maid, appeared on screen nearly two years later in February 1917.[26] Not nearly as well known, it provides fascinating comparisons with the first film.

The success of *The Birth of a Nation* lay not merely with the masterful work of the movie's director, D. W. Griffith, but also with its dramatic replication of Thomas Dixon Jr.'s 1905 novel *The Clansman: An Historical Romance of the Ku Klux Klan*. Not surprisingly, the cinematic Klansmen act heroically in Griffith's film, and audiences responded enthusiastically. Produced for over $100,000, *The Birth of a Nation* may have returned twenty million dollars from its distribution and possibly generated as much as one hundred million dollars in cash transactions, a financial bonanza that the cinema scholar James Monaco considers "an almost inconceivable amount for such an early film."[27] Desiring comparable success, Hollywood looked for additional historical epics, and Cecil B. DeMille at Famous Players–Lasky Studio decided to produce *A Mormon Maid*. A report in *Variety* recognized that this film provided "strait way drama of the strongest kind with not a single wasted foot, occupying the same relation to Mormonism that 'A Birth of a Nation' [sic] does to the colored question."[28] Supported by substantial advertising, *A Mormon Maid* attracted national attention in the press with its high quality production and its depiction of hooded evil Mormons on horseback who so resembled the KKK in their attire that the film's audience was informed that "this costume, but with the cross substituted for the eye, was later adopted by the Ku Klux Klan." In other words, for Hollywood's fake historical imagery, the evil secret sect of Mormon Danites could not wear crosses and could not be heroic like the KKK. The film does present a monogamous male Mormon hero in love with a young woman whose mother commits suicide after Brigham Young compelled her father to take a second wife. Although not unremittingly anti-Mormon, this cinematic melodrama does fit comfortably within the stream of more than forty major anti-Mormon films that appeared from 1905 to 1940.[29]

On the eve of World War II, Hollywood did produce *Brigham Young—Frontiersman* (1940) with a reported budget of $2,500,000 and an impressive cast that included Dean Jagger in the title role. Box office success did not follow, even with the film's grandly western theme and setting.[30] In fact, this positive treatment of Mormon history could not come close to matching the astounding success of perhaps the single most influential cinematic representation of Lost Cause history that had been released a year earlier, *Gone with the Wind* (1939). American audiences loved the fictional Scarlett O'Hara and Rhett Butler far more than the quasi-historical Brigham Young. Still, the tide of vehemently negative treatment of Mormon characters in film had at last started to ebb.

As for Latter-day Saints, their identification with a pioneer heritage marched forward throughout the twentieth century and into the early twenty-first century. Yet, not unlike the white South's evasion of the significance of slavery and its aftermath, Mormons showed little interest in the public recognition of the wars, diseases, and displacements that resulted for American Indians with the arrival of the pioneers. Mormons colonized Indian lands, thus becoming part of the larger "legacy of conquest," to use Patricia Nelson Limerick's phrase. When the occasion arose for grand monuments to the pioneer era, Indians received trifling representation. The two most prominent pioneer memorials in Utah give primacy to Brigham Young and his arrival in the valley of the Great Salt Lake. The first was erected as part of the sesquicentennial of the 1847 event, whereas the second celebrated the 1947 centennial. Only a single Indian figure appears on each monument situated below the heroic American Moses. The first statue may be readily viewed near Temple Square in downtown Salt Lake City, whereas the centennial monument anchors This Is the Place Heritage Park near the mouth of Emigration Canyon. The historian Cynthia Culver Prescott asserted that the artist Mahonri Young's design for This Is the Place represented a return to the "statuomania of the late nineteenth century," producing a monument "even more grandiose" than what the sculptor Cyrus Dallin had done in the 1890s for his depiction of Brigham Young. Prescott concluded that with the encouragement of church president Heber J. Grant, Mahonri Young "erected a monument that depicted LDS society in Utah as the fulfillment of American manifest destiny."[31]

In that nationalist spirit Mormons, especially in the Mountain West, continue to celebrate the 1847 arrival of the pioneers. The historian Jared Farmer observed that "LDS teenagers in Utah and Idaho are all but required to participate in at least one summer youth activity involving wagons or handcarts. Reenactments . . . cluster in July, when about 80 cities and towns in the Mormon heartland stage celebrations. The annual cycle of heritage climaxes on July 24, Pioneer Day—an official state holiday that eclipses Independence Day in many parts of Utah." The grandest celebration takes place in Salt Lake City with the Days of '47 Parade, purported to be the third largest annual parade in the United States.[32]

The Lost Cause has not retained as festive or positive an image. The rise of the civil rights movement, the impact of African American studies, and the ongoing cultural diversity of peoples within the South made the Lost Cause resemble a Last Stand for white supremacy. In New Orleans by the end of May in 2017, three monuments to Confederate leaders and a fourth to a violent Reconstruction-era insurrection carried out by racist whites had been taken down. In a remarkable statement, the city's mayor, Mitch Landrieu explained, "These statues are not just stone and metal. They are not just innocent remembrances of a benign history. These monuments purposefully celebrate a fictional, sanitized Confederacy; ignoring the death, ignoring the enslavement, and the terror that it actually stood for."[33]

Equally telling were the continuing battles over the display of the Confederate flag. This symbol of pride for white Southerners represented racial hatred toward African Americans in the minds of those no longer beguiled by Lost Cause romanticism. A significant turning point may have happened on June 14, 2016, when the Southern Baptist Convention (SBC) asked all Christians to stop displaying the Confederate battle flag because it offended millions of people who perceive it to be a "symbol of hatred, bigotry, and racism." Southern Baptists are possibly the largest Protestant denomination based in the United States with some 15.3 million members, of whom perhaps more than eighty percent are white. The church began in the mid-1840s with a split from northern Baptists over the issue of slavery and had a history of complicity with segregation in the South.[34] Yet, in the second decade of the twenty-first century this distinctly conservative religious denomination repudiated the most revered symbol of the Lost Cause.

Of course, many neo-Confederates, white supremacists, and regional heritage advocates will not heed the Southern Baptists, and even some Southern Baptist churches may not comply since they are independent congregations not required to follow SBC resolutions. Nonetheless, it seems worthwhile to consider that a century earlier in 1916, the acceptance of Lost Cause ideology had reached its apex and that public audiences easily accepted the heroic imagery of the KKK in novels and film. Now, a hundred years on, the Lost Cause seemed in obvious decline. Also, another major religious denomination with membership slightly larger than the SBC in 2016 at 15.6 million did not have to address any similar issue for its members.[35]

The Church of Jesus Christ of Latter-day Saints had effectively resolved its practice of polygamy more than a century earlier and had ended the exclusion of African heritage males from its priesthood in 1978. Clearly a conservative religious denomination in many social and political areas that today confronts protests from supporters of same-sex marriage, gay rights, women in the priesthood, and other issues, twenty-first century Mormons nonetheless in their own historical identity have not forged a Lost Cause symbolism. The church's April 2016 General Conference did not need to insist that offensive symbols of Mormon history be removed from public display. So statues of the Angel Moroni or Brigham Young and images of beehives and handcarts remained acceptable because they do not represent to millions a heritage of hatred, unlike the Confederate flag. Although American Indians have the right to object passionately, Mormons continue publicly to celebrate their pioneer ancestors. Unlike white Southerners, they have not wrapped themselves in a tattered symbol of failure and defeat. The seeds of such historical bitterness did not take root in the Great Basin Kingdom.

Notes

An earlier version of this essay first was published in the *Journal of Mormon History* 44, no. 2 (April 2018): 36–54. It is republished here by permission of the University of Illinois Press. The author wishes to thank Eric Eliason, Tom Alexander, Brian Cannon, Jared Farmer, and Cynthia Culver Prescott for their help and advice. He also wishes to dedicate this essay to the memory of Charles S. (Chas) Peterson and William A. (Bert) Wilson, who greatly expanded his understanding of Mormon history and culture as mentors, colleagues, and friends.

1. "Civil War Markers and Memorials," *The Encyclopedia of Arkansas History and Culture*, accessed August 23, 2016, http://www.encyclopediaofarkansas.net/encyclopedia/entry-detail.aspx?search=1&entryID=4794.

2. "The Battle of Jonesboro Remembered," KAIT Region8 News online, August 2, 2012, http://www.kait8.com/story/19184453/the-battle-of-jonesboro-remembered; "Jonesboro Group Fights for Confederate Flag," by Seth Stephenson, KAIT Region8 News online, June 27, 2015, http://www.kait8.com/story/29424397/jonesboro-group-fights-for-confederate-flag.

3. As noted below, the most important study for me is David W. Blight, *Race and Reunion: The Civil War in American Memory* (Cambridge, Mass.: Harvard University Press, 2001). Other books consulted for this essay include Rollin G. Osterweis, *Myth of the Lost Cause, 1865–1900* (Hamden, Conn.: Archon Books, 1973); Charles Reagan Wilson, *Baptized in Blood: The Religion of the Lost Cause, 1865–1920* (Athens: University of Georgia Press, 1980); Thomas L. Connelly and Barbara L. Bellows, *God and General Longstreet: The Lost Cause and the Southern Mind* (Baton Rouge: Louisiana State University Press, 1982); Gary W. Gallagher and Alan T. Nolan, eds., *The Myth of the Lost Cause and Civil War History* (Bloomington: Indiana University Press, 2000); David Goldfield, *Still Fighting the Civil War: The American South and Southern History* (Baton Rouge: Louisiana State University Press, 2002); Cynthia Mills and Pamela H. Simpson, eds., *Monuments to the Lost Cause: Women, Art, and the Landscapes of Southern Memory* (Knoxville: University of Tennessee Press, 2003); Caroline E. Janney, *Burying the Dead but Not the Past: Ladies' Memorial Associations and the Lost Cause* (Chapel Hill: University of North Carolina Press, 2008). Also see Grace Elizabeth Hale, "The Lost Cause and the Meaning of History," *Organization of American Historians Magazine of History* 27 (January 2013): 13–17. A recent publication that shows the continuing interest in understanding this topic is W. Stuart Towns, *Enduring Legacy: Rhetoric and Ritual of the Lost Cause* (Tuscaloosa: University of Alabama Press, 2012).

4. Caroline E. Janney, "The Lost Cause," *Encyclopedia Virginia* online, Virginia Foundation for the Humanities, accessed August 23, 2016, http://encyclopediavirginia.org/lost_cause_the#its1.

5. William Faulkner, *Requiem for a Nun*, act 1, scene 3 (1951).

6. Eric A. Eliason, "Pioneers and Recapitulation in Mormon Popular Historical Expression," in *Usable Pasts: Traditions and Group Expressions in North America*, ed. Tad Tuleja (Logan: Utah State University Press, 1997), 195.

7. Blight, *Race and Reunion*, 258–59.

8. Published annotated extracts from each of the two journals, written by William Z. Walker and Edward Jackson, may be found in Brian D. Reeves, "Two Massachusetts Forty-Niner Perspectives on the Mormon Landscape, July–August 1849," *BYU Studies* 38, no. 3 (1999): 123–44. The quotations are from Reeves's article. The originals are held in the L. Tom Perry Special Collections at the Harold B. Lee Library, Brigham Young University.

9. Augusta Cobb to Alexander and Mary Ann Badlam, July 20, 1849, in Laurel Thatcher Ulrich, *A House Full of Females: Plural Marriage and Women's Rights in Early Mormonism, 1835–1870* (New York: Alfred A. Knopf, 2017), 207; and Ulrich, *A House Full of Females*, 204–5.

10. John G. Turner, *Brigham Young: Pioneer Prophet* (Cambridge, Mass.: Harvard University Press, 2012), 197.

11. Steven L. Olsen, "Celebrating Cultural Identity: Pioneer Day in Nineteenth-Century Mormonism," *BYU Studies* 36, no. 1 (1996–97): 160.

12. Journal History of the Church, Church History Library, The Church of Jesus Christ of Latter-day Saints, Salt Lake City, can be accessed at http://eadview.lds.org/findingaid/CR%20100%20137 (accessed August 23, 2016).

13. In addition to the remarkable documentation in the Journal History of the Church, highlights from various annual Pioneer Days in Salt Lake City and elsewhere, including the dramatic events in 1857, are available in a pamphlet published by the Daughters of the Utah Pioneers, "Celebrating the 24th of July," compiled by Kate B. Carter, which originally appeared in *Heart Throbs of the West*, vol. 7, chap. 3 (September 1945).

14. Reid L. Neilson, *Exhibiting Mormonism: The Latter-day Saints and the 1893 Chicago World's Fair* (New York: Oxford University Press, 2011).

15. As reported in the *Deseret News* and preserved in the Journal History of the Church, the procession for the celebration of July 24, 1869, in Salt Lake City included "companies representing the various ways of immigration that have been used in times past to reach this Territory; there was the old slow-going ox team, the lighter mule team, the handcarts with the weary toilers, who dragged them across the plains a dozen or more years ago, again in harness for one short hour to show how the thing was done." See Volume 76 (July–September 1869, image 86) in Journal History of the Church. The driving of the golden spike had occurred the previous May 10 at Promontory Summit. Brigham Young did not attend this event, perhaps out of disappointment that the celebration and main rail route were not in Salt Lake City. Nonetheless, the LDS Church did send representatives. See Richard V. Francaviglia, *Over the Range: A History of the Promontory Summit Route*

of the Pacific Railroad (Logan: Utah State University Press, 2008), 132. Eventually, the completion of the first transcontinental railroad became part of the July 24 celebrations. Eric Eliason observed, "As the railroad closed off the time window of the 1847–69 pioneer era, it opened the possibility of a new progressive romanticism celebrating the modern world's arrival in Utah. Today the railroad can be seen on Pioneer Day as heralding the possibilities of Mormon/Gentile cooperation in Utah—a memory open for appreciation by a larger percentage of Utahans." See Eric Eliason, "The Cultural Dynamics of Historical Self-Fashioning: LDS Pioneer Nostalgia, American Culture, and the International Church," *Journal of Mormon History* 28, no. 2 (Fall 2002): 155.

16. Steven L. Olsen, "Pioneer Day," in *Utah History Encyclopedia*, ed. Allen Kent Powell (Salt Lake City: University of Utah Press, 1994), accessed August 23, 2016, https://www.uen.org/utah_history_encyclopedia/p/PIONEER_DAY.shtml.

17. Erastus Snow, *The Utah Pioneers: Celebration of the Entrance of the Pioneers into Great Salt Lake Valley, Thirty-Third Anniversary, July 24, 1880, Full Account of the Proceedings* (Salt Lake City: Deseret News Printing, 1880); and Kate B. Carter, "Celebrating the 24th of July," 96–98.

18. Stephen C. Taysom, "'There Is Always a Way of Escape': Continuity and Reconstitution in Nineteenth-Century Mormon Boundary Maintenance Strategies," *Western Historical Quarterly* 37 (Summer 2006): 202.

19. Anne Miller Eckman, "The Utah Pioneer Jubilee of 1897," in *Daughters of the Utah Pioneers Lesson for November 2010* (Salt Lake City: Pioneer Memorial Museum, 2010), 103.

20. Eckman, "Utah Pioneer Jubilee of 1897," 101; Anne Miller Eckman, "Joyful Jubilee," in *Daughters of the Utah Pioneers Lesson for February 2011* (Salt Lake City: Pioneer Memorial Museum, 2011), 254–300; and "This Is Still the Place: Utah's 1897 Pioneer Jubilee," online exhibit, Daughters of the Utah Pioneers, accessed August 23, 2016, http://www.dupinternational.org/jubilee/main.htm. Also see *Report and Financial Statement of the Utah Semi-Centennial Commission and Official Programme of the Utah Pioneer Jubilee Held at Salt Lake City, Utah, July 20 to July 25, 1897, in Commemoration of the Fiftieth Anniversary of the Arrival of the First Band of Pioneers in the Valley of the Great Salt Lake* (Salt Lake City: Deseret News Publishing, 1899).

21. Eckman, "Joyful Jubilee," 259–60. An image of the badge may be viewed online at "This Is Still the Place," accessed August 23, 2016, http://www.dupinternational.org/jubilee/main.htm.

22. *Deseret Evening News*, July 26, 1897, clipping in vol. 338 (July 24–31, 1897, images 184–87), Journal History of the Church, Church History Library, The Church of Jesus Christ of Latter-day Saints, Salt Lake City, accessed August 23, 2016, http://eadview.lds.org/findingaid/CR%20100%20137.

23. For an excellent overview of this debate see Nina Silber, "Reunion and Reconciliation, Reviewed and Reconsidered," *Journal of American History* 103 (June 2016): 59–83.

24. Karen L. Cox, *Dixie's Daughters: The United Daughters of the Confederacy and the Preservation of Confederate Culture* (Gainesville: University Press of Florida, 2003), 158; and Karen L. Cox, "Lost Cause Ideology," *Encyclopedia of Alabama* online, accessed August 22, 2016, http://www.encyclopediaofalabama.org/article/h-1643.

25. Linda Thatcher, "Daughters of Utah Pioneers," *Utah History Encyclopedia* online, accessed August 22, 2016, http://www.uen.org/utah_history_encyclopedia/d/DAUGHTERS_OF_UTAH_PIONEERS.shtml.

26. Tim Dirks, "The Birth of a Nation (1915)" *Filmsite Movie Review*, accessed August 22, 2016, http://www.filmsite.org/birt.html; and Richard Alan Nelson, "Commercial Propaganda in the Silent Film: A Case Study of 'A Mormon Maid' (1917)," *Film History* 1, no. 2 (1987): 157.

27. James Monaco, *How to Read a Film: Movies, Media, and Beyond*, 4th ed. (New York: Oxford University Press, 2009), 262. Also see Richard Brody, "The Worst Thing about 'Birth of a Nation' Is How Good It Is," *New Yorker*, February 1, 2013, http://www.newyorker.com/culture/richard-brody/the-worst-thing-about-birth-of-a-nation-is-how-good-it-is.

28. Review, "A Mormon Maid," *Variety* 45 (February 16, 1917): 23, quoted in Nelson, "Commercial Propaganda in the Silent Film: A Case Study of 'A Mormon Maid' (1917)," 154.

29. "Commercial Propaganda in the Silent Film: A Case Study of 'A Mormon Maid' (1917)," 150–54. Also see Jared Farmer, *Mormons in the Media, 1830–2012* (e-book, 2012), 144–45, accessed August 22, 2016, http://jaredfarmer.net/e-books/.

30. Harry Medved and Michael Medved, *The Hollywood Hall of Shame: The Most Expensive Flops in Movie History* (New York: Perigee Books, 1984), 205. The $2,500,000 cost of the film is reported in *Los Angeles Times*, September 3, 1940, p. 8.

31. Cynthia Culver Prescott, "Mormon Exceptionalism, Assimilation, and Americanness," chap. 4 in *Pioneer Mothers and the All-American Family: Memory in the Making of the Settlers' West* (Norman: University of Oklahoma Press, forthcoming). Citation with permission of author. For more insights about the "legacy of conquest," see Patricia Nelson Limerick, *The Legacy of Conquest: The Unbroken Past of the American West* (New York: W. W. Norton, 1987). Atop This Is the Place Monument, Brigham Young is flanked by Mormon leaders Heber C. Kimball and Wilford Woodruff. Below these three figures, at the base of the center column are Orson Pratt and Erastus Snow, members of a scouting party and the first to enter the valley on July 21, 1847. Scenes on the monument depict the Dominguez and Escalante expedition, mountain men, various explorers, wagon trains, and even the ill-fated Donner-Reed Party. Chief Washakie warrants a separate statue on the east side of the monument along with separate statues of five prominent mountain men and explorers: Etienne Provost, Peter Skene Ogden, Captain Benjamin Bonneville, Father Pierre-Jean De Smet, and John C. Frémont. See Tricia Smith-Mansfield, "This Is the Place Monument," *Utah History Encyclopedia*, https://www.uen.org/utah_history_encyclopedia/t/THIS_IS_THE_PLACE_MONUMENT.shtml.

32. Farmer, *Mormons in the Media*, 182–83. In present-day Utah, Pioneer Day is important, but it does not displace Independence Day in other locations. In Provo, Utah, for example, July Fourth is celebrated with a massive parade and an impressive fireworks event before a crowd that often exceeds more than sixty thousand people in Lavell Edwards Stadium at Brigham Young University. This set of events is known as "America's Freedom Festival at Provo," which has a website at https://www.freedomfestival.org/.

33. Peter Applebome, "New Orleans Mayor's Message on Race," *New York Times*, May 24, 2017, https://www.nytimes.com/2017/05/24/us/mitch-landrieu-speech-new-orleans.html.

34. Hannah Wise, "Southern Baptists Condemn Confederate Battle Flag as Racist," *Dallas Morning News*, June 14, 2016, http://www.dallasnews.com/news/religion/20160614-southern-baptists-condemn-confederate-battle-flag-as-racist.ece. Also see "Southern Baptists Oppose Confederate Flag, Talk Racial Unity," *New York Times*, June 14, 2016.

35. "2015 Statistical Report for April 2016 General Conference," April 2, 2016, http://www.mormonnewsroom.org/article/2015-statistical-report-april-2016-general-conference.

= 8 =

Whither Mormons' Lost Cause?

Collective Historical Memory in Comparison

Eric A. Eliason

Several years ago, I got a call from Clyde Milner, whom I had never met, but who was one of my idols as a graduate student. His much-thumbed *Oxford History of the American West* held pride of place on the closest bookshelf to my work space. He wanted to talk about my dissertation on LDS popular historical memory. I had assumed it went down the memory hole more than fifteen years before, right after it was written. Over lunch we discussed how collective memory is memorialized and ritualized and how pioneer commemorations such as July 24 celebrations helped reweave the Mormon story back into the central narrative of the United States, even though the people who actually trekked to Utah saw themselves as fleeing America. Yet the United States caught up with them, throwing its full military, political, legal, and cultural might into bringing Mormons into conformity with the will of U.S. politicians and their supporters. This was part of a larger Reconstruction project directed at not only Mormons but also American Indians and, most famously, the South. While the reconstruction of Mormonism was arguably the most successful of these three enterprises, LDS popular memory on this era is a virtual black hole of ignorance, unlike the "Lost Noble Cause" of neo-Confederates and their sympathizers, or for that matter the much-remembered (by American Indians) loss of land and sovereignty punctuated by infamous episodes such as the Trail of Tears and the Massacre at Wounded Knee. Why don't Mormons nurture the memory of their own loss of land and sovereignty? This essay proposes a few possibilities. In so doing, I occasionally slip from the detached scholarly tone I usually try to maintain in such venues. With Clyde's encouragement, and for the sake of elucidating certain key issues, I sometimes more forcefully articulate a pro-Deseret position than might be prudent within traditionally deferential and peaceable Mormondom.

The Role of the LDS Church

Central to understanding anything that happens in Mormon popular historical consciousness is a full consideration of the central role of the centralized hierarchy and pervasive authority of the Church of Jesus Christ of Latter-day Saints in the Mormon culture region. (Did you notice I said "central," or a variant, three times in one sentence? That was on purpose.) Except for a few divergent restorationist groups, Mormon identity and memory has been profoundly shaped by a long and well-developed tradition of top-down dissemination of ideas, policies, and priorities to all Mormons. I don't mean to imply anything sinister here, but only to make the ethnographic observation that devout Mormon identity by the choice of devout Mormons is closely bound to taking seriously the pronouncements of a leadership believed to be prophets of God. Mormons may even go further than asked here. An old saw goes, "Catholics doctrinally believe the Pope is infallible but don't act like it. While Mormons *don't* doctrinally believe the Prophet is infallible, but don't act like it." So, however the church decides to remember history is going to be very important to Mormon popular memory.

The Protestant South with its fragmented sects and uneven commitment to churches—despite the cultural power in recent decades of conservative evangelicals across denominations—has no central authority that could shape how people would think about sacred or quasi-sacred history. One church might decide nurturing a lost cause is a bad idea but could not stop others from taking it up. The unchurched or marginally churched might not listen anyway, or might just go to another church. Who cares what churches say on this topic anyway? Most Mormons would not be so cavalier.

What Lost Cause?

Many Mormons, even those familiar with the 1847–1905 period might earnestly wonder, "What lost cause?" Nothing ever happened that was not exactly what the Lord intended. We didn't lose anything. We moved forward obedient to the Lord's will. We stopped polygamy because President Wilford Woodruff got a revelation; government pressure had nothing to do with it. We would have gone on had the Lord asked. To entertain a notion of a lost cause would go against a strong perception, right or wrong, of not having bowed to federal pressure and of everything happening exactly according to the Lord's will as revealed to his prophets. Disinterested historians might agree in the broad outlines here, if not the theological framing. While the CSA has ceased to exist, the LDS hierarchy targeted by federal efforts trimmed only polygamy and theo-democracy, but kept, as Wilford Woodruff hoped,[1] missionary work, temples, and other church properties and programs. Church leadership bodies stayed intact and functioning throughout even the most difficult years of conflict—the logistical difficulties of the underground and the late-game excommunication of a few junior apostles notwithstanding. Even if we accept we lost something, we simply did not lose as big as the South, and we remain on a roll.

Missouri as Lost Cause

Another response to "Where is the Mormons' lost cause?" is "We do have one, but it is about Missouri, not Utah." The mobs, militias, expulsions, abandoned temples; Governor Boggs's extermination order, unheeded redress petitions, and Haun's Mill Massacre in Missouri are much more alive in Mormon minds than the Edmunds-Tucker Act, the Utah Commission, federal marshals on the prowl, the underground, safe houses, cohabs in prison stripes, and temples in receivership. We remember trying to build Zion in Missouri, that persecutions kicked us out, that this was, in part, God's punishment for our own sins, and we still nurture the vague hope that we may return to reclaim our birthright. And this is all canonized in the scriptural narrative of the Doctrine and Covenants. Our Utah experience has no scriptural analogue. We often trot out our typological Isaiah fulfillments of the "desert blossoming as a rose" and the establishment of the Salt Lake temple as the "mountain of the Lord's house."[2] But at the back of our minds, we all have long wondered if Utah is only a provisional Zion until we all take handcarts back to Jackson County, even as the expectation of this wanes further into the mists of memory, and the idea of Zion becomes, in emergent and prominent interpretations today, all of the Western Hemisphere or anywhere in the world where there is an LDS chapel. Or perhaps Zion is the righteous state of the community soul wherever there are any members at all.

Compared to Southern Lost Cause-ism, Mormon Missouri millenarian nostalgia/anticipation is pretty weak sauce. Tourists from Utah who leave the alpine snowcapped grandeur and fluttering aspen-rimmed crystal mountain streams of their homes to visit LDS Church history sites in the undifferentiated oppressive muggy mass of hot summer green supposed Eden in—according to folk theology—Missouri, often see their nostalgia wane even more. Over the decades, small handfuls of die-hard come-earliers have jumped the gun, bringing their food storage, vague employment plans, and idiosyncratic millennial expectations to Missouri. Locals call these zealots "gatherers." But they are few.

Mormons are Culturally Distinct from Southerners

There is a long, perhaps minority, tradition in the South of seeing the Civil War as divine retribution for the sin of slavery. This is not the lost cause narrative we are discussing here however. To Southern Lost Causers, Confederate efforts were noble, and the North won not by right but by might. Unlike this view, we Mormons often blame ourselves. Mormons don't have a lost cause *like* Southerners, rather, we have a lost cause *because of* Southerners—lawless Missouri pukes and proslavery vigilantes who burned us out of our homes in Jackson, Caldwell, and Clay Counties. Comparing Mormon and Southern historical experiences, cultural mores, and interactions with each other merits further investigation for answering why Mormons don't have a lost cause.

In the 1990s, my wife served as a copyeditor for a publication of all the redress petitions Mormons made against Missourians who destroyed and stole their property.[3] It makes for sad reading. "Lost: one horse, 30 acres burned. Lost: one house and one barn with tools and 20 bushels wheat stores." There are hundreds of such petitions. The books sold reasonably well for an obscure collection of primary sources. If there were to be a touchstone document set for the Mormon version of unfulfilled promises and unredressed wrongs from years ago like African Americans' "40 acres and a mule" or the Palestinians' "I want my house and date orchard back," the redress petitions would be it. But outside history buffs, no one knows about them. I know of no movement to "get our Missouri land back." By the way, through my wife, I would likely be a beneficiary if there were one. But living in Utah and having been to Missouri, I'm not interested, really. The Missouri experience could have been catechized into the centerpiece of a Mormon grievance culture as alive today as in the 1830s. But it is not. Whatever it might have been in the past is even more petered out now. The 1985 official hymnal downplayed grievances in many old hymn lyrics, including changing the line "remember the *wrongs* of Missouri" to "remember the *trials* of Missouri" in the hymn "Up Awake Ye Defenders of Zion."[4] Wrongs need be avenged; trials purify the soul.

Mormons have forgotten Albert Sidney Johnston's depredations against them in the Utah War; neo-Confederates honor him as a hero of the Lost Cause martyred at Shiloh. Why have we Mormons failed to thoroughly exploit the potential of our history? David Hackett Fischer may give us a clue in his fascinating *Albion's Seed*, which chronicles the transplantation of British regional cultures to regions of colonial America and the perpetuation of certain sets of values up to this day.[5] Mormons are not Scots-Irish Southerners culturally primed for hair trigger sensitivity and flamboyant responses to the slightest perceived insult.[6] We are sober New England Yankees, respectable north English tradespeople, and unassuming Danish farmers.

Mormon leaders' New England root culture values orderliness, piety, industry, self-discipline, self-improvement, thrift, circumspection, decorum, and a blend of attenuated non-aristo-phile hierarchy with a not-quite leveler sense of equality. Nathan Hatch pointed out long ago, and more recently Terryl Givens elaborated on, the curious mix of Joseph Smith extending the priesthood to all men but then organizing those men into clear lines of authority still seen today in the organizational leadership portraits published in every conference *Ensign* centerfold.[7] Notably the smiling faces on these charts seem, like most Mormons, comfortable in their role in the position in their hierarchy wherever it may be.

The ethnic core of Mormondom that still undergirds those leadership charts comprises mostly two waves of English immigrants, one in the 1600s that peopled New England, whose inhabitants then peopled the Western Reserve from whence many early converts came. The next wave of Englishness came via LDS missionary efforts from the 1830s to 1880s. For much of the nineteenth century, there were more Mormons in England than in Utah. Most of them eventually immigrated, making Utah today the most English-heritage state in a nation where German, African, Irish, and Mexican heritaged peoples each outnumber those who claim English ancestry.[8] Both English waves that fed into Mormondom came from parts of the British Isles that Fischer describes as having the mores that continue to be advocated by church leaders. Like New England Yankees, British Mormon converts tended to be opposed to slavery.

Conversely, Southerners have historically been disproportionately Scots-Irish borderlanders steeped in outlaw culture, dissolute, riotous, fatalistic, xenophobic, and uninterested in self-improvement. Nonetheless, they have cultivated a fiercely proud honor culture steeped in values of martial prowess and vigilante violence. Key to this has been nurturing an acute awareness and long memory of the slightest wrongs and the need to avenge them. Their history displays a comfort with inequality and dominance as long as they were on top, and a willingness to subjugate others, particularly to slavery. This is a very different stance toward the world. (If you are a Southerner and these observations seem like accusations that demand a response, you are proving my point nicely.) Clashing values helped lead to actual clashes in Missouri in the 1830s, Kansas in the 1850s, and along the whole of the Mason-Dixon Line in the early 1860s.

Notably, some Southerners were among nineteenth and early twentieth century LDS converts who gathered to Zion. LDS missionaries and members in the South were subject to beatings and murder and other persecutions long after such behavior died out everywhere else. These Southern converts were, perhaps tellingly, often kept at arm's length from Salt Lake City and called to settle in the remote Mormon culture region outpost of the San Luis Valley of Colorado.[9]

These views of ethnicity are largely retrospective and, while they may have applied somewhat in the past to non-Mormon Protestant Anglo-Americans, they do not represent how Gentiles viewed Mormon ethnicity at the time. Paul Reeve has shown how nineteenth-century conceptions of race were easily disconnected from ancestral history and allowed for quick degeneration, a process that especially applied to non-Christian theocratic polygamy-practicing Mormons who, in essence, turned themselves into benighted Africans and Asiatics.[10] Quite a different state of affairs from today where Mormons, in part through our own efforts such as the priesthood ban and flirtations with British Israelitism,[11] have endeavored to portray ourselves as the whitest white people who ever whited. And have succeeded just in time for this totally to not be cool anymore in our multicultural age.

Mormons' Weak Martial Culture and Mountain Meadows

Compared to Southern celebration of their own martial values and skill, Mormon military history reveals a meager heritage. Only history nerds know about Crooked River and its indeterminate outcome in a larger conflict we lost. The Nauvoo Legion always seemed more for public pageantry, and its only major engagement in Illinois, The Battle of Nauvoo, was a covering action under enemy artillery fire for a retreat to avoid civil war. We won Utah's Black Hawk War only after tremendous initial setbacks and after abandoning several towns. Brigham Young worked hard to make sure it did not draw federal attention, but it eventually required the arrival of the U.S. military to secure the peace. Despite several decades of veterans' organizations and parades in subsequent years, it has fallen down the memory hole today—completely uncelebrated.[12]

Perhaps our most glorious military victory was ridiculously against stampeding feral cows in the Battle of the Bulls in the Mexican-American War, in which the Mormon Battalion had no other engagements.[13] Our history contains strains of pacifism and nonlethal resistance. Our main historical *modus operandi* has been a preference for "retreat and rebuild" rather than "stand your ground."

There is of course one dramatic exception. Our greatest tactical victory in a campaign of otherwise disciplined nonlethal resistance during the Utah War was the Mountain Meadows Massacre.[14] It was a complex plan that relied on tight control and discipline and a great deal of luck to be pulled off as smoothly as it was. It was executed like clockwork and was totally successful in its immediate tactical objectives. Yet it was straightaway regarded as a disastrous strategic and moral mistake—now widely seen as the darkest of black marks on our history. We didn't tout it as a victory, but in our deep shame tried to blame it on the Indians and bury its memory. Compare this to the "battles," as they were initially called, of Bear River and Wounded Knee that came to be seen as massacres of women and children much like Mountain Meadows. At the time though, these two episodes were hailed as great victories, which produced many commendations for the military participants. But such were the standards to which we held ourselves, and such were the stringent double standards others applied to us at the time, that Mormons rightly understood that we, unlike the U.S. Army, would get no grace period in which to relish a victory over disarmed men, women, and children before the backlash laid in.[15]

It is impossible to celebrate any nineteenth-century Mormon resistance struggle with a military dimension no matter how restrained, nonlethal, and noble overall without the exceptional Mountain Meadows sticking its ugly head in and poisoning all remembrance. Perhaps this, as well, checks any lost cause sentimentality we may want to wallow in.

Our Lost Cause Falls Outside Our Typologically Constrained Historical Attention Frame

The events that reconstructed Mormonism into a shape preferred by U.S. politicians did not happen in Missouri or Illinois, from which we fled with our autonomy intact; they happened in Utah when we had nowhere left to run. In Utah, moralistic do-gooders and economic opportunists backed by federal power could hammer us until we resembled what they wanted. These actions happened outside the time period of Mormon historical consciousness, which begins in 1820 and ends in 1847. Joseph Smith's founding visions and the Great Trek make for a nice biblically typological recapitulation of the founding of Christianity and the exodus. No scripture emerged from the pioneer period, except one to organize wagon trains and one declaration devoid of doctrinal content that merely stopped polygamy; it was only seen fully as a revelation later and is still not even dignified by induction into full section status in The Doctrine and Covenants.

Maybe 1890 initiated our Babylonian exile? Are we still waiting for our Darius? Are we still living typologically? Not really. We have made our peace and have saved and expanded out temples. For decades we have swum in the American mainstream and touted our hyper-Americanism. Perhaps any given society, even one as history-conscious as ours, can only muster so much attention for its own past and must prioritize which eras it will focus on. The fascinating post-1847 period doesn't make the cut. History starts again with the 1960s renewal of rapid church growth. The international growth of the church, especially in Latin America, and the end of the priesthood ban on blacks have rekindled our historical imagination for a late-twentieth-century saga.

Perhaps we just don't have time for sections of our past that don't fit the narrative, especially if they raise difficult questions for our modern sensibilities and priorities.

Nineteenth versus Twenty-First Century Mormon Priorities

Many Mormons today have ambiguous, even negative, feelings about polygamy, theocracy, and state-run "cooperative" economies. They don't square with current political beliefs and religious practice. Like most people, Mormons can be presentist in projecting back onto the past the assumption that we always thought and did things the same. It is disconcerting to find this not the case. It is easier not to go there.

Lost Cause Southerners try to convince themselves that the Civil War—sorry, War Between the States—sorry, War of Northern Aggression—was not about defending slavery but about the nobler conceptions of states' rights and decentralized power. Noble goals perhaps, but what did Southerners intend to do with their decentralized states' rights? Answer: preserve slavery.

Maybe if we Mormons convince ourselves that our resistance was not about polygamy *per se* but about religious freedom and freedom of conscience, we would have a start on a noble lost cause. There would be some legitimacy to this as, unlike our Quaker-persecuting Puritan forefathers, Mormons have been pretty Kantian in holding to a categorical imperative perspective on religious freedom. Consider Joseph Smith's recently reiterated famous quotes:

> The same principle which would trample upon the rights of the Latter-day Saints would trample upon the rights of the Roman Catholics, or of any other denomination who may be unpopular and too weak to defend themselves. It is a love of liberty which inspires my soul—civil and religious liberty to the whole of the human race.

And the Nauvoo City Council ordinance reinstated with similar wording in Salt Lake City:

> Be it ordained by the City Council of the City of Nauvoo, that the Catholics, Presbyterians, Methodists, Baptists, Latter-day Saints, Quakers, Episcopals, Universalists, Unitarians, Mohammedans [Muslims], and all other religious sects and denominations whatever, shall have free toleration, and equal privileges in this city.[16]

And the scripturally enshrined Eleventh Article of Faith saying:

> We claim the privilege of worshiping Almighty God according to the dictates of our own conscience, and allow all men the same privilege, let them worship how, where, or what they may.

Such ideas inspired thinking in pioneer Utah that continues to this day in LDS defenses of religious freedom for those who would use that freedom to believe and act even in conflict with LDS values.[17] But going fully in this direction might entail returning to arguing, as church lawyers did before the Supreme Court with *Reynolds*, that marriage is an issue of individual conscience that the state has no business defining in one way or another. This might be hard to square with the church's position over the last few years. So, maybe the less we go there, the better.

LDS Lost Cause nurturing might also go crosswise with current church public relations goals. The polygamous underground, safe houses, daring escapes from federal marshals, flouting the law and going to jail for "the Principle" are difficult to square with the obedient-to-law image the church tries to convey to foster its worldwide missionary efforts. The famous, to historians at least, picture of George Q. Cannon posing proudly with his pals in prison stripes (figure 8.1) is probably not the image we want Chinese government officials to see as they consider whether allowing Mormons to worship freely in China would be disruptive to a well-ordered state. We have invested a lot and paid a steep price for our in-through-the-front door policy. We are stuck in the starting block in the race for converts (if there is such a thing) while Jehovah's Witnesses, Seventh

FIGURE 8.1. Charles Roscoe Savage, "Portrait of Mormon Polygamists in Prison, at the Utah Penitentiary," circa 1889.
Courtesy Church History Collections, The Church of Jesus Christ of Latter-day Saints and Intellectual Reserves, Inc.

Day Adventists, and numerous evangelical groups with far fewer persnickety qualms about ignoring the corrupt and oppressive whims of tyrannical states race ahead. They creatively find ways to get missionaries and materials into restricted environments; Mormons are obliged not to. Any memories of past Mormon civil disobedience and placing God's laws above man's is not particularly useful to the overriding goals of the moment—getting permission from governments for the church to operate in their countries.

Lost Causes and Christian Commitment

Lost causes are difficult to square with Christian commitment—turning the other cheek, rendering unto Caesar, if forced to go a mile then going twain, forgiving and forgetting, letting go of self-righteous grudge holding, and forgoing idolatrous adoration of old bearded generals, are all central tenets of pious Christian living. The Mormon West and evangelical South are rival regions, each making a vigorous claim to best represent authentic Christian religiosity. Perhaps I would be violating authentic Christian humility to even ask what the South's nurturing a Lost Cause versus the Mountain West's lack of one might tell us about where the real Christians live.

The Mormon Case for a Genuinely Noble Lost Cause

This having been said, a good case can be made for Mormondom having a better case for a truly noble lost cause than the South if we wanted one. We never fired on Fort Sumter. We didn't start anything. When invaded, we mostly followed a disciplined policy of nonlethal resistance—Mountain Meadows being the single and overshadowing exception. And our leadership maintained its loyalty to the United States throughout the Mormon conflict despite our differences. The first-ever telegraph out of Salt Lake City on July 23, 1861, from Brigham Young to President Lincoln read, "Utah has not seceded but is firm for the Constitution and laws of our once happy country."[18]

Much nineteenth-century political thought portrayed antislavery and antipolygamy efforts as emerging from the same reformist impulse and as enjoying the same moral mandate.[19] However, while antipolygamy and antislavery campaigns may have shared some of the same spirit and rhetoric of Victorian Protestant sensibility, their effects and moral basis were almost diametrically opposed. There are fundamental differences between the first and second "relic of barbarism" (of the Republican Party's first platform) and the regional governments that protected them.

In the South the slaves were in bondage; they were the least enfranchised people in the country. Their African religious expressions were suppressed and their Christian expressions forcibly channeled and constrained. The slaves were held down by the complex and effective exercise of threats and applications of physical terror—a system that survived in modified Jim Crow form long after it became illegal to own another person.[20]

On the other hand, unlike in the South, and contrary to popular literary stereotypes, no systematically organized posses chased after those who decided to leave Utah and plural marriage.[21] Rather than compelling people to stay, Brigham Young on several occasions invited the dissatisfied to leave the territory if they wished, even if it meant defaulting on loans from the church that had allowed them to emigrate to Utah. Some took up this offer and left for California gold fields or elsewhere, but most freely decided to stay.

Rather than being disenfranchised by Deseret, Mormon women, the alleged victims of "polygamic theocracy," were on the cutting edge of female suffrage in the United States. They were the first American women to vote in municipal elections.[22] In Deseret before "Americanization," Mormon women were freer to practice their religion and exercise their political rights than they were anywhere else in the United States. That Mormon women overwhelmingly practiced plural marriage as a religiously motivated personal choice is forcefully and frequently stated in their own writings, public and private.[23]

A central piece of the effort to establish full federal hegemony in Utah was to strip women of their franchise in order to reduce Mormon political power—an effort condemned by national suffrage leaders such as Elizabeth Cady Stanton and Susan B. Anthony—and then not only polygamist men but all Mormon men were to be disenfranchised. Federal action subjected Utah's populace to imprisonment and harassment and made them less free to practice their religion and exercise their civil rights. Mormons did not demand a level of religious tolerance that they were not willing to extend to others. Deseret law required, and Brigham Young forcefully advocated, religious freedom for everyone. He even set aside land for Salt Lake City's Catholic Cathedral.

It is ironic that this time period is often referred to as the "Americanization of Utah." People are not "Americanized" by taking away their most American of rights—the right to vote, the right to free exercise of religion, and the right to be free from unreasonable seizure and imprisonment. In sum then, Reconstruction in the South sought to *expand* the civil rights and freedoms of an oppressed formally enslaved minority while the reconstruction or "Americanization of Utah" *constricted* the civil rights and freedoms of an oppressed religious minority. In this sense, they were different endeavors entirely.

Forgotten Flags and Military Service: "If You Can't Beat 'Em, Join 'Em"

Despite having a moral case for a lost cause based on denial of religious liberty, Utah—not Deseret anymore—does not proclaim one. There is very little interest in it. This is evident by how few Mormons recognize this flag:

This is a common variant of the flag of the nascent State of Deseret snuffed out by federal power. I fly it from my house on Pioneer Day, Brigham Young's Birthday, and other such occasions. I live in a small town in Utah. Everyone on both sides of my street is Mormon. People ask me if it is the Greek or Israeli flag. Only one neighbor, a history buff, recognized it. The Stars and Bars of course are

FIGURE 8.2. Re-creation of an alleged Mormon flag, based on an 1877 description by Don Maguire. Were this a color image, the black would be a blue like that of the Israeli flag. Both this "Deseret flag" and the Israeli flag use this color because of its use traditionally in Hebrew scripture.
Courtesy of Wikimedia Commons.

immediately recognizable throughout the South (and the world for that matter) and are displayed all the time in all sorts of ways for all sorts of reasons.

But on any given Fourth of July in Utah, the Stars and Stripes come out in force, sometimes with the assistance of LDS deacons who plant flags in everyone's yard in the neighborhood. Who could be more patriotic than Utah Mormons? Well, curiously perhaps, Southerners and American Indians. Both groups serve disproportionately in the U.S. military, and rates of military service have been seen as a sign of the patriotism within a community.[24] Go to any Southern or American Indian cemetery and see how many American flags and military-provided gravestones you see. Few groups have clearer historical reasons to bear animus toward the U.S. military as Southerners, Indians, and Mormons, and many of those who serve today are descendants of those who fought against it. This may be in part due to the traditional warrior/honor culture of Southerners and Indians, where manhood is obtained through rites of passage that prove one's mettle, and the military provides a good opportunity for this. Recent studies have shown that it seems not due to the military providing opportunities for, or taking advantage of, the poverty stricken. Military recruits, at least in the last several decades, tend to skew more educated and upper-middle class than the general population.[25]

How much is it the hyper-Americanism of people who once fought against federal authority in an attempt to counter suspicions of lack of patriotism? Or how much is it "if you can't beat 'em, join 'em" and the opportunities this provides for taking control of instruments of power that once worked against you and making them your own. I am not sure, but it is interesting to think about.

The moment, if there ever was one, for a Mormon lost cause may be waning even more as the Mormon consciousness becomes more international. Converts internationally likely have little time for the historical minutiae not even interesting to Mormondom's American minority. My students from the eastern U.S. often feel nothing for, or even averse to, plains-crossing pioneer reverencing treks and talks, even though this has considerable official church sanction. It seems the fight for a Mormon lost cause, if there ever was one, is—I am not necessarily sorry to say—lost.

Notes

1. Doctrine and Covenants: Official Declaration 1, Cache Stake Conference, Logan, Utah, November 1, 1891, reported in *Deseret Weekly*, November 14, 1891.

2. Isaiah 35:1 and 2:1–5.

3. Clark Johnson, *Mormon Redress Petitions: Documents of the 1833–1838 Missouri Conflict*, Religious Studies Center Monograph Series, vol. 16 (Salt Lake City: Bookcraft, 1992).

4. Douglas Campbell, "Changes in LDS Hymns: Implications and Opportunities," *Dialogue: A Journal of Mormon Thought* 28, no. 3 (Fall 1995): 73.

5. David Hackett Fischer, *Albion's Seed: Four British Folkways in America* (New York: Oxford University Press, 1989).

6. Scots-Irish cultural impact is far larger than what Southerners' self-reported ethnic backgrounds might suggest. People of Scots-Irish descent tend to claim "American" as their only ethnic background, being either unaware of their deep ancestry, or unwilling to share it with busybody demographers, or both. (In contrast, western Mormons are likely the most ancestrally aware Americans, and tend to be eager to tell you the religious reasons why they are.) Also, well-known historical settlement patterns suggest many Southerners reporting "Irish" backgrounds spring not from the Catholic south but the Protestant north—hence Scots-Irish. Perhaps most significantly, Fischer's thesis does not posit that everyone who participates in a regional culture necessarily shares bloodlines, rather subsequent arrivals from elsewhere learn to conform to an influential founding population's values and mores. This well describes the South's relationship to the Scots-Irish. The English language's dominance in the United States—despite most Americans descending from non-English speaking peoples—is a good national example of the power of a founding and dominant group's cultural impact.

7. Nathan Hatch, *The Democratization of American Christianity* (New Haven, Conn.: Yale University Press, 1991); Terryl Givens, *People of Paradox: A History of Mormon Culture* (New York: Oxford University Press, 2012).

8. "People of German Ancestry Dominate U.S. Melting Pot," *Voice of America*, December 19, 2014, http://blogs.voanews.com/all-about-america/2014/12/19/people-of-german-ancestry-dominate-us-melting-pot/.

9. Patrick Mason, *The Mormon Menace: Violence and Anti-Mormonism in the Postbellum South* (New York: Oxford University Press, 2011).

10. Paul Reeve, *Religion of a Different Color: Race and the Mormon Struggle for Whiteness* (New York: Oxford University Press, 2015).

11. See for example the influential book by later church president Joseph Fielding Smith surmising that the geographic distribution in the British Isles and Nordic countries of Mormon missionary success demonstrates the presence of the blood of Israel in those lands. *Man, His Origin, and His Destiny* (Salt Lake City: Deseret Book, 1954).

12. John Alton Peterson, *Utah's Black Hawk War* (Salt Lake City: University of Utah Press, 1999).

13. Norma Ricketts, *Mormon Battalion: United States Army of the West, 1846–1848* (Logan: Utah State University, 1997).

14. This action focused on an overland party from Arkansas that was not part of the invading U.S. forces but that Mormons feared might assist them. That they were Southerners, neighbors of Missourians, rumored to be bragging about killing Joseph Smith probably didn't help their case either.

15. Ronald W. Walker, Richard E. Turley, and Glen M. Leonard, *Massacre at Mountain Meadows* (New York: Oxford University Press, 2011).

16. "Religious Freedom Ordinance in Relation to Religious Societies, City of Nauvoo, (Illinois) Headquarters of The Church of Jesus Christ of Latter-day Saints, March 1, 1841," in "Church Points to Joseph Smith's Statements on Religious Freedom, Pluralism," December 8, 2015, http://www.mormonnewsroom.org/article/church-statement-religious-freedom-pluralism.

17. In the 1990s the LDS Church supported the Religious Freedom Restoration Act (RFRA) even though it would protect the religious use of narcotics such as cannabis, peyote, and DMT-containing plants not part of LDS worship and condemned by many Mormon religious conservatives. "Elder Oaks Testifies Before U.S. Congressional Subcommittee," *Ensign*, July 1992, https://www.lds.org/ensign/1992/07/news-of-the-church/elder-oaks-testifies-before-u-s-congressional-subcommittee?lang=eng.

18. Twila van Leer, "Telegraph Link Electrified the Nation," *Salt Lake Tribune*, January 28, 1996, https://www.deseretnews.com/article/468297/TELEGRAPH-LINK-ELECTRIFIED-THE-NATION.html.

19. See for example the preface of A. G. Paddock's *The Fate of Madam La Tour: A Story of the Great Salt Lake* (New York: Fords, Howard, and Hulbert, 1881), 366, which touted itself as doing "for Mormonism what 'Uncle Tom's Cabin' did for Slavery." Harriet Beecher Stowe equated the antipolygamy crusade with antislavery in her "introductory preface," to Mrs. T. B. H. Stenhouse, *Tell It All: The Story of A Life's Experience in Mormonism* (Cincinnati: Queen City Publishing, 1874), no page numbers given for the introductory preface.

20. On historical understandings of American slavery see for example Peter J. Parish, *Slavery: History and Historians* (New York: Harper and Row, 1989). On the religious situation of slaves see Albert J. Raboteau, *Slave Religion: The "Invisible Institution" in the Antebellum South* (Oxford: Oxford University Press, 1978).

21. Leonard J. Arrington and Jon Haupt, "Intolerable Zion: The Image of Mormonism in Nineteenth Century American Literature," *Western Humanities Review* 22 (Summer 1968): 243–60.

22. Seraph Young was the first woman to vote after the passage of the Utah State suffrage bill. Richard Poll and Thomas Alexander, *Utah: The Right Place* (Logan: Utah State University Press), 180.

23. For a general overview of Mormon defenses of plural marriage see B. Carmon Hardy, "The Blessings of the Abrahamic Household," in *Solemn Covenant: The Mormon Polygamous Passage* (Urbana: University of Illinois Press, 1992): 84–126; and David J. Whittaker, "Early Mormon Polygamy Defenses," *Journal of Mormon History* 11 (1984): 43–63. For female defenses of polygamy see Helen Mar Whitney, *Plural Marriage as Taught by the Prophet Joseph: A Reply to Joseph Smith, Editor of the Lamoni (Iowa) "Herald"* (Salt Lake City: Juvenile Instructor Office, 1882). Also see Helen Mar Whitney, *Why We Practice Plural Marriage: By a "Mormon" and Mother* (Salt Lake City: Juvenile Instructor Office, 1884). Claudia L. Bushman, ed., *Mormon Sisters* (Cambridge, Mass.: Emmeline Press, 1976) provides a number of essays that give insight into the political and social views of women regarding polygamy and feminism. See especially Stephanie Smith Goodson, "Plural Wives," 89–112, and Judith Rasmussen Dushku, "Feminists," 177–98.

24. Despite Mormons' reputation for patriotism and generally promilitary attitudes, many LDS young men opt for missions in their fighting-age years, marry and start families younger, and are more likely to go to college. Even with these significant deterrents to military service, we Mormons hold our own proportionally in military service rates. "While Romney Didn't Serve in Military, Many Mormons Do," Reuters, November 2, 2012, http://www.reuters.com/article/us-usa-campaign-mormons-military-idUSBRE8A11HA20121103. There are some segments of the military like the Army Green Berets and the Air Force officer corps that seem to be disproportionately Mormon.

25. Stephen J. Dubner, "Who Serves in the Military Today?" *Freakonomics*, September 22, 2008, http://freakonomics.com/2008/09/22/who-serves-in-the-military-today/; "Who's Volunteering for Today's Military, Myths vs. Facts," Military.com, http://www.military.com/Recruiting/Content/0,13898,062006-who-joining-marines-today-myth-fact,,00.html?ESRC=recruiting.nl.

= 9 =

The Mormon Cause, Lost and Found

Jared Farmer

The Lost Cause is a weaponized story about the Civil War and its aftermath. For most of the twentieth century, a coalition of white Americans deployed it in service of a *winning* cause. Although Confederates had surrendered in defeat, their postbellum sympathizers prevailed in the memory war. Their fallacious and malicious interpretation of Reconstruction provided a justification for white supremacy in the former Confederate states, and an apology for white privilege across the entire United States. Even after the hard-won successes of the civil rights movement—and the revolution it inspired in the historical discipline—an army of Southerners defended the old narrative regime, conferring the honorific "heritage" upon this historiographical hatemongering.

At first glance, Utah Mormons would seem to have common ground with Southerners as white regionalists with legacies of "peculiar institutions." Like the South, Utah was "defeated" and "reconstructed" by the federal government—indeed, by feds aligned with the party of Lincoln. Before the war, Republicans rhetorically connected Utah to the South—another bastion of another barbaric "relic"—and after the war, they followed through politically. Unfree marriage, like unfree labor, had to be vanquished by liberty.

However, the absence of *military* loss and *sovereign* defeat deprived Utah Mormons of various memory-rich possibilities: a prophet who actually earned the title general; a Nauvoo Legion that grew into a regular army; a Council of Fifty that became a war council; a polygamist resistance that went down fighting instead of hiding; tactical losses that could be glorified as deeds of courage, honor, and sacrifice; battlefields that could be consecrated as sacred ground; fallen boys who could be heroized with tombstones and statues; women and children who could be valorized as domestic defenders or homefront victims; and Deseret battle flags that could be waved and planted. In short, the storehouse of "useful" material for Dixie-style memorialization in the newly forty-fifth state was quite bare. It remains so. Not even stalwart Daughters of the Utah Pioneers sing out: "Remember Echo Canyon!" LDS martyrology remains mired in Missouri and Illinois (and, to some extent, Winter Quarters, Nebraska, and Martins Cove, Wyoming). In public memory, Mormons stopped dying of unnatural, unjust causes once they arrived in the Great Basin. The most terrible massacres in territorial history—Mountain Meadows, Circleville, Bear River—featured Mormon aggressors or beneficiaries, and for over a century the LDS Church did nothing to commemorate the victims or the sites.

Instead of Johnny Reb's gray kepi in the attic, Mormons have flowery sunbonnets. In the Mormon culture region, "heritage" connotes westering, wagoning, handcarting, Dutch-oven cooking, road cutting, cabin raising, tabernacle building, town planning, tree planting, crop irrigating, and so on. The Turnerian figure of the pioneer overshadows everything, including the Civil War, and everyone, including the state's Native peoples. Brigham Young inaugurated Pioneer Day practically from the moment he colonized Ute and Shoshone land for his Zionist project. Whereas expulsion from Jackson County was remembered as a trail of despair, evacuation from Nauvoo was reconceived as a trail of hope—an accelerated exodus leading to a promised land. Pioneerism repaired the group identity of displaced American Mormons, survivors of trauma and schism, and forged a congruent identity for emigrating British and Danish Mormons. It was a mission in ethnogenesis.

In retrospect, Latter-day Saints could not have chosen a safer theme for internal commemoration in the national context of settler colonialism. Although U.S. Protestants maligned Mormonism as the definition of un-religion—too illegitimate to earn pejoratives like heretical religion, or even false religion—the vocabulary and values of pioneerism provided a racial common cause, and conveyed to Mormons a kernel of Americanness that no amount of Orientalization could eradicate. Even the most censorious opponents of LDS theocracy and polygamy could praise Mormon settlers for "reclaiming the waste desert land" with irrigation, for making it "blossom as a rose." In reference to irrigation, outsiders lauded Saints for their communalism, cooperation, and consensus—the same qualities that presumably made the LDS Church a political threat. Mormons and non-Mormons alike encouraged the false historical memory that the Pioneer Camp of 1847 had encountered an arid wilderness devoid of trees—and people. This triumphal and implicitly racist story appealed to a broad section of Anglo-Americans.

Latter-day Saints of the 1890s—the critical decade for neo-Confederate myth-making—had no incentive to promulgate a competing narrative of religious subnationalism. Such a story would have validated past accusations, hardly unfounded, of their theocratic ambitions. A new lost cause about the State of Deseret would have stymied the ongoing cause of Utah statehood. Whereas white Southerners, using race, could and did convert plenty of Northerners to their Lost Cause, Latter-day Saints, using religion, could not expect to find any allies among American Protestants. Better to subsume LDS kingdom-building, increasingly a metaphor, under American pioneering. This narrative strategy took stage at the Columbian Exposition in Chicago in 1893, when the soon-to-be State of Utah bravely erected a pavilion. The exhibition included looted Indian (*not* Lamanite) artifacts—an ethnographic move that placed Mormons within "white civilization"—and a statue of Brigham Young as a pioneer (*not* potentate). Mormons recapitulated this Americanist theme on Statehood Day in 1896, when they literally wrapped the Salt Lake Temple in the Stars and Stripes.

On the legal path to statehood, Utah Mormons encountered an insurmountable drawbridge. Only Congress could open the castle: territories, unlike states, have no rights under the U.S. Constitution. Whereas Southern states claimed state sovereignty (including secession power) under the federal system, and then national sovereignty under their own Confederate constitution, Utah Territory (1850–96) remained an unambiguous dependency. Absent the Second Coming, the legislative branch reigned supreme, and Congress decreed that Utah (and Arizona, and New Mexico) had to wait in federal purgatory. On the administrative level, the General Land Office delayed opening for business in Utah until 1869, leaving early Mormon land claims in limbo. Latter-day Saints watched in frustration as Congress sawed off a chunk of Utah Territory, and promptly awarded statehood to less populous and barely developed Nevada. Like a schoolchild held back year after year at the discretion of a principal, Utah squirmed in its outgrown kiddie seat. Long after Lincoln went to war to prevent the Confederate states from *leaving* the Union, after those defeated and occupied states submitted revised constitutions, and even after "redeemed" states eviscerated those revisions, the Republican Party still waged political, judicial, and financial war to prevent Utah Territory from *joining* the Union. The Supreme Court with *Reynolds v. U.S.* (1879) provided the vise; Congress used the Edmunds Act (1882/87) as the hammer.

As opposed to their elite Southern counterparts, LDS hierarchs ultimately decided to participate in their own reconstruction, internalizing the federal project. The process of unmaking the kingdom was reluctant, tactical, and dissembling at first, hedged on widespread expectation that the Millennium would begin in 1891 (based on a Joseph Smith prophecy) or 1893 (with the completion of the Salt Lake Temple). However, by the 1907 conclusion of the Reed Smoot hearings—a gauntlet of humiliation—church leadership had turned coerced accommodation into self-transformation. A progressive version of Mormonism came into being, and with it an inevitable externality: fundamentalism.

One should not minimize the psychic pain of the "Great Accommodation" for LDS leadership and laity. During the Brigham Young period, Mormonism had evolved from a society with closeted polygamy to an out-and-proud polygamous society. For elite, educated Mormons—the main participants and defenders of "the Principle"—giving up celestial marriage felt like giving in to the world. As in the South, nonelites participated in the "peculiar institution" at lower rates, yet the practice, and its slow dissolution, affected every extended family. The emotional costs of renunciation were somewhat offset by economic and political gains. Once the United States secured multiple disavowals of theocracy and plural marriage, it essentially allowed the LDS Church to run the show in Utah. Although Mormons had to remake their religion radically (again), they only had to make minor adjustments to Utah's power structure. In terms of political economy, the end of church-sponsored polygamy was hardly comparable to the end of Confederate-sponsored slavery. Unlike emancipation, the "liberation" of Mormon women did not result in human property transferal.

The Americanization of Utah was less regime change than power play. Congress in the end deemed the "Mormon Problem" (an erstwhile religious "empire," "monarchy," or "caliphate" full of undesirable immigrants) less problematic than New Mexico and Arizona with their larger native-born Hispanic and Native populations. Likewise, the racial status of Utah Saints—for even rhetorically racialized Mormons presented as white—allowed the territory to graduate from congressional guardianship more quickly and thoroughly than the Uintah and Ouray Indian Reservation, effectively a lesser Utah. Because of their whiteness, foreign-born Mormons received the right to naturalize before Indians, and many

Utah citizens received land rights and self-determination at the direct expense of reservation Utes with the allotment of the Uintah Basin in 1905.

The Beehive State's population structure encouraged majoritarianism. In contrast to white Democrats throughout the former Confederacy, Utah Mormons after 1896 did not at the state level portray themselves as a beset minority. Indians hadn't obtained franchise under the Fifteenth Amendment, and non-Mormons didn't make up a significant voting bloc outside Salt Lake City and a few mining towns. Unlike segregationists, who needed a solid South in the U.S. Senate to protect "home rule," the post-Manifesto LDS Church could dominate a normalized two-party (Democratic-Republican) system without resorting to electoral shenanigans. Gratuitously, Utah, like other western states, would go on to institute a small version of Jim Crow, targeting Indian voters in San Juan County, the place where Utah Natives had greatest potential power. Mainly, though, the enduring political dominance of the LDS Church in the State of Utah was a function of the demographic and cultural strength of its membership. By design or by accident, Mormon pioneerism relegated second-class cultural citizenship to all "Gentiles" (though non-Mormon mining magnates had other routes to influence).

As it ossified, the pioneer master narrative presented two long-term problems to the LDS Church: 1) It did not translate to converts outside the United States in the post-"Gathering" era; 2) It could not incorporate the period between the death of Brigham Young in 1877 and the confirmation of President David O. McKay (pioneer of the modern missionary program) in 1951. In official church history, this transformative era barely registers. Mormon novelists avoid it, too. The laity fills the lacuna with family history. In the safe space of genealogy, post-pioneer Saints can share private stories of "The Raid" without the public embarrassment of explaining or excusing plural marriage. For example, in the self-published memoir of my maternal grandfather, Walter Edward Clark (1889–1987), I read the following:

> Neither Father nor Mother were molested by U.S. Marshals, unlike many others living in polygamy. Polygamous relationships were not publicized. In fact, it was not generally known exactly where we fit into the Clark clan. My grandfather Clark spent a period of time in the penitentiary because he had two families and my father paid his father's fine. My grandfather Alfred Randall was spotted for arrest for the same reason. He had five families. One day a marshal found him at home. Grandfather Randall quickly invited the marshal to view his orchard and picked a box of choice fruit, and handed it to the marshal saying, "Take this home to your family." The marshal reported, "I could not arrest a man like him."

Grandpa goes on to say that "some of the marshals were honorable men." His was not the stuff of scalawags, carpetbaggers, and snot-nosed Yankees. Mormons like Elder Clark turned histories of structural oppression into stories of personal inspiration. Hard work and quick wits supposedly saved my great-great-grandfather, whose appearance as an orchard keeper trumped his secret life as a harem keeper; the Turnerian phenotype overrode the Orientalist stereotype.

Institutions can radicalize or moderate memory. In the Mormon culture region, the LDS Church is the great influencer of public *and* personal memory, and its influence comes as general moderation and selective suppression. The twentieth-century church had no reason to advance a lost cause counterpoint to the myth of pioneering. The reality of fundamentalism poisoned the memory of plural marriage. Twentieth-century Mormons developed an intense allergy to ridicule, and strived to disassociate themselves from modern cohabs who seemed to embody nineteenth-century stereotypes. Through the Church Educational System, the Missionary Training Center, and Sunday school lesson books approved by "Correlation," Mormon baby boomers grew up on historical lies, for instance, that Joseph Smith married just once, and that only 2 to 3 percent of Latter-day Saints in Utah Territory practiced polygamy.

The web made such lying unsustainable, and the LDS Church made a necessary if belated U-turn with the inauguration of the Joseph Smith Papers Project (2008) and the online "Gospel Topics Essays" (2014) drafted by a revitalized Church History Department. Simultaneously, the internet opened a thousand new doors to self-learning and grassroots miseducation. As seen every day in the "Bloggernacle," the Mormon laity is not completely obedient to official memory or theology. This is true on the LDS left and especially the far right. Many individual Saints still nurture aggrieved and apocalyptic beliefs based on nineteenth-century ideas about the "Kingdom of God." Drawing upon Joseph Smith's canonized "Civil War Prophecy" and the apocryphal "White Horse Prophecy," a millenarian minority still anticipates the demise of the United States and the rebirth of theocracy, perhaps even a return to Missouri, the once and future Eden. Unavoidably, Mormon "survivalists" and "preppers" now borrow some of their ideas and methods from militia movements, sovereign citizens, Tea Partiers, white nationalists, and neo-Confederates they encounter online. However, there is no formal outlet for such religious beliefs, and the modern LDS Church discourages the substance if not the practice of folk prophecy.

Despite all the historical and institutional factors moderating against a "Mormon Lost Cause," I detect the existence of three politicized stories of governmental tyranny in contemporary Mormondon. That is, I count three communities of memory that have publicized narratives of historical injustices against local rights. Each of these stories currently exists in a different stage of life. The oldest is hyperlocal, ultraconservative, sectarian, and faltering. The middle-aged example is regional, rightist, partisan, and entrenched. The youngest is cosmopolitan, progressive, pan-religious, and embryonic.

1. Fundamentalism

Members of the Fundamentalist Church of Jesus Christ of Latter-day Saints may not be "Mormons"—on this semantic point they and the LDS Church agree—but they share allegiance to Joseph Smith and Brigham Young. The largest, most controversial, and most visible of the many post-Manifesto splinter groups, the FLDS Church nurtures a lost cause narrative of the government's own conception. At multiple points, law officers heartlessly disrupted the sectarian community, yet didn't have the heart to destroy it, thus giving members a persecution story valuable for remobilization. True believers will never forget the 1953 "raid" (and a similar action in 2008), plus the appearance of prophet-president Warren Jeffs on the FBI's "Most Wanted" list, and his long-term sentence to prison.

Unlike so many Smith-ites who practice down-low polygamy in suburbia, the FLDS Church maintains "the Principle" in defiance of state and federal law in small towns it owns outright through its "United Effort Plan." This territorial dimension—albeit on a small scale—gives a nineteenth-century cast to this ongoing conflict, as does the church's pioneer dress code. The twin enclaves of Colorado City, Arizona, and Hildale, Utah, would be more sympathetic to defenders of civil liberties if FLDS patriarchs weren't culpable of systematic sexual and emotional abuse of women and minors (not to mention racist comments on miscegenation that attracted scrutiny from the Southern Poverty Law Center). A characteristically western irony of the FLDS Church's antigovernment stance is its historic reliance on government benefits, including benefits fraud.

2. Public Land

In Utah, less than 30 percent of the land has become privatized—the third lowest percentage in the Union, after Nevada and Alaska. Utah's federal property—more than 60 percent of the state—is managed by various agencies, including the Bureau of Land Management (BLM), which controls almost 23 million acres, or 42 percent of the Beehive State. When contemporary politicians speak of "public land," they mean BLM land. The BLM and its precursor, the U.S. Grazing

Service, have been the focus of rural western ire since the 1930s. In the 1970s and 1990s, Nevada led the Sagebrush Rebellion, hoping to extinguish BLM title, thus massively increasing state property for lease or sale.

More recently, the State of Utah has taken up this losing cause of state sovereignty under the banner of the "land transfer movement." In 2012 Utah's (Mormon) governor signed the Transfer of Public Lands Act, passed by the (90 percent majority Mormon) legislature, which issued an imperious and meaningless deadline to the federal government to cede jurisdiction. The state's legal argument came from a wishful reading of the Enclave Clause of the U.S. Constitution and a fairytale reading of the Utah Enabling Act (1894) by which Congress ostensibly "promised" to dispose all public land. According to a 2012 poll, 77 percent of Utah's Mormons supported transfer, compared to 34 percent of non-Mormons. Subsequent polling found a much higher approval in Utah for liquidating BLM land than in other western states. Utah's land-transfer movement overlaps with its antiwilderness crusade. Particularly in San Juan County—the section of Utah where pioneerism *and* anti-Indianism took deepest root—the federal designation of BLM roadless areas contravenes a sacralized heritage of trail building.

Although the LDS Church does not take positions on public land issues, it bears some responsibility for the political climate. The patriarch of "Mormon Constitutionalism" was W. Cleon Skousen, an anti-Communist ideologue championed by LDS apostle-cum-prophet Ezra Taft Benson long before Mormon convert Glenn Beck via Fox News made him a posthumous bestseller. The ideas of Skousen and Benson—including literalist, militaristic readings of the Book of Mormon—influenced the worldview of the Bundy family, who, in armed standoffs in Nevada and Oregon, declared that the government has no authority over public land. From the fringes of power at the Bundy ranch to the corridors of power in Salt Lake City, the story of patrimony lost to the federal government through unconstitutional "land grabs" is now Republican orthodoxy. Morally—if not politically—this narrative would be more powerful coming from American Indian tribes.

3. Religious Freedom

After 9/11, and especially after the election of Donald J. Trump on a platform of nativist white Christian nationalism, Islamophobia became normalized in "Red" America. Alarmed by this outcome, "progressive" Mormons took the moral high ground by highlighting the LDS experience of state-sponsored religious intolerance. It wasn't so long ago, they reminded Americans, that Mormonism, now mocked for being the Wonder Bread of religions, was attacked—rhetorically *and* legally—as a violent, un-American ideology inimical to Christianity and democracy. Nineteenth-century anti-Mormon imagery lifted from anti-Islamic imagery: Joseph Smith as a Koranic prophet, Brigham Young as an Ottoman sultan, and so on.

In the *anni mirabiles* 2016–17, a cohort of mostly youngish Mormon intellectuals announced their solidarity with Muslim immigrants and American Muslims in op-eds, blog posts, and amicus briefs. The church itself issued a series of statements condemning xenophobia and bigotry, and through BYU's International Center for Law and Religion Studies at the J. Reuben Clark Law School, continued to support activist scholarship on religious freedom. For self-serving as well as selfless reasons, the proselytizing church worries about the political persecution of religious minorities—whether they be Jehovah's Witnesses in Russia, Yazidis in Iraq, or Falun Gong in China. Before Trump carried Utah, albeit narrowly, Latter-day Saints (and their would-be ensign-bearer, Mitt Romney) had positioned themselves as potential leaders of a moral alternative to the "Christian right" in conservative U.S. politics. That has not (yet?) happened. Nonetheless, one can imagine future BYU students wearing T-shirts with George Q. Cannon in his jailhouse stripes next to a phrase like "Prisoner of Conscience" or "Unlawful Detainee." Such a sentiment would represent the opposite of fundamentalism. Progressive Mormons are glad their church gave up polygamy, yet somewhat paradoxically they hope to use the history of the government's victimization of polygamists to promote religious tolerance.

Within Mormonism, this kind of creative inversion appeared earlier during the debate surrounding the legalization of gay marriage. After the LDS gerontocracy bet it all on "traditional marriage" in California in 2008, it lost many youthful members who saw contemporary homophobia as history-denying hypocrisy. Gay Mormons and their feminist allies found ironic inspiration in ancestors having experimented with triad relationships, not to mention founding mothers of the Relief Society having found joy in huddling together in same-sex meetings for the sharing of revelations and the laying on of hands. MAKE MORMONISM QUEER AGAIN! As lost causes go, Saints could find worse.

Contributors

Editors

Clyde A. Milner II is founding director of the PhD program in Heritage Studies and professor of history emeritus at Arkansas State University. Retired to Albuquerque, New Mexico, he is a visiting scholar in history at the University of New Mexico. Prior to Arkansas State, Milner was on the Utah State University history faculty where, for eighteen of his twenty-six years there, he edited the *Western Historical Quarterly*. He has written or edited eight books, including the coedited *Oxford History of the American West* (1994) and *As Big as the West: The Pioneer Life of Granville Stuart* (2009), coauthored with his wife, Carol O'Connor.

Brian Q. Cannon is professor of history at Brigham Young University, where he directed the Charles Redd Center for Western Studies from 2003 to 2018. He has written or edited six books and more than two dozen articles and book chapters on western, Mormon, and rural history topics, including *The Awkward State of Utah: Coming of Age in the Nation, 1896–1945*, coauthored with Charles S. Peterson. He is past president of the Agricultural History Society and of the Mormon History Association and serves on the editorial boards of *Agricultural History* and the *Utah Historical Quarterly*.

Contributors

Cathleen Cahill is associate professor of history at Pennsylvania State University. A former Clements Fellow at Southern Methodist University's Clements Center, she received her doctorate from the University of Chicago and taught previously at the University of New Mexico. A U.S. social history specialist, she is author of *Federal Fathers and Mothers: A Social History of the United States Indian Service, 1869–1933*, which won the 2011 Labriola Center American Indian National Book Award and was a finalist for the Weber-Clements Book Prize. She is at work on her second book, "Raising the Banner: Women of Color Challenge the Mainstream Suffrage Movement," and is coeditor with Kent Blansett and Andrew Needham of the forthcoming collection of essays "Indian Cities: Histories of Indigenous Urbanism."

Brett D. Dowdle is a historian with the Joseph Smith Papers Project in Salt Lake City, Utah. He received his doctorate in American history from Texas Christian University in 2018. His dissertation, titled "'Beyond the Pale of Human Sympathy': Utah and the Reconstruction of the American West, 1856–1890," examines the role of reconstructive policies in shaping nineteenth-century Mormonism. He lives in Orem, Utah, with his wife, Ashley.

Eric A. Eliason is a folklore professor at Brigham Young University, where he has published on Mormon, Mountain West, Caribbean, Russian, English, Mexican, military, hunting, and biblical cultural traditions. His publications include *Latter-day Lore: Mormon Folklore Studies*, coedited with Tom Mould (2013), *Black Velvet Art* (2011), and *To See Them Run: Great Plains Coyote Coursing* (2015). His service in Afghanistan and the Philippines as a U.S. Army Special Forces chaplain for the Utah National Guard is featured in *Hammerhead Six: How Green Berets Waged an Unconventional War against the Taliban to Win in Afghanistan's Deadly Pech Valley* (2017).

Jared Farmer is an expatriate of Provo, Utah. Professor of history at Stony Brook University, he holds degrees from Utah State University, the University of Montana, and Stanford University. He is the author of three books, including *On Zion's Mount: Mormons, Indians, and the American Landscape* (2008), which received the Francis Parkman Prize from the Society of American Historians. A past winner of the Hiett Prize in the Humanities, Farmer is presently an Andrew Carnegie Fellow.

Crystal N. Feimster is an associate professor in the American Studies Program and the departments of African American Studies and History at Yale University and an associate professor of history in the School of Philosophical Historical and International Studies (SOPHIS), Faculty of Arts at Monash University. She received a doctorate in history from Princeton University and is the author of *Southern Horrors: Women and the Politics of Rape and Lynching* (2009). She is at work on her second book, "Truth Be Told: Rape and Mutiny in Civil War Louisiana."

Angela Pulley Hudson is professor of history at Texas A&M University and author of *Real Native Genius: How an Ex-slave and a White Mormon Became Famous Indians* (2015), which won the 2016 Evans Biography Prize from the Mountain West Center for Regional Studies, and *Creek Paths and Federal Roads: Indians, Settlers, and Slaves and the Making of the American South* (2010). She serves on the editorial board of the *Journal of the Civil War Era* and is senior editor of Native American history for the *Oxford Research Encyclopedia in American History*. With Andrew Frank and Kristofer Ray she coedits the "Indians and Southern History" series from the University of Alabama Press.

Anne Hyde is professor of history at the University of Oklahoma and editor-in-chief of the *Western Historical Quarterly*. Her most recent books include *Shaped by the West* (2018), coauthored with William F. Deverell, and *Empires, Nations, and Families: A New History of the North American West, 1800–1860* (2012), which won the Bancroft Prize from Columbia University and the John W. Caughey Prize from the Western History Association.

Patrick Q. Mason is Leonard J. Arrington Chair of Mormon History and Culture and associate professor of Religious Studies and History at Utah State University. He is the author or editor of multiple books and articles, including *What Is Mormonism? A Student's Introduction* (2017), *The Mormon Menace: Violence and Anti-Mormonism in the Postbellum South* (2011), and, with John Turner, *Out of Obscurity: Mormonism since 1945* (2016).

Brent M. Rogers is the associate managing historian for the Joseph Smith Papers Project and an instructor of history at Brigham Young University, Salt Lake Center. He received his doctorate from the University of Nebraska and is author of *Unpopular Sovereignty: Mormons and the Federal Management of Early Utah*

Territory (2017), which received the Charles Redd Center–Phi Alpha Theta Book Award, the Mormon History Association's Best First Book Award, and Utah State Historical Society's Francis Armstrong Madsen Best History Book Award. His *Utah Historical Quarterly* article, "A 'Distinction between Mormons and Americans': Mormon Indian Missionaries, Federal Indian Policy, and the Utah War" (Fall 2014), won the Western History Association's 2015 Arrington-Prucha Prize.

Rachel St. John is associate professor of history at the University of California, Davis. A native of the San Bernardino Mountains in Southern California, she received her doctorate from Stanford University. She spent eleven years on the East Coast at Harvard University and New York University before returning to California to join the faculty at UC Davis in 2016. She is author of *Line in the Sand: A History of the Western U.S.-Mexico Border* (2011) and is at work on a study of the diverse range of nation-building projects that emerged across North America in the nineteenth century.

Christine Talbot is associate professor and coordinator of Gender Studies at the University of Northern Colorado, where she has served for ten years. Previously, she was a visiting assistant professor at Dickinson College in Carlisle, Pennsylvania. She earned a graduate certificate in Women's Studies and received her doctorate in history from the University of Michigan. She teaches courses in feminist and queer theories, the history of feminism, intersectionality, and gender studies. Her book, *A Foreign Kingdom: Mormons and Polygamy in American Political Culture, 1852–1890* (2013) examines the national controversy over the Mormon practice of plural marriage.

Elliott West is the Alumni Distinguished Professor of History at the University of Arkansas and past president of the Western History Association. In his work in Native American and western social and environmental history, he has written six books. Two, *The Last Indian War: The Nez Perce Story* (2009) and *The Contested Plains: Indians, Goldseekers, and the Rush to Colorado* (1998), have received the Western History Association's John W. Caughey Prize. His *Contested Plains* also won the Francis Parkman Prize and three other major awards. Twice named as his university's best teacher of the year, he was one of three finalists in 2009 for the Robert Foster Cherry Award for the best classroom teacher in the nation.

Index

Adams, Anne P., 63
African American rights, 80, 111, 131–34, 142, 147n66, 156–57
Aikau, Hokulani K., 43–44
Alton, Illinois, 93
American Indian removal. *See under* forced migration
Anderson, Thomas, 89
Angel Moroni, 213
Anthony, Susan B., 158, 230
anti-Mormonism, 19–22, 30–34, 40–41, 54, 96–98, 100–102, 136, 139, 210–11, 243
Apaches, 130
Arrington, Leonard J., 69
Arthur, Chester A., 98, 138
Ashley, James M., 132

Babbitt, Almon, 206
Bagley, George A., 154
Bannock Indians, 147n60
Bargain of 1877, 184

Basso, Keith, 37–38
Battle of Nauvoo, 224
Battle of the Bulls, 225
Bear River massacre, 167, 225, 236
Beck, Glenn, 242
Belisle, Orvilla, 73, 75–78
Benson, Ezra Taft, 242
Bentley, Nancy, 72, 75
Berwanger, Eugene, 176
Bill of Rights, 132–33, 136
Birth of a Nation, 111, 210–11
Black Hawk War, 224
Blair, Austin, 133
Blight, David, 204–5, 210
Boggs, Lilburn, 29, 221
Book of Mormon, 21–23, 242
Bottoms, Michael, 185
Bourne, George, 58–60, 62–63, 65–66, 70
Brigham Young—Frontiersman, 211
Brigham Young University, 217n32
Brimhall, Flora Robertson, 197
Brown, Gillian, 63

INDEX

Brown, John, 94
Brown, Richard Maxwell, 92
Buchanan, James, 17, 79, 88, 95, 121–23, 172, 182, 197
Buffalo Bill Cody's Wild West Show, 6, 160
Bundy ranch, 242
Bureau of Land Management (BLM), 241–42
Byrd, Jodi A., 20

Cahill, Cathleen, 111, 245
Caldwell County, Missouri, 222
Camp Douglas, 88, 126
Camp Floyd, 88, 123, 145n37, 197
Canada, 64, 90, 189
Cannon, Brian Q., 195, 244
Cannon, David, 197
Cannon, George Q., 135–36, 227, 243
Carleton, James H., 130
Carlisle Indian School, 169
Carson, James Taylor, 36–37
Carthage Jail, 200
Cass, Lewis, 24, 38, 119
Catholicism, 113, 118, 152–55, 162–66, 173–74, 220, 227
Cavanaugh, William, 90, 100–101, 104
Cherokee Indians, 17, 19, 24–27, 30–31, 37, 39–40, 44n1, 46n27
Chicago World's Fair 1893, 207–9
Child, Lydia Maria, 61–62, 64–65, 67, 70, 83n65
China, 169, 227, 243
Chinese Exclusion Act, 170–72
Chinese immigrants, 4–6, 112–13, 140, 152–55, 169–72, 189
Choctaw Indians, 21
Christenson, Joseph, 199
Church Educational System, 240
Church History Department, 206, 240
Circleville massacre, 236
civil rights movement, 212, 235
Civil War, 2–4, 112–14, 116–17, 124–28, 202–4

Clansman, The, 111, 211
Clark, Walter Edward, 239–40
Clay County, Missouri, 92–93, 222
Cleveland, Grover, 98, 139–40, 208
Cobb, Augusta, 206
Colorado City, Arizona, 241
Columbian Exposition, Chicago, 1893, 237
Committee on the Territories, 120, 132–33, 144
Compromise of 1850, 163
Confederacy, 8–9, 113–14, 181–84, 235–39; in modern culture and historical study, 202–4, 210–14; monuments in honor of, 203, 210, 212–13. *See also* neo-Confederates
Connor, Patrick Edward, 89, 126–28, 145n37, 172
Corrill, John, 96
Cott, Nancy F., 79
Council of Fifty, 236
Cox, Karen L., 210
Cragin, Aaron H., 133
Crooked River, 224
Crounse, Lorenzo, 135–36
Cullom, Shelby, 133
Cumming, Alfred, 79, 95, 196

Dakota Uprising, 185
Dall, Caroline W. Healey, 59
Dallin, Cyrus, 212
Danites, 97–98, 211
Daughters of the Utah Pioneers, 210, 236
Dawes Allotment Act, 172
Dawes Severalty Act, 168
Daynes, Kathryn, 149n97
Dean, Joseph, 197–98
Delano, Columbus, 168
Delaware Indians, 21, 27, 47n32
Deloria, Vine, Jr., 37
DeMille, Cecil B., 211
Democratic Party, 79, 102, 119–22, 132, 134, 136, 165, 239

Department of Utah, 123, 128, 131
Deseret, 4–5, 7–9, 17, 58, 163, 206, 220, 230, 236–37
Devens, Charles, 99
Dixon, Thomas, Jr., 111, 211
Dole, William P., 128–29
Douglas, Stephen A., 119, 122–23, 132, 144n22, 145n29
Dowdle, Brett D., 3–6, 42, 112–14, 150, 187, 245
Downs, Gregory, 186
Doyle, Arthur Conan, 98
Dred Scott decision, 112
Drum, Richard C., 127
Drummond, William W., 121
Du Bois, W. E. B., 111–14
Dunklin, Daniel, 100–101
Dunning, William A., 111, 158
Dunning School, 111, 158–59

Eaton, John, 49n81
Edmunds, George F., 138
Edmunds Act, 138, 171, 238
Edmunds-Tucker Act, 140–41, 171, 221
Eliason, Eric A., 8, 50n99, 50, 195, 198, 204–5, 216n15, 219, 245
Emigration Canyon, 212
Emmons, David, 164
Enforcement Acts, 134
Evans, John, 167
Evarts, William, 139–40

Faragher, John Mack, 10, 41, 81n4, 81, 187
Farmer, Jared, 8–9, 29, 43, 47n41, 48n68, 195, 197, 199–200, 212, 235, 245
Faulkner, William, 204
Feimster, Crystal N., 111, 246
Ferris, B. G., 75
Fifteenth Amendment, 42, 132, 156, 183, 186, 239
Fillmore, Millard, 94
First Presidency, 103–4, 198, 209
first Reconstruction, 102

Fischer, David Hackett, 223, 232n6
Fisher, Philip, 63
flag of Deseret, 205–6, 230–31, 236
flags: Confederate, 202–3, 213–14; Mormon, 230; Mormon flag illustration, 231
Fletcher, Margaret, 73
Floyd, John B., 118
Fluhman, Spencer, 41, 96
Foner, Eric, 111, 159, 173, 186
forced migration: of American Indians, 7, 16, 20–21, 24–44, 128–29, 167–69, 187; of Mormons, 16, 19–22, 28, 31–35, 38–39, 171, 229, 236; removal comparison of each group, 7, 19–21, 30–34, 39–44
Fort Bridger, 123, 126, 195
Fort Douglas, 114, 124, 126–28, 131
Fort Sumter, 229
Fourteenth Amendment, 112, 132, 166–67, 170, 186
Fourth of July. *See* July Fourth
Freedmen's Bureau, 80, 131
Fuller, Metta Victoria, 58, 71, 73–74, 77–78
Fundamentalist Church of Jesus Christ of Latter-day Saints (FLDS), 241

Gaines, Edmund P., 48n48
Garfield, James, 138
gathering, 23, 27–28, 33–34, 39, 239
gay rights, 213, 243
General Land Office, 237
Givens, Terryl, 57, 99, 223
golden spike, 207, 215n15
Gone with the Wind, 211
Goodnow, Frank, 94
Gordon, Sarah Barringer, 29, 55, 57, 81n12, 88, 136, 184
Goshute Indians, 130, 147n60
Gospel Topics Essays, 240
Grande, Sandy, 40
Grant, Heber J., 200, 212

Grant, Ulysses S., 130, 134–35, 146n54, 158, 168
"Great Accommodation," 238
Green, Frances H., 66
Green, Nelson Winch, 57
Griffith, D. W., 111, 211
Grimsted, David, 93

Hahn, Steven, 157, 184
Hamblin, Jacob, 24
handcarts, 207, 212, 214–15, 221
Harpers Ferry, 94
Harrison, Benjamin, 98, 198–99
Hatch, Nathan, 223
Hatfield, Maud, 73
Haun's Mill Massacre, 221
Haupt, Jon, 69
Hayes, Rutherford B., 89, 98, 134, 137–39
Higginson, Thomas Wentworth, 70
Hildale, Utah, 241
Hill Cumorah, 7
historical trauma, 39, 50n98
Hobbes, Thomas, 90–91, 100, 105n6
Homestead Act, 125, 131
Hudson, Angela Pulley, 6–7, 16–17, 19, 184, 186–87, 246
Husband, Julie, 62–63
Hutchings, Elias, 30, 32
Hyde, Anne, 15, 29, 95, 246

Illinois, 2, 7, 15–17, 19, 28–34, 38–40, 76, 96–97, 151, 171, 195–96, 200, 224, 236
immigration: of Catholics, 165–66; of Chinese, 170, 189; of Mormons from Europe, 139–41, 236
Independence, Missouri, 22
Independence Day. *See* July Fourth
Indian Appropriations Act, 146n55
Indian boarding schools, 173
Indian removal. *See under* forced migration
internet, effects on LDS Church, 240

Jackson, Andrew, 24, 26, 38
Jackson County, Missouri, 7, 50n99, 96–97, 221–22, 236
Janney, Caroline E., 203–4
Jefferson, Thomas, 25–26
Jenkens, Jennifer L., 70
Jepson, James, 197
Johnson, Andrew, 158
Johnson, Kimberley S., 94
Johnston, Albert Sidney, 207, 223
Jones, Evan, 31
Jones, John H., 49n80
Jones, Ray, 203
Jonesboro, Arkansas, 202–4
Joseph Smith Papers Project, 240
July Fourth, 206, 208, 212, 217n32, 217n32, 231
July 24, 206–9, 212, 215n15, 216n15, 219. *See also* Pioneer Day
jury, polygamists serving on, 133, 135, 138

Kaplan, Amy, 69
Kickapoo Indians, 27, 47n32
Kimball, Heber C., 196, 217n31
Ku Klux Klan, 156, 211, 213

Lamanites, 7, 21–24, 28–29, 32–33, 43, 48n68
Lamar, Howard, 119, 176n38
Larson, Lorena Eugenia Washburn, 198
Lasser, Carol, 65, 67
Lee, Robert E., 203–4
Lewis, James, 196
Liberia, 64, 189
Limerick, Patricia Nelson, 212
Lincoln, Abraham, 93–94, 122, 124–27, 129, 145n29, 182, 229
Little, James, 34–35
lost cause, Mormon, 8, 205, 213, 220–32, 237, 240–43
Lost Cause, Southern, 8, 195, 203–5, 210–13, 222–23, 226, 229
Lost Tribe of Israel, 23

Lost Tribes thesis, 23, 46n20
Lott, John, 196
Lovejoy, Elijah, 93
Lundstrom, Mormon August, 197

Maine, Henry Sumner, 55
Manifesto, 103–4, 141, 197–200, 205, 208; Second, 199
marriage: ideas about, 53–65, 73–80; laws on, 124, 126–27, 132–42, 199–200, 227, 238; modern views on, 213, 240, 243; plural (*see* polygamy); among slaves, 58–66
Martin, Joel W., 26
Martins Cove, Wyoming, 236
Mason, Patrick Q., 4–7, 18, 42, 88, 184, 186–88, 246
McDougall, James A., 127
McKay, David O., 239
McKenney, Thomas, 41
McLeod, Norman, 127–28
Mexican, 118–19, 163, 165, 185, 189, 204, 223
Mexican Americans, and rights, 163, 185, 189
Mexican-American War, 17, 118–19, 165, 225
Mexican Army, 17
Mexico: and American Indians, 161; and Confederates, 181, 183, 189; and Mormons, 118, 171, 181, 183, 189, 199
Miles, Tiya, 39
military, Mormons in, 234n24
Milner, Clyde A., II, 8–9, 195, 198, 200, 202, 219–20, 244
Missionary Training Center, 240
mission work, 21–25, 41, 43, 99, 170, 173, 223–24, 227–28
Missouri: forcing Mormons out of, 6–7, 15–17, 29–35, 44n1, 50n99, 92–93, 96–97, 100–101, 195–96, 221–25, 240; life of Mormons in, 22, 28–35, 96–97, 100–101, 195–96

Molina, Natalia, 113, 152
Monaco, James, 211
monuments, of pioneers, 209, 212, 217n31
Mormon Battalion, 225
Mormon Maid, A, 211
Morrill, Justin Smith, 79, 120–21, 126, 135, 145n29
Morrill Anti-Bigamy Act, 79, 114, 124–27, 132–33, 138, 171, 183
Mountain Meadows Massacre, 8, 96–97, 179n106, 196, 224–25, 229, 236
Murray, Eli H., 208
Muslims, 153, 227, 243

Nast, Thomas, 154–55, 174
Nauvoo, Illinois, 6–7, 31, 34, 78, 97, 227, 236
Nauvoo City Council ordinance, 227
Nauvoo Legion, 97, 224, 236
Navajos, 17, 130
Neilson, Reid L., 207
neo-Confederates, 213, 219, 223, 237, 240. *See also* Confederacy
New Jerusalem, 22–23, 27
Nez Perce Indians, 167, 189
Nez Perce War, 160
Novkov, Julie, 80, 102
Nuevo Mexicanos, 161, 163

O'Connor, Carol, 202
Ojibwas (Anishinaabes), 21
Olsen, Steven L., 206, 208
Omaha Indians, 28, 36, 47n41
Orientalism, 69–71, 78, 240
Ottawa Indians, 21
Ouray Indians, 238

Pacific Railroad Act, 125–26
Paddison, Joshua, 169, 185
Paiute Indians, 97, 130
Panic of 1873, 170
Patten, David, 196
Perkins, John, Jr., 181, 189

Peteetneet, 129
Pierson, Michael D., 53–54, 62, 68–69
Pilgrim Fathers, 208
Pioneer Camp of 1847, 237
Pioneer Day, 9, 204–7, 212, 215n13, 216n15, 217n32, 230, 236. *See also* July 24
plural marriage. *See* polygamy
Poland, Luke, 135
Poland Act, 135–36, 138, 171
polygamy, 6, 88, 182–83, 188, 204–5, 226, 229–30, 243; altered history of, 240; announcement of, 71; cessation of, 4, 8, 80, 89, 103–4, 141–42, 197–200, 220–21; clandestine, 238–39, 241; and comparison to slavery, 6, 54–55, 58–59, 72, 79; fictional portrayals of, 53–59, 68–69, 71–80, 81n12; and government intervention, 79, 98–99, 120–24, 127, 132–34, 138–40, 144n22, 145n29; laws against, 126–28, 132–33, 135–41, 149n97, 154, 171–72, 181; perceived dangers of, 53–55, 57–58, 64, 68, 71–80, 99, 120, 138; and slavery, 5, 18, 52–55, 58, 71, 78–79, 120, 124, 154
Pony Express, 208–9
popular sovereignty, 79, 88, 92–93, 114, 117, 119–22, 137, 144n22, 162
Porter, Joy, 23, 46n20
Potawatomi Indians, 21
Pratt, Orson, 33, 208, 217n31
Pratt, Parley P., 30, 45n13, 196, 205
Pratt, Richard Henry, 42, 169
Prescott, Cynthia Culver, 212
Promontory Summit, 207, 215n15
Prosser, William F., 173
Protestants, 49n74, 107n45, 152–58, 162–65, 169–70, 173–74, 236–37
Provo, Utah, 217
Prucha, Francis, 168

Randall, Alfred, 239
Reconstruction: and American Indians, 89, 152, 167–69, 207, 219; expanded definition of, 2–10, 20–21, 40–44, 80, 111–14, 152–60, 164–74, 182–89; in the South, 42, 80, 88–89, 102, 111–14, 116–17, 130–36, 142, 152, 156–60, 171–74, 185–89, 230; in the West (concept of), 88–89, 96, 102, 156, 160–64, 173–74, 184, 188, 230
Reconstruction Acts, 130–31
Reconstruction era, 2–3, 20, 113, 116, 141–42, 156, 158, 186
Reeve, Paul, 20, 29, 41, 224
Religious Freedom Restoration Act, 233n17
Republican Party, 5, 52–55, 78–79, 102, 116–26, 130–36, 158, 166, 182–83, 235, 238, 242
Reynolds, George, 136
Reynolds v. United States, 99, 136–38, 227, 238
Richards, Franklin, 197
Richardson, Heather Cox, 159
Ridge, John, 31, 46n27
Ridge, Major, 31
Rifkin, Mark, 34
Robinson, Joseph, 198
Rockwood, Albert, 97
Rogers, Brent M., 4–6, 42, 113–14, 116, 182, 246
Romney, Miles Park, 181, 189, 243
Rusling, James F., 124, 154

Salt Lake City, 88, 104, 126, 206, 208–9, 212, 215n15, 229–30
Salt Lake Temple, 221, 237–38
Sánchez-Eppler, Karen, 61
Sand Creek Massacre, 167
San Juan County, Utah, 239, 242
San Luis Valley, Colorado, 224
Sanpitch (Ute leader), 129
Sauk and Fox Indians, 30, 38
Schenck, Robert C., 172
Scots-Irish, 195, 223, 232n6
Scott, Winfield, 30, 145n29

Seneca Nation, 21
Seward, William, 173
sexuality, 6, 53–59, 62–80
Shaffer, J. Wilson, 130
Shawnee Indians, 21
Sherman, William Tecumseh, 3, 113–14, 150–53, 174
Shoshones, 130, 147n60, 236
Sinha, Manisha, 56
Skousen, W. Cleon, 242
slavery, 3–6, 26, 52–81, 111–14, 119–26, 154–56, 162, 181–83, 203–4, 212–13, 222–26, 229–30
Smith, Caleb B., 129
Smith, Ettie V., 57
Smith, George A., 196
Smith, Hyrum, 196
Smith, Joseph, Jr.: and American Indians, 23, 27, 29, 32; and beliefs, 21, 23, 48n68, 102–3, 200, 209, 223, 225–27, 238, 240–41; death of, 29, 89, 97–98, 196; and forced migration, 22, 32, 35, 93, 97; portrayals of, 73, 99, 240
Smith, Joseph F., 199, 209
Smith, Joseph Fielding, 233n11
Smoot, Reed, 199, 238
Snow, Erastus, 217
Sons of Confederate Veterans, 203, 210
Southern Baptists, 213
Southern Paiutes, 147n60
Sowiette (Ute leader), 129
Spanish-American War, 104
Spanish Fork Treaty, 129
Standing Army of Israel, 4
Stanley, Amy Dru, 185
Stanton, Edwin, 158
Stanton, Elizabeth Cady, 158, 230
Statehood Day, 237
states' rights, 27, 117, 143n13, 143, 183, 204, 226
Stenhouse, Fanny, 79
Stevenson, Edward, 198
St. John, Rachel, 5, 10, 18, 113, 181, 247

Stowe, Harriet Beecher, 56–57, 63–64, 67–68, 70–71, 79–80, 233n19
Sumner, Charles, 79, 94
Supreme Court, 25, 99, 112, 136–37, 141, 227, 238

Talbot, Christine, 5–6, 18, 42, 52, 113, 182, 247
Talmage, James E., 200
Tanglen, Randi Lynn, 49n74
Taylor, Melanie Benson, 44
Taysom, Stephen C., 200, 208
telegraph, 96, 126, 129, 208, 229
Temple Square, 212
Tenure of Office Act, 158
This Is the Place Heritage Park, 212, 217n31
Thomas, James F., 93
Thomas, Robert K., 37
Thomson, Janice, 4
Tompkins, Jane, 56
Trail of Tears: Cherokee, 8, 19, 39–40, 44n1, 219; Mormon (concept of), 7, 20, 40
Transfer of Public Lands Act, 242
Treaty of Guadalupe Hidalgo, 95, 116, 161, 163, 165–66
Treaty of New Echota, 31
Trump, Donald J., 242–43
Turner, Frederick Jackson, 160, 207
Turner, John G., 206
Turnerian theories, 207, 236, 240
Twain, Mark, 158
Twelve Apostles, Council of, 103, 205
twin relics of barbarism, 5, 18, 52–56, 64, 68, 78–79, 120–26, 154

Uintah Basin, 239
Uintah Indian Reservation, 114, 129–30, 147n60, 238
Ulrich, Laurel Thatcher, 206
Uncle Tom's Cabin, 56, 63, 67–68, 70, 233n19

United Confederate Veterans, 210
United Daughters of the Confederacy, 210
U.S. Army: and American Indians, 17, 130, 167, 185; and Mormons, 15, 17, 101, 207
U.S. Census Bureau, 95
Utah Commission, 138, 221
Utah Enabling Act, 242
Utah Expedition, 95, 184
Utah Organic Act, 132
Utah Pioneer Jubilee, 208–9
Utah statehood, 42, 104, 114, 125, 132, 137, 144n22, 163–66, 205–9, 237
Utah Territory, 17, 102, 114, 117, 120–28, 131–35, 138–39, 163, 182, 196, 237–40
Utah War, 5, 8, 79, 94–96, 114, 122–28, 172, 179n106, 180n106, 182, 195–96
Utes, 129–30, 146n55, 147n60, 236, 239

van Deusen, Increase, 72
van Deusen, Maria, 72
voting rights, 3, 184–85, 189; of African Americans, 131, 156; of Mormons, 89, 135, 138–39, 199, 230, 234n22, 239; of women 140, 199, 230, 234n22

Waite, Morrison R., 136
Walker, Francis A., 150, 152
Ward, Austin, 74
Ward, Maria, 57, 71–74, 76–77
War Department, 126, 131
Warren, Louis, 6

Weber, Max, 90–92
Wells, Daniel H., 88
Wells, Heber Manning, 208
West, Elliott, 1, 16, 20, 108n49, 113, 134, 152, 159–60, 162, 184–85, 188–89, 247
Western Reserve, 21, 93, 223
White, Richard, 6, 118, 141, 163
White Horse (Omaha leader), 36
Whitmire, Eliza, 30
Wills, John A., 52–53
Wilmot, David, 119
Wilmot Proviso, 119, 124
Winter Quarters, Nebraska, 28, 31, 34, 39, 44n1, 47n41, 236
Wirt, William, 46n27
Wolfe, Patrick, 40
Woodruff, Wilford, 80, 103–4, 141–42, 197–200, 217n31, 217, 220–21
Woodward, C. Vann, 159
Wounded Knee, 220, 225
Wyandotte Indians, 21

Yellowstone National Park, 178n80
Young, Ann, 34
Young, Brigham, 17, 29, 34, 47n41, 74, 76–77, 79, 88, 97–98, 119, 121–22, 127, 129, 196, 204–6, 208–9, 211–13, 215n15, 217n31, 224, 229–30, 236–39, 241, 243
Young, Mahonri, 212
Young, Seraph, 234n22

Zion, 7, 22–23, 27–28, 50n99, 97, 104, 198, 221–22, 224, 240

www.ingramcontent.com/pod-product-compliance
Lightning Source LLC
Chambersburg PA
CBHW020834160426
43192CB00007B/646